TAOISM

BOOKS BY EVA WONG

Cultivating Stillness

Cultivating the Energy of Life

Feng-shui

Harmonizing Yin and Yang

Holding Yin, Embracing Yang

Lieh-tzu

A Master Course in Feng-shui

Nourishing the Essence of Life

The Pocket Tao Reader

Seven Taoist Masters

Tales of the Dancing Dragon: Stories of the Tao

Tales of the Taoist Immortals

Taoism: An Essential Guide

Teachings of the Tao

TAOISM

An Essential Guide

Eva Wong

SHAMBHALA
Boston & London
2011

Shambhala Publications, Inc.
Horticultural Hall
300 Massachusetts Avenue
Boston, Massachusetts 02115
www.shambhala.com

9 8 7 6 5 4 3 2 1

Printed in the United States of America

⊛ This edition is printed on acid-free paper that meets the
American National Standards Institute Z39.48 Standard.
♻ This book was printed on 30% postconsumer recycled paper.
For more information please visit www.shambhala.com.
Distributed in the United States by Random House, Inc.,
and in Canada by Random House of Canada Ltd

Library of Congress Cataloging-in-Publication Data
Wong, Eva, 1951–
Taoism: an essential guide/Eva Wong.
p. cm.
Includes bibliographical references and index.
ISBN 978-1-59030-882-0 (pbk.: alk. paper)
1. Taoism. 2. Tao. I. Title.
BL1920.W66 2011
299.5′14—dc22
2010049929

FRONT COVER:
"Spring Dawn Over the Elixir Terrace." China, Yuan dynasty, ca. 1369.
Hanging scroll; ink on paper. Image: 24¼ x 10¼ in. (61.6 x 26 cm).
Overall with mounting: 87½ x 17⅝ in. (222.3 x 44.8 cm). Overall with
knobs: 87½ x 20⅝ in. (222.3 x 52.4 cm). Photographed by Malcolm
Varon. Image © The Metropolitan Museum of Art / Art Resource, NY.

Contents

Part Three: Taoist Practices

List of Illustrations and Tables

Taoism

Introduction

MANY PEOPLE WILL EXPERIENCE, at least once in their lifetime, the urge to venture beyond the everyday world of the mundane into the world of the spirit. These journeys into the spiritual world often take us into a universe we normally do not encounter in our daily lives, and allow us to explore regions of our consciousness that we have not before known.

This book is a guide to the spiritual landscape of Taoism. In it you will encounter events in the history of Taoism, meet the sages who wrote the Taoist texts, be introduced to the various schools of Taoist thinking, and get a feel for what it means to practice Taoism today.

The spiritual landscape of Taoism is a kaleidoscope of colors and sounds. It is also a land of silence and stillness. It can be friendly and attractive, and at the same time challenging and dangerous. In this book, you will be traveling through the spiritual terrain of Taoism. On your journey, you will see shamans dressed in animal skins dancing the patterns of the stars as they fly to the sky and tunnel beneath the earth; you will see talismans displaying symbols of power that are designed to heal, protect, and ward off malevolent spirits; you will see people sitting, standing, or sleeping in unusual postures, cultivating the breath of life and longevity; you will see colorful tapestries, images of deities and immortals, huge brass cauldrons, altars with

1

sticks of incense, and oil lamps burning eternal flames. On this journey, you will see, etched on bamboo sticks, hexagrams, the symbols of change, used by diviners to interpret the pattern of events in the universe; you will also see ordinary people tending the aged and the sick, teaching the young, and helping others who are less fortunate than themselves; you will hear the loud clang of cymbals and drums, the shrill and melodious sound of flutes, and slow, rhythmic voices chanting to the beat of a wooden block. You will hear the silence of a meditation hall, the soft gait of feet walking on the flagstones of monastic cloisters, and the occasional sound of a bell amid the rustle of leaves. All these are features in the spiritual landscape of Taoism—a tradition of wisdom accumulated over thousands of years that has changed human consciousness, and yet been changed by it.

This book is a guide, and a guide differs from a textbook or an anthology of translated texts.

First, a true guide is based on the personal experience of someone who has traveled the terrain; one cannot write a guide about places one has not been to. Information contained in a guide is not based on book knowledge alone but on experience.

Second, a true guide has a perspective and does not pretend to be objective. What is seen is never independent of the observer. As a guide to the spiritual landscape of Taoism, this book shows things that I have experienced and enjoyed.

Third, a true guide does not pretend to be complete. Any landscape, physical or spiritual, is rich beyond imagination. This book is meant to give you enough information to get started. It is a map and field guide to a territory; it is not the territory itself.

Finally, a guide alerts travelers to possible dangers. The spiritual landscape is both attractive and forbidding, and travelers need to be aware of hazards along the way. Therefore, throughout the book, I shall point out which are the safest paths and which are the hazardous routes in the spiritual terrain of Taoism.

This book is divided into three parts: History of Taoism, Systems of Taoism, and Taoist Practices.

History of Taoism

It is important to know the history of a wisdom tradition and be connected to its origins. Part One presents a brief history of Taoism.

We begin by looking at how the shamans of ancient China laid down the foundations of Taoism. Several thousand years ago, before there was the idea of *the Tao* and before a philosophy was built around it, tribal leaders made offerings to the sky, earth, mountains, valleys, and rivers to renew the bond between humanity and the sacred powers. They danced movements of power that took them to distant realms to gain knowledge and wisdom. We can still see some of these practices today in Taoist religious ceremonies and in the "moving meditation" and exercises of internal health.

Next we turn to the Classical Period—that span of Chinese history between the eighth and third centuries BCE. During this time lived some of the greatest philosophers of China: Lao-tzu, Confucius, Han-fei-tzu, Chuang-tzu, Sun-tzu, and Mo-tzu. This era gave us the *Tao-te ching* and its philosophy of nonaction (*wu-wei*) and harmonious living. The *Tao-te ching* is still the most widely translated Chinese book, and for many Westerners the book that gave them their first glimpse of Taoism.

The history of Taoism took an interesting turn between the first and seventh centuries CE: a form of Taoism that combined magic and devotion emerged. Under the influence of a charismatic spiritual leader, Chang Tao-ling, Taoism became a religion. Chang's descendants completed the transformation of Taoism from a philosophy to an organized religion, creating a system of rituals, liturgies, and a priesthood. Others, inspired by Chang's form of Taoism and impressed by Buddhism's growing collection of scriptures, compiled a large number of "sacred" texts and claimed that these writings were transmitted by the deities. These scriptures are some of the oldest texts in the Taoist canon.

While the peasants followed the popular religious leaders and entrusted their welfare to talismans and amulets, the middle class and nobility were attracted to another kind of Taoism. Around the end of the third century CE, a noblewoman by the name of Wei Hua-ts'un founded the Shang-ch'ing (High Pure) school of Taoism. The Shang-ch'ing practitioners visualized images of deities, invoked the deities' names, drew talismans, and entered into a mystical union with the sacred powers. Although this form of Taoism is now rarely practiced, its influence can be seen in today's Taoist sacred ceremonies and health arts.

Parallel to the rise of Taoist mysticism was the development of Taoist alchemy. Alchemical Taoism is concerned with cultivating health, longevity, and immortality, and is divided into external and internal alchemy. The School of External Alchemy believed that immortality could be attained by ingesting the appropriate minerals and herbs. It emerged in the third century CE and rose to the height of its development in the seventh and eighth centuries CE. The School of Internal Alchemy did not believe in ingesting external substances and held that longevity and immortality could be attained by transforming body and mind from within. The beginnings of internal alchemy could be traced to the third century CE. However, the movement did not come into its own until external alchemy declined, around the tenth century CE. Alchemical Taoism introduced the idea of ch'i, or internal energy, and was responsible for giving Taoism its reputation as an art of health and longevity.

Finally we look at the synthesis of classical Taoist philosophy, internal alchemy, Buddhism, and Confucianism. By the eleventh century CE, alchemical Taoism had sunk into a quagmire of esoteric terminology and abused practices. Tired of the empty jargon and realizing that spiritual development required a balance of physical health and mental clarity, sages like Wang Ch'ung-yang, Chen Hsi-yi and Lü Tung-pin began to teach a form of Taoism that advocated the cultivation of both body and mind. Inspired by the Confucian philosophy of the original nature of goodness and the Zen techniques of stilling the mind, a synthesis of the three philosophies—Confucianism, Buddhism, and Taoism—was reached. This form of Taoism is found in the teachings of two major Taoist sects today: the

Complete Reality School (Ch'üan-chen) and the Earlier Heaven Way (Hsien-t'ien Tao).

Systems of Taoism

Part Two discusses different paths within Taoism. Although these paths are sometimes called schools, their teachings are not mutually exclusive.

Magical Taoism, the Way of Power, is the oldest form of Taoism practiced today. In Magical Taoism, power from the natural elements and from the spirits, immortals, and deities is invoked and channeled by the practitioner. Talismans are an important part of Magical Taoism: power can be channeled into objects for protection and healing. This path of Taoism is the least known to Westerners, and is often shrouded in mystery and misunderstanding. It is also the most demanding and difficult path to follow.

Divinational Taoism, the Way of Seeing, is based on understanding the workings of the universe and seeing the patterns of change. Celestial divination is based on skylore and the observation of the sun, moon, and stars; terrestrial divination is based on earth science and the observation of the features of landforms. Divinational Taoism believes that seeing and understanding the patterns of the universe will help us live in harmony with change, and to live in harmony with change is to live according to the principles of the Tao.

Ceremonial Taoism, the Way of Devotion, believes that the destiny of humanity is governed by sacred powers. By performing the correct ceremonies, humanity enters into a bond with the sacred powers and receives blessings and protection from them. Liturgies and rituals are integral to this form of Taoism. There is a clear distinction between practitioner and believer. In Ceremonial Taoism, the practitioner is a person trained to perform the ceremonies; the believer is the individual who trusts the leader of the ceremony to represent him or her before the sacred powers.

Internal-Alchemical Taoism, the Way of Transformation, advocates changing mind and body to attain health, longevity, and immortality. Central to its beliefs is the idea that internal energy, or ch'i, in the body is the foundation of health. Thus, Internal-Alchemical Taoism advocates cultivating, gathering, and circulating energy. Of all the paths of Taoism, this one is the most dangerous.

Action and Karma Taoism, the Way of Right Action, focuses on accumulating merit by doing charitable works. Its origin lies in the traditional Chinese belief that good deeds bring reward and unethical deeds invite retribution. After Buddhism was introduced into China, the belief in karmic retribution was incorporated into this form of Taoism. Action and Karma Taoism became a sophisticated system of ethics in which the rewards of an ethical life are health and well-being.

Taoist Practices

In Part Three we look at four kinds of practices: meditation, cultivation of the body, sacred ceremony, and the magical arts.

There are many forms of Taoist meditation, different sects practicing different styles. Sometimes, even within the same sect, the form of meditation changes as the practitioner advances spiritually. For example, Shang-ch'ing meditation uses visualizations to help the practitioner achieve a mystical union with the deities. Insight meditation, or internal observation, another style of Taoist meditation, is very similar to Buddhist vipassana meditation. A form of quiet sitting, like Zen meditation, is used by Taoists of the Complete Reality School to still the mind and tame the emotions. There are also forms of Taoist meditation for gathering, cultivating, and circulating internal energy. These types of meditation are most similar to kundalini yoga.

Taoism's preoccupation with physical health has inspired the development of techniques that cultivate the body. The best-known of these techniques is *ch'i-kung*, or the work of energy. Some ch'i-kung techniques are breathing exercises; others involve massaging various areas of the body; some are static postures, not unlike those of hatha yoga; and some incorporate methods of circulating energy into natural activities such as sitting, standing, walking, and sleeping. Another method of cultivating the body is known as tendon-changing. This technique is said to have been introduced by Bodhidharma, the Buddhist, to the Shaolin Temple in the fourth century CE. Designed to strengthen and relax the muscles, tendons, and ligaments, these exercises were originally used by Buddhist monks to prepare themselves for long sessions of zazen, or sitting meditation. The techniques were adopted by the Taoists, who saw their value in strengthening the muscular and skeletal system. Internal martial arts, such as t'ai-chi ch'uan and pa-k'ua chang, are also methods of cultivating the body. These systems of movement are designed to correct unhealthy body postures and facilitate the natural flow of energy.

Ceremony is an important part of Taoist practice. All Taoist ceremonies are preceded by rituals of purification designed to cleanse the bodies and minds of the participants. Ceremonies are performed to honor the deities and renew the bond between humanity and the sacred powers. Typically, a ceremony involves chanting, invocation, and other ritualistic performances, such as dancing and drawing talismans.

The final category of Taoist practices is the magical arts. The most popular form practiced today is talismanic magic. Using symbols and words of power written on a strip of paper, this magic invokes the deities and spirits to heal and protect, warding off malevolent forces. The preparation and use of talismanic magic require not only skill but also trust in the known and unknown powers of the universe.

Each chapter in this guide is divided into two sections: the first presents an introductory survey of the subject matter; the closing section contains a list of recommended readings to help you in your exploration of Taoism.

This guide will have been successful if it stimulates your interest. It will also have been successful if it tells you that an investigation of Taoism is not what you want—and in that case, you can stop immediately and save your resources. Most of all, this guide will be successful if you enjoy what you see in your travels.

As with visiting unknown regions of the world, when you journey through a spiritual landscape, you must let go of expectations. Be prepared to be rattled, enticed, excited, awed, and dumbfounded. There is no set way on how you should react to what you see. The richness of a spiritual tradition is best experienced when you let your thoughts, feelings, and senses participate fully.

The information in this guide is not the final word: it is impossible to document every detail in a spiritual landscape; moreover, as more people connect with the spiritual terrain, better guides will be written. Meanwhile, I hope you will enjoy this spiritual armchair journey. May this guide serve you well!

PART ONE

HISTORY OF TAOISM

1
Shamanic Origins
(3000–800 BCE)

F IVE THOUSAND YEARS AGO, a tribal people settled along the shores of the Yellow River in northern China. These people had not developed a national identity, nor did they venture far from the banks of the river that carved its path through the dusty plateau. Their daily activities consisted of hunting, fishing, tending their herds, and planting small plots of wheat and millet. At night they gathered by their fires and looked up into the mysterious dome of faint, twinkling lights. Sometimes the howling of wild animals in the dark would remind them of having lost their herds to powerful beasts; at other times they would recall fleeing from the raging river that overflowed its banks and wiped out their crops. But they would also talk about how their chiefs pursued the wild animals and fought back the floods. These chieftains possessed unusual powers: they had mastery over the elements, the rivers bent to their will, plants and animals yielded their secrets to them, they talked with invisible powers, and they traveled across the sky and beneath the earth to gather knowledge that would help the tribe. The greatest of these chiefs was Yü.

The Legendary Yü

Legends tell us that Yü was no ordinary mortal. He had no mother and he came directly from the body of his father, Kun. Kun was

11

selected by the tribal leader, Shun, to battle the floods. When Kun failed, he was punished by the powers, and his dead body was left abandoned on a mountain side. For three years, Yü lay inside his father's dead body. When Kun was revived, he was transformed into a brown bear, and he opened up his own belly and brought out his son, Yü. Immediately, Yü also changed himself into a bear, and we are told that, throughout his life, Yü shape-shifted between man and bear, and always walked with a shuffle that was known as bear's gait. In the Chou dynasty, a thousand years after the legendary times of Yü, priests still dressed in bearskins and grunted and shuffled as they danced the gait of power to honor Yü the Great.

We are told that, when Yü grew up, he carried on the work of his father. Yü was able to succeed where his father had failed because the sacred powers gave him the mythical book *Shui-ching* (The Book of Power over Waters). Yü also journeyed frequently to the stars to learn from the celestial spirits. The Pace of Yü (fig. 1.1), a dance of power that carried Yü to the sky, is preserved in the Taoist texts. These movements were danced by generations of Taoist priests, mystics, and sorcerers, and by the practitioners of the internal martial arts today.

Yü was able not only to assume the shape of animals, he also trusted and understood them, and in return they yielded him their secrets. When the flood waters receded, Yü saw a tortoise emerge from the river. On its shell was the pattern of the Lo-shu pa-k'ua that described the nature of flux and change in the universe. This pattern was to become the basis of the divination arts of China.

Everything that legend has attributed to Yü characterizes him as a shaman. Mircea Eliade, in his classic study on shamanism, described the following features as part of the shamanic experience: flight to the sky, the journey underground, the dance of power, ecstasy and sudden revelation, the power to converse with animals, power over the elements, healing, and knowledge and use of plants. In fact, in ancient Chinese society, there was a class of people, called the *wu*, whose abilities resembled those typically attributed to sha-

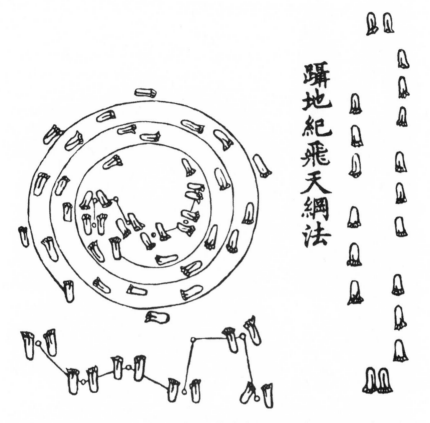

FIGURE 1.1. The Pace of Yü. Also called the Steps of Yü. From the *T'ai-shang chu-kuo chiu-min tsung-chen pi-yao* (The Great One's True Secret Essentials of Helping the Nation and Saving the People). The pattern on the right—called the Steps of the Celestial Ladder—is used to lift the dancer up to the sky. The pattern at the foot of the illustration traces the configuration of the Northern Bushel (the Big Dipper)—a pattern used to take the dancer to the Northern Bushel stars. In the pattern at top left—the spiral—the dancer starts at the outermost part of the circle and spirals progressively toward the center—traveling to the North Pole Star and the Northern Bushel stars. The inscription (center) reads, Method of Walking the Earth's Pattern and Flying Through the Celestial Net.

mans. This has led Eliade to identify the wu of ancient China as shamans.

Yü was a wu, or shaman, and he lived in a society where shamans were important members of the tribal community. His father, too, was a shaman capable of shape-shifting into a bear. Shun, the tribal king who rewarded Yü's success in taming the flood with a kingship, was also a shaman. It was said that Shun was the first person to journey to the sky, and he was taught by the daughter of his predecessor, Yao.

Shamanism in Literate China

Shamanism entered a new phase in ancient China with the development of literacy and a sedentary society. By the twelfth century BCE, in the early part of the Chou dynasty, kings and nobles employed shamans as advisers, diviners, and healers. Shamanism became an institution, and shamans were expected to exercise their ability as a duty. Shamans employed by the state or by individuals were expected to fulfill certain functions, and failure in an assignment was often punishable by death. The historical records of the Chou dynasty document many failures of shamans, suggesting that many so-called shamans did not have the powers of Yü. Although they dressed in bearskins and danced the Pace of Yü, these ceremonial shamans did not acquire the power of the animal spirit in the dance.

Duties of Shamans in Chou Society

During the Chou dynasty, the duties of the shamans were inviting the spirits, interpreting dreams, reading omens, rainmaking, healing, and celestial divination.

1. *Inviting the spirits.* A major task of the shamans of the Chou dynasty was to invite the spirits to visit the mortal realm and offer themselves as a place for the spirit to stay temporarily. The visitation of the spirit generally began with a dance, which put the shaman in

a trance and allowed the spirit to enter the shaman's body. This is different from possession, in which the spirit enters the body of the possessed, which then causes the trance. The shaman's trance is the state of consciousness necessary for the visitation, rather than the result of the visitation. As Eliade asserts, this is the hallmark of a shamanic experience, making shamans different from psychic mediums and sorcerers whose magic is based on possession.

2. *Interpreting dreams.* Dreams are considered to be carriers of omens, and one of the shaman's tasks is to interpret these messages from the spirits. In ancient China, the dream was also linked to the shaman's journey to the other realms. The ceremony of summoning the soul of the dead was conducted by a shaman called "the dream master." This suggests that although dreams of nonshamans were messages from the spirits, they were not under the dreamer's control, whereas the dreams of the shamans were journeys to other realms of existence in which the shamans were in full control of the dream journey.

3. *Reading omens.* Another task of the shaman was to observe the changes in nature, predict the course of events, and decide whether it was auspicious or not to engage in a certain activity. Thus, shamans in the Chou dynasty were adept in the knowledge of the *I-ching* (the classic work of divination from ancient China known as the Book of Change) and were the forerunners of diviners.

4. *Rainmaking.* It was also the task of the shaman to pray for rain. The rainmaking ceremony involved dancing and singing. The Chinese word for spirit (*ling*) consists of three radicals: one meaning *rain*, another (showing three mouths), *chanting*, and the third, *shaman*. Often, the shaman would be exposed to the sun, using his or her suffering to "persuade" the sacred powers to send rain. Although the specifics of the ceremony have changed down the years, praying for rain has continued to be an integral part of Chinese religious ritual, and today the ceremony is performed by Taoist priests.

5. *Healing.* Healing was another major task of the shaman. In the earliest times, this was primarily the responsibility of the shamaness. We are told that, in the healing ceremony, the shamaness grasped a

green snake in her right hand and a red snake in her left hand and climbed into the mountains to gather the herbs that would restore life and health to a sick or dying person.

The ancient Chinese believed that illness was the result of malevolent spirits invading the body; it was therefore logical that the task of healing should fall on the shoulders of the shaman, who had the ability to deal with both good and malevolent spirits.

6. *Celestial divination.* During the latter part of the Chou dynasty, celestial divination was very popular. It was believed that, given harmony in the skies, there would be peace, prosperity, and harmony on earth. The key to peace and prosperity lay in following the Celestial Way, or will of heaven, and for the Celestial Way to be followed, the meaning of celestial phenomena must be interpreted; thus, shamans were employed in the court to observe the skies and interpret celestial events.

The Shamanic Tradition of Southern China

When shamanism declined in the mainstream society of the Chou dynasty, pockets of shamanic culture remained in regions around the river valley of the Yang-tze and China's southeastern coast (for a map of China, see appendix 2). These areas were occupied by three feudal kingdoms: Ch'u, Wu, and Yüeh.

The land of Ch'u was situated along the Yang-tze valley—a region considered barbaric and primitive by the sophisticated northerners of the ruling dynasties. Vast cultural differences existed between the north (Yellow River valley) and the south (Yang-tze valley): the people of Ch'u were passionate; the northerners were reserved; when the northern people abandoned their beliefs in the spirits of the land after they had developed literacy, the southern people continued to believe in the powers of nature.

The lands of Wu and Yüeh, farther to the east, were even more removed from the mainstream of Chou civilization. The shamans of Yüeh used incantations and mantras to ward off malevolent spirits, restrain wild animals, and battle other humans. Moreover, it was in

Wu and Yüeh that talismans were used as objects of power. These talismanic scripts later became an integral part of Taoist magic and sorcery.

Throughout China's history, even after the the kingdoms of Ch'u, Wu, and Yüeh disappeared as political entities, their regional cultures continued to influence the wider culture's philosophy, religion, and spiritual practices.

The Legacy of Shamanism in Later Developments of Taoism

The most obvious incorporation of shamanic practices into Taoism was found in the religious and magical aspects of Taoism that emerged in the Han dynasty (206 BCE–219 CE). Like the Yüeh shamans, Taoist magicians used incantations and talismans to ward off malevolent spirits and heal the sick. Indeed, the use of water and mirrors to combat malevolent and destructive forces, which can be traced back to the Yüeh shamans, is seen in the practice of Taoist magic today.

Another legacy of shamanism is the Pace of Yü and the flight to the stars. This aspect of shamanism found its way into a form of Taoist mysticism known as Shang-ch'ing Taoism in the fourth century CE and inspired writings that would become a major part of the Taoist canon.

The shamanic journey underground would also become central to Taoist magic and mysticism in the hands of Tung-fang Shuo, a Han dynasty Taoist, who wrote a guide to journeying through the roots of China's five sacred mountains. Today, we find elements of these underground journeys in Taoist ceremonies: priests still enter the underworld to rescue dead souls who have been abducted by malevolent spirits.

An even greater influence on Taoism came through shamanism's impact on the philosophy of Lao-tzu and Chuang-tzu. This influence is often unrecognized, because many scholars consider the Tao-chia (philosophical Taoism) and the Tao-chiao (religious Taoism) as opposing branches of Taoist thinking. A little-known entry in Ssu-ma Ch'ien's monumental work of history titled *Shi-chi* (Historical Records) in the biography of Lao-tzu, reads, "Lao-tzu was a native of Ch'u, of the county of Fu, of the village of Li." Lao-tzu, the founder of the philosophy of Taoism, lived in a society that had a strong shamanic culture. Moreover, several prominent Chinese scholars have also recently noted similarities in language construction between the *Tao-te ching* and the literature of the Ch'u culture.

Similarly with Chuang-tzu: the *Lü-shih ch'un-ch'iu* (Lü's Spring and Autumn Annals), a history of the Spring and Autumn Period of the Chou dynasty (770–476 BCE) written during the Warring States (475–221 BCE), tells us that Chuang-tzu came from the township of Mong, in Sung, a vassal state of Ch'u. Ssu-ma Ch'ien, the Grand Historian, concurred; Chuang-tzu, he wrote, was a native of Sung, a small kingdom that got amalgamated into the state of Ch'u. In the next chapter we shall see how Lao-tzu's and Chuang-tzu's philosophy grew out of the shamanic culture that prevailed in regions south of the Yang-tze.

FURTHER READINGS

Michael Harner's book *The Way of the Shaman* is probably the best introduction to the theory and practice of shamanism. Harner, who received his training from South American shamans, presents shamanism in a way that is very accessible to people who have no previous knowledge of the discipline.

For more detail about shamanic practices of various cultures, Mircea Eliade's classic work, *Shamanism*, is still the most authoritative source around. However, unlike Harner's work, which focuses on the *practice* of shamanism, Eliade's research is purely scholastic.

Of all the Chinese sources, the *Ch'u-tz'u (Songs of the Land of the South)* is the most colorful and fascinating. Four poems in the collection have a strong shamanic flavor: "The Nine Songs," "Summoning the Soul," "Far-off Journeys," and "Questions to Heaven." The tales of Yü the shaman are found in the poem "Questions to Heaven." There is a full translation of the *Ch'u-tz'u*, titled *The Songs of the South*, by David Hawkes.

Another translation of one of the poems, titled "Far-off Journey," can be found in Livia Kohn's Taoist anthology *The Taoist Experience*. I prefer Kohn's translation over that of Hawkes: Kohn conveys a better feel of the original.

2

The Classical Period
(700–220 BCE)

WE NOW MOVE to historical time. A thousand years have passed since Yü the Great danced his gait of power, traveled among the stars, and journeyed beneath the earth. By now, the tribes who lived along the banks of the Yellow River have built cities and have become citizens of a large and prospering empire. Families who had helped the king secure his power were given lands and titles. The kings were no longer shamans; the duties of performing the sacred rites have been delegated to professionals—shamans employed by the court. The king was involved in only two ceremonies—the most important, those of Spring Planting and Autumn Thanksgiving.

As long as the emperor was powerful and assertive, the feudal system worked well. The nobles helped with local administration and defended the nation against border tribes. These tribespeople were becoming envious of the wealth of the Chou empire. But not all the emperors were conscientious and virtuous, and after three hundred years of strong and centralized rule, things fell apart for the ruling house.

In 770 BCE, the political and social structures of the Chou empire were disintegrating. For the next five hundred years, the people of China would live through political chaos and civil war. This era of internal war began with the Spring and Autumn Period (770–476

BCE), when powerful feudal lords expanded their territory through military conquest and political intrigue, to be followed by the Warring States Period (475–221 BCE), when the large number of feudal states was reduced to seven superpowers. The period ended when one of the seven, Ch'in, defeated its rivals and reunited China.

Within this period of five hundred years lived the greatest philosophers that China, and the world, had ever known: Confucius and Mencius, the upholders of social order and virtue; Mo-tzu, the philosopher of universal love and self-sacrifice; Han-fei-tzu, the legalist; Kung-sun Lung, the sophist; Sun-tzu, the military strategist; and the giants of Taoist thinking, Lao-tzu, Chuang-tzu, and Lieh-tzu.

This part of the history of Taoism is known as the Classical Period, so named because the three classics of Taoism—*Lao-tzu* (also known as *Tao-te ching*), *Chuang-tzu*, and *Lieh-tzu*—all came from this time. The Classical Period can be divided into two parts—one earlier, in the Spring and Autumn Period, and the other later, coinciding with the Warring States Period.

The Political and Historical Background of the Spring and Autumn Period (770–476 BCE)

The distinguishing feature of the Spring and Autumn Period is the rise of semiautonomous feudal states. By about 800 BCE, the nobles who had been given titles and land for helping the Chou establish its dynasty had become so powerful that they lived like petty kings. Five great noble houses emerged: Ch'i, Ch'in, Sung, Chin, and Ch'u. They were known as the Five Warlords of the Spring and Autumn Period.

During the Spring and Autumn Period, the great feudal lords used their resources to build military strength and expand their territory, subjugating the smaller fiefs. In the beginning of the Spring and Autumn Period, there were some one hundred and forty feudal states; three hundred years later, when that period ended, only forty-four were left.

These warlords were fully aware that a strong state was not built by military power alone. Diplomacy and statesmanship were equally important. How and where would they find qualified political advisers?

The demand for political and military advisers produced a new social class that was unique to the latter part of the Chou dynasty. These were the mercenary statesmen and itinerant advisers who traveled from one state to another, offering their skills. Fame, wealth, and power that had been limited to the hereditary nobility were now accessible to common citizens. Of course, politics was a risky business, for intrigues were rampant and competition was fierce. An adviser could be in favor one day and out of favor the next. While many were attracted by fame and power, some truly had the vision of building a better society, and tried to counsel the rulers to be virtuous and benevolent. Confucius was one of them; Lao-tzu was another.

Classical Taoism in the Spring and Autumn Period: Lao-tzu and the Tao-te ching

Lao-tzu is generally acknowledged as the founder of the philosophy of Taoism. We know little more about Lao-tzu the person than what has already been mentioned: he was named Li Erh and was a native of the southern feudal state of Ch'u; he was born into the educated upper class and held a minor government post, serving as a librarian in the imperial archives. We do not know his reasons for retirement from the civil service, but we could guess that, like Confucius, he became disillusioned with the political intrigues and the ruthlessness of the feudal lords. The next thing we hear about Lao-tzu is more legendary than historical: it was said that he came to some kind of enlightenment, traveled to the western frontier, and disappeared (or became immortal). Before his departure, he dictated a treatise of five thousand words to a frontier guardsman (called a gatekeeper). The treatise is now known as the *Tao-te ching*, or *Lao-tzu*, and the gatekeeper was Wen-shih (also known as Wen-tzu), who became the first disciple of Lao-tzu.

The *Tao-te ching* is the first text of Taoism, and it is certain that the book was written by more than one person. Most historians and scholars now agree that the *Tao-te ching* was a product of the Spring and Autumn Period. Like its contemporaries, the text discussed statecraft and offered political alternatives. It was only in the Taoism of the *Chuang-tzu* and the *Lieh-tzu* that noninvolvement was advocated. The Taoists of the *Tao-te ching* were not social dropouts. For them, the sage was an individual who understood the natural way of things (the Tao) and lived in harmony with it; therefore, changes in society must come from changes within individuals, and changes in individuals could come only from following the principles of the Tao. It is this feature that distinguished the Taoism of the *Tao-te ching* from the teachings of Confucius. For Confucius, a peaceful and harmonious society was one in which people observed and followed the correct rituals and codes of interpersonal behavior; it did not matter what the nature of the universe was. For the Taoist philosophers, understanding the natural order of things was paramount, because only by knowing the principles of the Tao could people live in harmony.

The Teachings of the Tao-te ching

ON THE TAO

The Tao is the source of life of all things. It is nameless, invisible, and ungraspable by normal modes of perception. It is boundless and cannot be exhausted, although all things depend on it for existence. Hidden beneath transition and change, the Tao is the permanent underlying reality. These ideas will become the center of all future Taoist thinking.

Although the Tao is the source of all life, it is not a deity or spirit. This is quite different from the shaman's animistic view of the universe. In the *Tao-te ching*, the sky, the earth, rivers, and mountains are part of a larger and unified power, known as Tao, which is an impersonal and unnamed force behind the workings of the universe. However, in the *Tao-te ching*, this unnamed and unnameable power is not entirely neutral; it is benevolent: "The Celestial Way is to benefit others and not to cause harm" (chapter 81, *Tao-te ching*); and since the "Celestial Way follows the Way of the Tao" (chapter 25, *Tao-te ching*), we can assume that in the *Tao-te ching*, the Tao is a benevolent force.

ON SAGEHOOD

Some parts of the *Tao-te ching* show strong influence from the shamanic culture of Ch'u; they are to be found in the discussions on sagehood and on cultivating life.

Recall that Lao-tzu was a native of Ch'u. The students who recorded his teachings were most likely natives of the same region. Philosopher-teachers of the Spring and Autumn Period rarely established schools outside their native states: most of their students came from the local or neighboring towns. That is why the students of Confucius, who was a native of the state of Lu, and lived and taught there, were called the "gentlemen of Lu." Similarly, the students of Lao-tzu were most likely people from his native state of Ch'u. This has led many Chinese scholars to assert that Taoism was rooted in the culture of the south, because Lao-tzu and Chuang-tzu were natives of Ch'u and their followers came from the same cultural background.

The Taoist sage had abilities similar to those of the shaman of Yü's times. He or she was immune to poison, talked to the animals, and had a body that was as soft as an infant. Sexual energy was strong, and the sage practiced methods of prolonging life. These shamanic qualities of the sage remain a permanent feature of Taoism up to this day.

The Taoist sage was also a very involved member of the community; in fact, Taoist sages made ideal rulers. One of the most famous ideas of Taoism, and also the source of a lot of misunderstanding, is *wu-wei*. This word, used in describing the sage and often translated as nonaction, gives the impression that the Taoist sages "did nothing." This is inaccurate, and could not be used to describe all Taoists. Wu-wei had different meanings for different Taoist philosophers.

The wu-wei of the *Tao-te ching* is different from the wu-wei of *Chu-ang-tzu*, which is different again from the wu-wei of *Lieh-tzu*.

Wu-wei in the *Tao-te ching* is "going with the principles of the Tao," and the path of the Tao is a benevolent one. Thus, wu-wei in the *Tao-te ching* is not "doing nothing"; it is not even the noninterference advocated in the *Chuang-tzu*. In the *Tao-te ching*, wu-wei means not using force. The sagely ruler who cares for his subjects in a nonintrusive way also practices wu-wei. Far from doing nothing, the Taoist sage of the *Tao-te ching* is an active member of society and is fit to be a king.

ON CULTIVATING LIFE

In the *Tao-te ching*, the sage is one who cultivates life. The *Tao-te ching* describes two methods of cultivating life: physical techniques and attitude.

The physical techniques included regulation of breath, physical postures that are the precursors of calisthenics, and possibly techniques of retaining and cultivating sexual energy for the return to youth and vitality.

On the matter of lifestyle and attitude, the *Tao-te ching* states that desire, attachment to material things, and activities that excite the mind, rouse the emotions, tire the body, and stimulate the senses, are all detrimental to health.

In the early form of Classical Taoism, it was possible to be active in politics and not sacrifice physical and mental health. The problem arises only when one gets attached to fame and fortune and does not know when to stop. The message in the *Tao-te ching* is: Cultivate the physical and mental qualities of the sage; get involved and help in a nonintrusive way; retire when the work is done.

The *Tao-te ching* values shamanic qualities and personal power, but it does not share the animistic worldview of the shamans. Instead of accepting a world of diverse spirits, it sees the Tao, a unified and unnameable force, as the underlying reality of all things.

The philosophy of the *Tao-te ching* grew out of the Spring and Autumn Period; however, it was also a cultural product from the region of Ch'u. In shedding the shamanic world of diverse spirits and retaining the personal power of the shaman, the *Tao-te ching* represents a transition from shamanic beliefs to a philosophical system with a unified view of the nature of reality (the Tao), the sage, and the cultivation of life.

The Political and Historical Background of the Warring States Period (475–221 BCE)

As the Spring and Autumn Period was drawing to a close, in 475 BCE, there were forty-four feudal states. In 390 BCE, this number was reduced to seven large states and three small ones. With fewer small states to act as buffers between the large and powerful ones, territorial expansion came to a halt, because military conquest would henceforth involve a major confrontation between superpowers. However, with the Chou imperial lands reduced to the size of a small county, the possibility for another entity to conquer the rival powers and establish a unified rule became a possibility; thus, the demand for quality statesmen, diplomats, and military advisers in the Warring States Period surpassed even that of the Spring and Autumn Period. In fact, many of China's most famous philosophers lived during the Warring States Period. They included Mencius, the successor to Confucius, Mo-tzu who taught self-sacrifice and universal love, Kung-sun Lung, the legendary Kuei-ku Tzu, from whose school came some of the best military strategists and diplomats, and Chuang-tzu and Lieh-tzu, the Taoists.

By the time of the Warring States Period there had been more than three hundred years of war and political conflict, and some people were beginning to be convinced that any reform within the government was hopeless. Everywhere they looked they saw power-hungry nobles and unscrupulous ministers waiting for the chance to conquer their rivals. These people did not want to be involved in politics; in fact, they believed that the pursuit of fame and fortune was inherently opposed to the cultivation of health and longevity. Chuang-tzu was one of them, and he was open in his critique of all those who served the interests of the feudal lords. Lieh-tzu, another Taoist philosopher, also advocated noninvolvement, and both men regarded social conventions as the greatest enemy of personal freedom and integrity.

Classical Taoism in the Warring States Period

With Chuang-tzu and Lieh-tzu, Classical Taoism entered a new phase. Several features distinguished the Classical Taoism of the Warring States from the philosophy of the *Tao-te ching*:

First, the talk of sagely rulers and ideal governments is gone. Politics were dirty and dangerous; fame and fortune were not worth the sacrifice of freedom and longevity. Even the Yellow Emperor, a most respected figure in Chinese history, was called a meddler of people's minds. In fact, all the Confucian models of a benevolent ruler, like Yao and Shun, were mocked. This was very different from the Classical Taoism of the Spring and Autumn Period.

Second, the sage was no longer interested in ruling a country, or even offering his skills to one. In the *Tao-te ching*, the sage minimized his desires, lived simply, and attained longevity, while functioning as the head of the state. In the Warring States, the Taoists of the *Chuang-tzu* and *Lieh-tzu* believed that political involvement and longevity were inherently incompatible. With this change in the image of sagehood, the meaning of wu-wei also changed. Wu-wei now meant noninvolvement, or letting things be. The sage was no longer involved with or concerned about the matters of the world. While other people trapped themselves in fame, fortune, and socially accepted behavior, the sage ignored them, and was completely free.

Third, the Taoism of the Warring States came up with a different conception of the Tao. In the *Tao-te ching*, although the Tao was not a deity or a spirit-being, it had a benevolent nature. This quality disappeared in the *Chuang-tzu* and the *Lieh-tzu*. The Taoist philosophers of the Warring States saw the Tao as a neutral force. It was still the underlying reality of all things, but it was no longer a benevolent force. Moreover, the Tao had no control over the course of events: what would happen would happen, and nothing could be done to facilitate it or prevent it.

However, despite the differences, the Taoism of the Warring States Period and of the *Tao-te ching* had much in common. The Tao was still that nameless, formless source that was the foundation of all existence. It could not be perceived through normal sensory channels nor understood by rational thinking. The individual who understood the nature of the Tao and its workings was an enlightened being, or sage.

In the *Tao-te ching*, the Tao was regarded as the origin of all things; thus, everything shared a common ancestry. This thinking was developed further in the Taoism of the Warring States Period to imply that all things had equal standing in the universe. No one thing was more valuable than another, and no one species of animal (including humans) was more privileged than another. This famous "principle of the equality of all things" was introduced in the *Chuang-tzu*.

Like the *Tao-te ching*, the *Chuang-tzu* and *Lieh-tzu* contained descriptions of the sage that were unmistakably shamanic. The sage had power over the elements, communicated with animals, could soar through the skies, and perform incredible feats of power. The authors of the *Chuang-tzu* and *Lieh-tzu*, however, were not sympathetic to the "institutional" form of shamanism. Their views of shamans and sorcerers as charlatans are often taken to mean that Classical Taoism was hostile to shamans, but this is quite contrary to the truth: it was only the superficial form of shamanism that they had no patience for.

In the *Chuang-tzu* and *Lieh-tzu*, we continue to see the emphasis on caring for the body. Like the Taoists of the *Tao-te ching*, the Taoists of the Warring States Period advocated living a simple lifestyle with minimal desire, believing that too much excitement and satisfaction of the senses could harm body and mind. However, in the *Chuang-tzu* and *Lieh-tzu*, social and cultural norms were also condemned. Rules and regulations were obstacles to the freedom of expression and thinking and living in harmony with the Tao, or the natural way.

By the end of the Warring States Period, Classical Taoism became a voice speaking out against hypocrisy. Since society was corrupt, the only way not to be entangled in the web of truths and lies was to stay out. Thus, an alternative lifestyle, that of the hermit or recluse, emerged. Later, this lifestyle would be adopted not only by Taoists but by some of the greatest poets and artists of China. Far from being seen as escaping responsibility, hermits became the symbol of personal integrity, and their lifestyle an expression of individual freedom.

We have looked at more than five hundred years of Classical Taoist philosophy and seen how, in its early phase of development, Taoism was a voice that advocated reform with the hope of building a better society; and how, during the Warring States, Taoism lost some of its early ideals and began to take a negative view of politics, culture, and social rules, and simultaneously increased its emphasis on individual freedom and the cultivation of life. By the late Han (circa third century CE) and the Wei and Chin dynasties (in the fourth and fifth centuries CE), its distrust of the establishment—political, social, and cultural—was complete. However, whether it was optimistic or pessimistic, idealistic or disillusioned, active or escapist, Taoism was always a voice that spoke for the preservation of the natural way of the Tao.

FURTHER READINGS

There are many translations of the *Tao-te ching*. I find Wing-tsit Chan's classic translation still one of the best, because it retains the simplicity and clarity of the original text. Chan's translation is to be found in his collection of Chinese philosophical texts, *A Source Book in Chinese Philosophy*. For those interested in Chinese philosophy in general, this is a good book to have.

Recently, archaeologists in China have discovered another version of the *Tao-te ching*—the Ma-wang-tui text, titled *Te-tao ching*. There are some differences between this version and the standard one of the Taoist canon. The differences are interesting, but overall each version gives the same feel for the teachings of Lao-tzu's Taoism. The translation by Robert Henricks, titled *Lao-tzu te-tao ching*, is the best rendition in English of the Ma-wang-tui text.

Burton Watson's *The Complete Works of Chuang-tzu* is still the best translation of the *Chuang-tzu*. Not only is it readable, it is also scholarly, without being scholastic. I also like Watson's approach to reading the *Chuang-tzu*—an approach he discusses in the introduction to his *Complete Works*.

The *Lieh-tzu* is one of my favorite Taoist texts. Its down-to-earth approach and its literary style make it one of the best presentations of Taoist teachings. In my *Lieh-tzu: A Taoist Guide to Practical Living*, I have tried to present the voice of Lieh-tzu—to let him speak as he would to us in our times. This is a book to enjoy, and it can help you through the ups and downs of everyday life.

Another Taoist book that belongs to this period is the *Wen-tzu*. A translation of this text by Thomas Cleary is titled *Further Teachings of Lao-tzu: Understanding the Mysteries*. The *Wen-tzu* appears to be a continuation of the legacy of the *Tao-te ching*. Like the *Tao-te ching*, it has a dual focus—on government and statecraft, and on sagehood and the cultivation of life. Read the *Tao-te ching* before the *Wen-tzu*. You may also want to have both texts available so that you can compare them. Cleary's translation of the *Wen-tzu* reads well and introduces a great classic of Taoism that until recently escaped the attention of the Western public.

3

The Transformation of Taoism from Philosophy into Organized Religion (20 BCE–600 CE)

IF THE PERIODS known as Spring and Autumn and the Warring States were the golden age of Taoist philosophy, then the era between the beginning of the Eastern Han dynasty (25–219 CE) and the end of the Southern and Northern dynasties (304–589 CE) was the golden age of Taoist religion. During this era, Taoism became an organized religion, instituted a priesthood, developed a set of sacred ceremonies and scriptures, and acquired a large number of followers.

The Beginnings of Religious Taoism in the Western Han (206–8 BCE)

Although it is often said that Chang Tao-ling singlehandedly changed Taoism from philosophy to religion in the Eastern Han dynasty (25–219 CE), this statement is exaggerated. Had the historical conditions that facilitated the transformation of Taoism from philosophy to religion not been in place, Chang Tao-ling's efforts would not have succeeded.

Several factors facilitated the transformation of Taoism from philosophy to religion, and these foundations were laid during the late Warring States and the early (or Western) Han.

The unification of China by the Ch'in dynasty brought an end to the demand for mercenary statesmen and itinerant political advisers.

The Han dynasty that followed the Ch'in also ruled a unified China. Moreover, the early Han emperors were determined not to repeat the mistakes of the Chou dynasty: they centralized the government and stripped the nobility of their power; thus, mercenary statesmen could no longer make their living by offering advice to the feudal lords. Many itinerant political advisers were trained in the arts of longevity, healing, and divination, and when military and political advice was no longer in demand, the wandering philosophers offered their other skills: divination, healing, and the arts of longevity. Thus was born in the Ch'in and early Han dynasties a unique social class. This class of people were the *fang-shih*, or "masters of the formulae."

In the early Han, the fang-shih could be divided roughly into two groups: those who specialized in magic, divination, and healing, and those who specialized in the arts of longevity and immortality. The middle and upper classes were preoccupied with longevity, but the peasants and other less fortunate social classes had no use for that kind of luxury. For them, life was so miserable that longevity meant only prolonged suffering; what they wanted was assurance that storms and drought would not destroy their harvest, and that they would have a large and healthy family to work the fields. The fang-shih who answered their needs were the workers of magic. Their magic was called talismanic magic because it used symbols and words of power to invoke the spirits to heal and to protect.

Another factor that facilitated the transformation of Taoism from philosophy to religion was a belief in a hierarchy of spirits and the practice of honoring them with offerings. This primitive form of organized religion was advocated by Mo-tzu, who generally is better known for his teachings of universal love and self-sacrifice. During the late Warring States, the followers of Mo-tzu (the Mohists) had developed systematic procedures for making offerings to the sacred powers. Throughout the Warring States, there were shrines devoted to honoring the guardian spirits of a location, such as a mountain pass or a valley. The Mohists, moreover, trained people to tend them. The Mohists lost their influence in the Han dynasty, but the shrines remained. Thus, when Taoism began to have its shrines and religious leaders, it was only continuing an already established tradition.

Another condition that facilitated the transformation of Taoism into a religion was the decline of state-organized ceremonies. During the Chou dynasty, the state ceremonies were performed by shamans employed at the court. When the shamans lost the personal power they had held in prehistoric times, they could no longer fulfill the spiritual needs of the people. As time went on, the real meaning of the ceremonies was forgotten: the festivals became celebrations without spiritual value. The final blow to the state-organized ceremonies came from the early Han emperors, who decided to promote Taoism. The state-employed shamans ceased to exist and their positions in the imperial court and with aristocratic families were replaced by the fang-shih.

The disappearance of the court shamans and traditional ceremonies in the Han dynasty allowed religious Taoism, as a form of organized religion, with ceremonies, to develop and take hold. Religious Taoism made its appearance in the Eastern Han (25–219 CE) and reached the height of its development in the Wei (220–265 CE), Chin (265–420 CE), and the Southern and Northern dynasties (304–589 CE).

Taoism Becomes an Organized Religion:
Eastern Han (25–219 CE)

In 150 CE, the Han emperor set up a shrine for Lao-tzu and conducted official ceremonies for honoring him. There are two kinds of shrines in Chinese culture: those that honor ancestors and those that honor the sacred powers. Since Lao-tzu was not an ancestor of the Han emperor, we must conclude that it was as a sacred power that he was honored. Thus, Lao-tzu had been transformed from a historical figure to a deity, or sacred power. This does not mean, however, that Lao-tzu was worshiped in the way that worship is understood in Judeo-Christian religions. In Chinese culture, the making of offerings to sacred powers or ancestors is not equivalent to worshiping them.

Ceremonial offerings at shrines have led many Westerners to believe that the Chinese worship their ancestors. This is a misunderstanding. Ancestors are remembered and honored with offerings; they are not worshiped. Similarly, making offerings to the sacred powers is a way of honoring and thanking them for protection and help.

An understanding of this relationship that the Chinese people have with the sacred powers is central to understanding the beliefs and practices of religious Taoism. Although religious Taoism introduced new deities and spirits, the cultural meaning of ceremony and offering remained unchanged throughout Chinese history.

The appearance of imperial shrines dedicated to Lao-tzu made it natural to invest Lao-tzu with a title and identify him as the chief deity of a religion. This was what Chang Tao-ling did toward the end of the Eastern Han dynasty.

Chang Tao-ling came from the southern part of China, a region where, as we have noted, shamanism and the belief in magic had always been strong. Historical records tell us that Chang was trained in the Confucian classics, but toward his middle years became interested in the teachings of Lao-tzu and the arts of longevity. It was said that he traveled and lived in Shu, the western part of China, to learn the secrets of immortality. The region of Shu occupies modern-day Szechuan and parts of Yunnan province. This area is isolated from the rest of China. Szechuan is a river basin surrounded by mountains; its only access is through the gorge where the river flows out. Szechuan has a culture of its own, and during the time of Chang Tao-ling was populated by tribes who still practiced shamanism in the ancient way. Yunnan is even more remote and mountainous. To its people who lived in its isolated villages, spirits were real, and magic was a central part of their lives.

Chang Tao-ling claimed that the teachings were revealed to him by Lao-tzu, who also gave him the power to heal the sick and ward off malevolent spirits. We can never know the truth of this claim, but it is likely that Chang apprenticed himself to the master shamans of Shu and acquired their skills. As a native of the south, Chang was probably also familiar with the talismanic magic that came from the old Wu and Yüeh cultures that had survived even after these king-doms met their end in the late Spring and Autumn Period.

Using talismanic water to heal the sick, Chang Tao-ling won a large following in Szechuan and the southern regions of China. Talismanic water is water that contains the ashes of a talisman that was burned ceremonially. The talisman is a strip of yellow paper with a special script written on it in red (fig. 3.1). Most of the scripts are incantations or invocations of spirits and deities. This is how the power of the deity is channeled into the talisman. When a sick person drinks talismanic water or is sprinkled with it, the power of the deity will enter the patient and fight off the malevolent spirits that cause the illness.

Chang Tao-ling organized a religion around himself, invested Lao-tzu with the title T'ai-shang Lao-chün (the Great Lord on High), and he and his descendants became the cult's leaders. This religious movement was named the Way of the Five Bushels of Rice, because

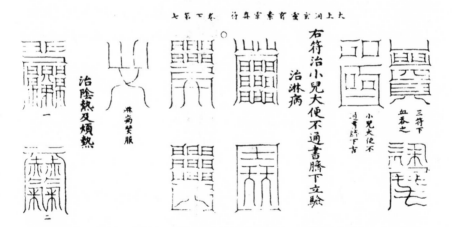

FIGURE 3.1. An example of a Ling-pao talisman of healing, from the *T'ai-shang tung-hsüan ling-pao su-ling chen-fu* (The Great One's True Basic Spirit Talismans of the Mysterious Cavern). The group of talismans on the right is for curing children's intestinal problems and constipation; the middle group is for curing gonorrhea; the group on the left is for curing fevers. Used by the Celestial Teachers.

initiation into the organization required a donation of five bushels of rice.

In the hands of Chang Tao-ling, Taoism became a religion. It had a founder, Lao-tzu, who as T'ai-shang Lao-chün was also its chief deity. It had the beginnings of a priestly leadership, Chang Tao-ling and his sons calling themselves the Celestial Teachers and becoming the mediators between the deities and the believers. And, most important of all, this religion served the spiritual needs of the common people.

Chang Tao-ling's movement would have remained a regional cult if his grandson, Chang Lu, had not developed political ambitions and pushed his influence into the central part of China. Moreover, several events cleared the way for the descendants of Chang Tao-ling to establish a fully organized religion complete with papal-like leadership, priesthood, scriptures and liturgy, rituals and ceremony, and magic.

The first event was the appearance of a book, the *T'ai-p'ing ching* (The Book of Peace and Balance), the first known "revealed" scripture in Taoism. While the Taoist classics such as the *Tao-te ching* and *Chuang-tzu* were philosophical treatises written by mortals, the authority of the *T'ai-p'ing ching* was attributed to the deities, known as Guardians of the Tao. *T'ai-p'ing ching* not only described a utopian ideal, it had all the features of a Taoist religious text. It invested deities with titles that had obvious Taoist references, such as Great Mystery, Primal Beginning, and so on; it had a theory of the creation of the universe; it emphasized the importance of ceremony and discipline; it described a system of reward and punishment; and, most importantly, it associated health and longevity with religious observances.

The second event that contributed to the success of Chang Tao-ling's descendants was the popularity of talismanic magic among nearly all the social classes. For a long time, historians had thought that only the poor and illiterate peasants believed in talismanic magic. In the next chapter, we shall see that talismans and invocations form a major part of Shang-ch'ing Taoism, a movement of religious Taoism among the aristocracy in the Wei and Chin dynasties (220–420 CE).

The third factor that helped the fortunes of the followers of the Celestial Teachers was a series of episodes in the dynastic history of China. This happened in the Chin dynasty. We shall look at these events in the following section.

The Golden Age of Taoist Religion:
Wei (220–265 CE), Chin (265–420 CE), and
Southern and Northern Dynasties (304–589 CE)

This was the golden age of Taoist religion. It was also the age of great chaos. During this period, China was broken into many small kingdoms, and—in the context of Chinese history—dynasties came and went in little more than the wink of an eye. Within a span of four hundred years, no less than twenty-five dynasties rose and fell, most of them with a life span of only twenty to fifty years. That Chinese historians were able to sort out and record what went on in this period is to be commended.

When the Han dynasty ended in 219 CE, China was divided into three warring kingdoms—Wei, Shu, and Wu—who fought each other for more than forty years. The Shu having been conquered by the Wei, the Wei dynasty took over (220–265 CE), and during the Wei, Chang Lu, the grandson of Chang Tao-ling, increased the influence of the Celestial Teachers movement. Chang Lu's religious organization was officially recognized by the state of Wei as the Cheng-i Meng-wei (Central Orthodox) school of Taoism. It was also during the Wei dynasty that a book titled *T'ai-shang ling-pao wu-fu ching* (The Highest Revelation of the Five Talismans of the Sacred Spirit) appeared. It is the earliest known Ling-pao (Sacred Spirit) text and the first of many Ling-pao texts that would be collected in the Taoist canon. The *Wu-fu ching* had the features of a religious scripture: talismans of protection, incantations, invocations of deities, a description of the administrative structure of the celestial realm, techniques of meditating and visualizing the deities, and vari-

ous recipes for ingesting herbs and minerals for immortality. Moreover, many talismans of protection were attributed to Yü the Great.
Whether or not Yü was actually the author of these talismans is not
important; the fact that the authority of Yü was invoked is significant, however, because it connected religious Taoism to the shamanism of the ancient times.

The Wei dynasty was toppled by the Ssu-ma clan who established
the Chin dynasty (265–420 CE) and united China by wiping out the
kingdom of Wu. The founder of the Chin dynasty came to power by
killing off his opponents, and his descendants continued to use force
and brutality even after unification and peace. The Chin emperors
also gave the Ssu-ma clan members favored treatment. This angered
the nobles who although not belonging to the Ssu-ma clan had
helped the Chin rulers gain power. Thus, even in the beginning of
the Chin dynasty, the ruling house had lost the support of many
powerful nobles. When the border tribes invaded Chin, the capital
city fell, and the lands north of the Yang-tze came under the rule of
tribal kingdoms. This ended what is now called the Western Chin
dynasty (265–316 CE). It lasted only fifty-two years.

The Chin imperial house fled south with those followers who had
remained loyal and founded the Eastern Chin (317 CE). Among its
supporters were Sun Yin and Lu Tun, two practitioners of Chang
Tao-ling's form of Taoism, which was now called the Way of the
Celestial Teachers (T'ien-shih Tao). Although neither man belonged
to the Ssu-ma clan, each received high honors for helping the Chin
royal house establish its new rule. The religious organization that
they belonged to, the Celestial Teachers Way, also received imperial
patronage, and the social status and influence of the Celestial Teachers thence increased rapidly. A body of sacred texts appeared, formed
around the *Wu-fu ching* and called the Ling-pao scriptures. These
texts, mentioned above, were said to have been revealed by the Taoist deities to leaders of Celestial Teachers Taoism, and they contained invocations, talismans, and descriptions of ceremonies. Many
Ling-pao scriptures are still used today in the practices of the Celestial Teachers, or the Central Orthodox (Cheng-i Meng-wei) School.

After the Chin royal house fled south, the lands north of the Yang-tze were divided into small tribal kingdoms, which fought each other. Some of the stronger kingdoms attempted to cross the river and invade Eastern Chin; they failed, however, because in its early years Eastern Chin was strong and prosperous. The dynasties of the northern kingdoms were short lived, and only two of them managed to unite the tribes under a single rule. One of them was the Northern Wei (386–534 CE).

The kings of Northern Wei conquered the rival kingdoms, and, for that time in China's history, held on to their rule for an unusually long time. This was because they adopted the language, culture, and customs of central China. Thus, the conquered peoples did not feel that they were under a foreign yoke. Moreover, Northern Wei had a prosperous trade relationship with distant nations via the silk route, and for a while it was a center of cultural exchange and learning. Buddhism flourished: monasteries were built and Sanskrit scriptures were translated into Chinese. And it was in Northern Wei that the liturgies of religious Taoism were systematized.

K'OU CH'IEN-CHIH

K'ou Ch'ien-chih was a Taoist scholar and priest who lived in Northern Wei at the height of its prosperity and power. Originally trained in Celestial Teachers (or Central Orthodox) Taoism, K'ou was adept at that school's liturgies and magical practices, and Taoist historians today still marvel at his accomplishments.

K'ou Ch'ien-chih established the northern branch of the Celestial Teachers school, became the spiritual adviser to the Northern Wei emperor, and wrote and compiled liturgies that are still widely used in Taoist religious ceremonies. His branch of Celestial Teachers Taoism emphasized ceremonies and liturgies—a sharp contrast to the original Celestial Teachers, whose major focus was talismanic magic. Inspired by the Buddhist disciplines of abstinence, K'ou came up with a list of dos and don'ts for practitioners of the Taoist religion. These included what foods to abstain from and when to abstain from them, what kinds of offerings were legitimate, and what types of behavior were demanded by Taoist practice. He attacked the popular cults for using alcohol, meats, hallucinogens, and sexual orgies in the ceremonies, using the slogan, "purifying the spiritual practices and reestablishing morality." He designated festival days for the major Taoist deities, prescribed the ceremonies that should be performed on those days, and wrote the music and liturgies for them. It is not too far-fetched to say that K'ou Ch'ieh-chih is the father of Taoist ceremonies.

The Northern Wei emperor was so impressed with K'ou that he gave him the title of Celestial Teacher and appointed him spiritual adviser. In 420 CE, the emperor took the title True King of the T'ai-p'ing Way and made K'ou Ch'ieh-chih's form of Central Orthodox Taoism the state religion.

LU HSIU-CHING

Although 420 CE was a great year for the northern branch of the Celestial Teacher Taoism, it was fateful for the Eastern Chin dynasty, in the south. Barely one hundred years after the Chin royal house had crossed the river to reestablish its rule, the dynasty fell. In 420 CE, the Eastern Chin dynasty ended and was replaced by the Sung (not to be confused with the Sung dynasty that later ruled over a united China). This Sung dynasty was the first of what Chinese historians call the Southern dynasties, as opposed to the Northern dynasties.

The Southern dynasties were kingdoms that occupied lands south of the Yang-tze; the Northern dynasties (like Northern Wei) occupied China north of the river. Between 420 and 589 CE, six dynasties came and went in the south, most of them the result of military coups, with the commanding general of the imperial army or the royal bodyguard killing the emperor and replacing him as ruler. During this period, southern China was plunged into political chaos.

The period of the Southern and Northern dynasties would be remembered only as a time of political and social disorder if all that had happened was the rapid succession of dynasties; however, this was also the period of the flowering of the Taoist religion. In the

Sung of the Southern dynasties lived one of the most important figures of religious Taoism—Lu Hsiu-ching. Lu is credited with compiling the first collection of Taoist scriptures that would become the core of today's Taoist canon.

Lu Hsiu-ching was trained in the Central Orthodox School of Taoism. A scholar and an adept in talismanic magic, he came from an established family in southeast China. Moreover, he had the combination of his regional culture's belief in talismanic magic and an aristocrat's attraction toward ceremonial details. We are told that Lu received a classical education and was knowledgeable in the Confucian classics, the *I-ching*, the Taoist classics, and the Ling-pao scriptures. He gained the respect and favor of the Sung court, revised the rituals and magical practices of the Celestial Teachers, and became known as the founder of the southern branch of Celestial Teachers Taoism.

During Lu's time, the number of Taoist books had multiplied. There were the old classics like the *Tao-te ching, Chuang-tzu,* and *Lieh-tzu;* there were books on alchemy and techniques of immortality passed down by the fang-shih; there were the Ling-pao scriptures, which in Lu's time numbered about fifty volumes; there was a new crop of texts called the Shang-ch'ing scriptures, which contained the teachings of the mystical form of Taoism (which will be dealt with in more detail in the next chapter); and there was also the *T'ai-p'ing ching,* which was more voluminous than the one we have now.

Inspired by the compilation of the Buddhist scriptures into a canon, Lu Hsiu-ching set out to collect and catalog the Taoist texts. In 471 CE, he published the first Taoist canon. It was divided into seven sections. The three major sections were the Cavern of the Realized (Tung-chen), the Cavern of the Mysteries (Tung-hsüan), and the Cavern of the Spirit (Tung-shen). The four minor sections were Great Mystery (T'ai-hsüan), Great Balance (T'ai-p'ing), Great Pure (T'ai-ch'ing), and Orthodox Classics (Cheng-i).

Lu's contribution was not limited to compiling the Taoist scriptures; like K'ou Ch'ieh-chih, in the north, he also wrote liturgies, set down the correct procedures for performing the sacred ceremonies, and systematized the liturgies.

When Lu Hsiu-ching died in 477 CE, Taoism had become a formidable influence in southern China. Due to his efforts, the Central Orthodox form of Taoism (the Celestial Teachers Way) became a respected and organized religion accepted by all strata of society. Moreover, Lu had brought together into the one canon teachings of the three major forms of Taoism of his time: the arts of longevity of the alchemists, the magic and ceremonies of the Celestial Teachers, and the mysticism of the Shang-ch'ing school. In chapter 4, we will examine the important Shang-ch'ing school.

FURTHER READINGS

Henri Maspero's work *Taoism and Chinese Religion* is still the most complete and authoritative work on the history of the Taoist religion. It looks at the mythology of China and its influence on Taoist religious beliefs, covers the development of Taoist organized religion, and examines the spiritual techniques of cultivating life and longevity. It is truly a great book.

Maspero's work is not the kind of book that you will want to read in one sitting; it is good to have around so that you can refer to it from time to time. A scholarly work, it nevertheless does not get bogged down in details. One does not have to be a specialist or researcher in the field to enjoy it. Book 1, "Chinese Religion in Its Historical Development," and book 5, "Taoism in Chinese Religious Beliefs of the Six Dynasties Period," are the most relevant to topics covered in this chapter.

Kristofer Schipper's delightful *The Taoist Body* presents a clear and concise approach to Taoist religion and religious practices. Schipper's chapter 1, which is a brief introduction to the nature of Taoist religious beliefs, and chapter 7, which discusses how Lao-tzu became the embodiment of the nature of the Tao, give further information on the topics discussed in this chapter. Later in the *Guide*, I will direct readers to other chapters of Schipper's.

Chapter 2 of Michael Saso's book *Blue Dragon, White Tiger* gives a list of events (with dates) in the history of Taoism. The list begins with the Spring and Autumn Period and brings readers all the way into the twentieth century, covering up to 1979. It is a good quick-reference resource, but you need to be familiar with the events before you can fully make use of this information.

Readers desiring more light on this period of Taoist history, and curious about other Taoist religious or revealed texts, can find a selection in Livia Kohn's *The Taoist Experience*. This anthology contains, in translation, the following texts related to the transformation of Taoism from philosophy to religion:

Scriptures Create the Universe: Scripture of How the Highest Venerable Lord Opens the Cosmos (reading #5)

Numinous Treasure—Wondrous History: A Short Record of the Numinous Treasure (#6)

The Three Caverns: The Ancestral Origin of the Three Caverns of Taoist Teaching (#9)

The Transformations of Lao-tzu: On the Conversion of the Barbarians (#10)

4

The Rise of Mystical Taoism
(300–600 CE)

THE WORLD OF Shang-ch'ing Taoism: a world where guardian spirits live inside the human body; a world where mystics fly to the sky and journey among the stars; a world where people absorb the essence of the sun and moon to cultivate immortality; a world where the highest attainment in life is to merge with the Tao in bliss and ecstasy. . . .

Mysticism and Shang-ch'ing Taoism

Shang-ch'ing Taoism is often called Mystical Taoism. Mysticism has been defined in many ways. *The Oxford English Dictionary* once called it a "self-delusion or dreamy confusion of thought" and "a religious belief to which these evil qualities are imputed." Modern views now recognize that, to understand mysticism, we need to understand the nature of mystical experience.

Although most studies of mysticism are based on mystical experiences found in Christianity (Catholicism and Protestantism), with a few from Hinduism, Buddhism, Islam, and Judaism, they can still help us to understand the form of Taoism that has been called "mystical." However, to equate the beliefs and practices of the mysticism found in the Judeo-Christian religions (or even in the ancient Greek religions) with Taoist mysticism is misleading. Chinese history and cultural background have created a form of mysticism that is unique among the world's spiritual traditions.

Contemporary scholars of religion have identified several features of mysticism:

1. *The cognitive component:* the belief system and worldview of mysticism. There are several beliefs that form the core of mysticism. First, mystics believe there is an underlying unity behind all things. This is commonly called the One and it is the true reality. Second, this One, or the underlying reality, cannot be perceived or known by ordinary experience. Third, this One is present in us, and by realizing it internally we can be united with everything around us. Finally, the goal of human life is to achieve unity with this One.

2. *The emotional component:* feelings that accompany the mystical experience. Bliss, joy, ecstasy, sexual excitement, and intoxication have all been used to describe the feelings of mystical experience.

3. *The perceptive component:* any visual, auditory, or other sensations that accompany the mystical experience. A heightened awareness of the surroundings and of auditory and visual images is experienced when the underlying reality of the One is directly perceived without the intrusion of rational thinking.

4. *The behavioral component:* actions that induce the mystical experience or are the result of it. The mystical experience involves action. Some actions function to induce the experience (such as, Dervish dancing in Sufism, or Islamic mysticism; body postures in yoga; and the rituals of Shang-ch'ing Taoism); other actions result from the mystical experience (such as, walking through fire; speaking in special languages).

There are many similarities between mysticism and shamanism. Each involves an ecstatic experience, transformed perception, feats of power, and a union with a force that takes the individual to a more complete existence than the mundane self. But mysticism and shamanism are not identical. For a long time, it was believed that the difference between the shamanic and mystical experience was that the former required disciplined training and was induced by systematic procedures, whereas the latter was spontaneous. When it became known that Sufism and yoga both employ systematic techniques to induce mystical experience, this criterion no longer held. In fact, Shang-ch'ing Taoism is another case where the mystical experience is induced by systematic procedures that can be practiced only after rigorous training.

I believe that what distinguishes mysticism from shamanism is the nature of the union between the practitioner and the sacred powers. In mysticism, the union is between two parts of ourselves—the cosmic and the mundane. The greater, or cosmic, power is a part of us. Whether we are separated from it because of cultural and social influence or because of the dominance of analytical thinking, it is still inside us. Therefore, one function of mysticism is that of undoing the conditions that separate ourselves from ourselves.

Shamanism, on the other hand, sees the greater or cosmic power as part of the external world. Thus, "it" has to be invited to enter the shaman before a union can be achieved. Sometimes the power comes to visit the shaman; for example, when the *awen* visits the Celtic bard, or when the nature spirits come to "court" with the Ch'u shaman. At other times, the shaman goes to the spirits by flying to their dwellings in the stars or journeying into their homes in the depth of the earth. In each case, the sacred power that the shamans wish to be united with is outside, not within.

Shang-ch'ing Taoism, with its belief that the deities, or the cosmic powers, are resident in the human body, identifies it as a mystical practice. However, the shamanic influence in Taoism had always been strong, and its imprint on Shang-ch'ing Taoism is unmistakable. In fact, this unique form of Taoism has both the features of mysticism and shamanism—the belief in the deities within and the journey to the other worlds.

The Predecessors of Shang-ch'ing Taoism

Shang-ch'ing Taoism was reputed to have been founded by Lady Wei Hua-ts'un during the early part of the Chin dynasty. Lady Wei received a revelation from the Guardians of the Tao (the deities) and recorded their teachings in a book titled *Shang-ch'ing huang-t'ing nei-ching yü-ching* (The Yellow Court Jade Classic of Internal Images of the High Pure Realm) in 288 CE. However, the two most important ideas of Shang-ch'ing Taoism—the notion of Keeping the One and the belief that there are guardian spirits in the body—were known as early as the Eastern Han dynasty. They can be found in parts of the *T'ai-p'ing ching* that are preserved in the *T'ai-p'ing ching ch'ao:* "If the body is still and the spirit is held within, then illness will not multiply. You will have a long life because the bright spirits protect you."

A commentary on the *Tao-te ching* by Ho-shang Kung (the River Sage), believed to have been written in the Han dynasty, also refers to Keeping the One: "If people can cultivate the spirit [i.e., the One], they will not die. By 'spirit' I mean the spirits of the five viscera. In the liver is the human spirit, in the lungs is the soul, in the heart is the seed of the immortal spirit, in the spleen is the intention, and in the kidneys is the generative energy. If the five viscera are injured, then the five spirits will leave." (Ho-shang Kung's Commentary on the Tao-te ching). That this idea of Keeping the One appeared in a commentary on a text of classical or philosophical Taoism is significant. It provides a continuity between classical Taoist philosophy and Taoist mysticism.

If the principal ideas of Shang-ch'ing Taoism were present well before the Chin dynasty, why did it have to wait until the Chin and the Southern dynasties to become a major movement in Taoism? To understand this, we must look at the lineage of Shang-ch'ing Taoism and the transmission of its scriptures in the Chin and Southern dynasties.

Shang-ch'ing Taoism in the Chin Dynasty (265–420 CE)

Lady Wei is reputed to have been the founder of Shang-ch'ing Taoism, but it was Yang Hsi who was responsible for spreading its teachings. The Shang-ch'ing texts tell us that Yang Hsi received a

vision from Lady Wei (who had become an immortal) and then
"wrote" the scriptures under the influence of a cannabis-induced
trance. The scriptures were then transmitted to Hsü Hui and Hsü
Mi (a father and son). The early Shang-ch'ing scriptures, in addition
to the *Huang-t'ing nei-ching yü-ching*, are the *T'ai-shang pao-wen*
(The Sacred Writ of the Most High), *Ta-tung chen-ching* (The True
Scripture of the Great Cavern), and the *Pa-su yin-shu* (The Hidden
Book of the Eight Simplicities).

The early proponents of Shang-ch'ing Taoism were related to each
other by clan or marriage; all were members of established families
in southeast China. Many of them were descendants of the fallen
aristocracy of the state of Wu of the Three Kingdoms. Lady Wei was
the daughter of a high-ranking priest of Celestial Teachers Taoism
and was herself initiated into the priestly order. Yang Hsi and Lady
Wei came from the same county, and their families, Yang and Wei,
had a long-standing friendship. As for Hsü Hui and Hsü Mi, the
father and son, they were related by marriage to the famous Ko family, whose members were known for their alchemical experiments
and expertise in the arts of longevity. Two of the best-known members of the Ko family were Ko Hung, who wrote the *P'ao-p'u-tzu*
(The Sage Who Embraces Simplicity), a Taoist encyclopedia, and
Ko Hsüan, who was instrumental in collating the Ling-pao scriptures. These two families, Ko and Hsü, were also linked through marriage to another established family of the region, the T'ao family.
Later, in the Southern dynasties, a descendant of the T'ao family,
T'ao Hung-ching, would become one of the greatest scholars and
practitioners of Shang-ch'ing Taoism.

Thus, the founders of Shang-ch'ing Taoism came from the aristocracy of the county of Wu, near the capital of the Eastern Chin dynasty, and the supporters of Shang-ch'ing Taoism were members of
the nobility and the artistic community of the capital. One of the
most famous followers of Shang-ch'ing Taoism was the calligrapher
Wang Hsi-che, who penned a copy of the *Huang-t'ing wai-ching
ching* (The Yellow Court Classic of External Images).

The early form of Shang-ch'ing Taoism incorporated many beliefs and practices of Celestial Teachers Taoism. It used talismans and adopted the Yüan-shih T'ien-tsun (Celestial Lord of the Great Beginning), another name for Lao-tzu, as its highest deity. It incorporated the *T'ai-p'ing ching*, the *Cheng-i fa-wen* (The Principles and Scripts of the Central Orthodox), the *T'ai-shang ling-pao wu-fu ching* (The Highest Revelation of the Five Talismans of the Sacred Spirit), and other Ling-pao texts into its corpus of sacred scriptures. The scriptures that were distinctly labeled as Shang-ch'ing texts numbered around fifty during the Eastern Chin.

However, two features of Shang-ch'ing Taoism distinguished it from Celestial Teachers Taoism. The first was the belief that Keeping the One and holding the guardian deities would lead to health and longevity: orthodox members of the Celestial Teachers Way were not sympathetic to the notion of Keeping the One as a method of attaining health; they maintained that talismans and incantations were *the* way to cure illness. The second feature separating Shang-ch'ing Taoism from Central Orthodox Taoism was the use of talismans: the Celestial Teachers used talismans for curing illness, exorcism, and for protection against malevolent spirits, whereas the Shang-ch'ing Taoists used them primarily for invoking and visualizing the deities inside the body and for journeying to other realms of existence.

As time went on, these differences between the two forms of Taoism overshadowed their similarities, and Shang-ch'ing Taoism began to pull away from Celestial Teachers Taoism and became a unique and distinct lineage. However, the separation of Shang-ch'ing Taoism from Central Orthodox did not invite hostility from the organized branch of religious Taoism. Unlike what happened in other cultures, where the mystics' worldview and experience of union with the sacred powers often made them heretics in the eyes of organized religion, especially in Christianity and Islam, in China, this was not so. I think there are several reasons for this.

First, the Chinese culture had always tolerated diversity in religious and spiritual practices. In the history of China, most emperors were content to leave religious groups alone as long as they did not have political ambitions. The emperors who favored one religion over others appointed personal spiritual advisers, but did not attempt to integrate state and religion. The zealous emperors who ordered religious persecution did not rule for long.

Second, there is a saying among Taoists, "In Taoism there are no heretics; there are only sects." Throughout the history of Taoism, differences in beliefs and practices have produced a diversity of sects that respected and tolerated each other.

Third, because of a specific historical circumstance, during the Chin dynasty, Shang-ch'ing Taoism found a receptive following among the artistic community and the upper class. When the Chin dynasty fled south, the capital was built in a region where several powerful and established families controlled the finance and commerce of the region; thus, although the empire was ruled by the Chin, members of the royal family and their entourage from the north were more like foreigners and refugees than established kings. The Ssu-ma clan was no longer strong enough to use force to subdue the powerful families of the south. But, most importantly, the Chin ruling house realized that destroying these families would destroy the economy of the empire, and an unusual relationship was therefore formed between the imperial house and the upper class: the established families of the southeast, although allowed to retain their lands and commercial enterprises, were not given high-level positions in the government; thus, families like the Wei, Yang, Hsü, and Ko were rich but politically powerless. Denied the road to high politics, many of them turned toward the arcane arts and dabbled in spiritual practices. Being wealthy, they had both the time and resources for such pursuits.

Fourth, the belief in spirits and talismanic magic had always been strong in southeast China. The region also had the heritage of the shamanic culture of Ch'u, Wu, and Yüeh, dating back to the sixth century BCE. Many founders of the Shang-ch'ing movement were already familiar with the talismanic magic and arcane arts of the Celestial Teachers; therefore, the shift from using talismans for healing to using them for achieving ecstatic union with the deities did not require a lot of retraining.

Finally, the regions south of the Yang-tze had always been the hotbed of new ideas and creative thinking. The northern Chinese are typically more conservative and traditional; the southerners are bolder in experimenting with new ideas and adopting them. It was in the south that Chang Tao-ling's religion of Taoism was first accepted, and, even before that, the philosophy of Lao-tzu and Chuang-tzu was more popular in the south than in the north. Shang-ch'ing Taoism, with its conception of guardian spirits inhabiting the human body, its vivid visualizations of images of deities, and its ecstatic flight to the celestial realm, could only have come from southern China. Moreover, only the people of the south could have taken it seriously and not dismissed it as wild fantasy.

By the end of the Eastern Chin dynasty, Shang-ch'ing Taoism had developed a sizable body of scriptures and a large following among the upper class. Its sacred scriptures were first kept by the Hsü family: toward the end of the Eastern Chin, they were under the custodianship of Hsü Mi's son Hsü Huang-wen, whose wife was the great-great-granddaughter of Ko Hung. Thus, the Ling-pao scriptures, the Shang-ch'ing scriptures, and the T'ai-ch'ing scriptures of the alchemists all came into the possession of the Hsü family.

This circumstance would have provided an excellent opportunity for the three traditions of Taoism—Ling-pao, Shang-ch'ing and T'ai-ching (alchemist)—to be unified, but the political situation did not allow this to happen. In 404 CE, the Hsü family was involved in an uprising and had to flee the capital. Then, in the political chaos that surrounded the fall of the Eastern Chin in 420 CE, many Shang-ch'ing scriptures were lost, and after the death of Hsü Huang-wen in 429 CE, the Shang-ch'ing scriptures were no longer under a single custodianship. Scattered among a number of followers, the scriptures were edited and revised. Some texts were hoarded by individuals and these texts perished when that person died; others were revised to suit the religious orientation of those who claimed possession and authority to transmit them. Many texts were written during those times and put forward as works revealed by the deities.

During the Southern dynasties, there were more than one hundred volumes of texts that claimed Shang-ch'ing lineage. However, these texts and those of the Ling-pao and the T'ai-ch'ing scriptures were scattered, and only the effort of one of the greatest scholars and Taoist adepts of the Southern dynasties, T'ao Hung-ching, brought them together again. T'ao Hung-ch'ing collated the Shang-ch'ing scriptures and began a revival and reformation of Shang-ch'ing Taoism that would forever change the Taoist spiritial tradition.

Shang-ch'ing Taoism in the Southern Dynasties (420–589 CE)

T'ao Hung-ching was born in the Sung of the Southern dynasties, in 456 CE, and died in 536 CE, in the Liang dynasty. T'ao came from one of the great families of southeast China; his grandfather held a respectable position in the Sung government. When the Sung dynasty fell and was replaced by Ch'i, the T'ao family lost its fortunes; however, an emphasis on education and learning was an important part of the family tradition, and T'ao Hung-ching was brought up in an atmosphere that encouraged mastering a wide range of knowledge.

During the Southern Ch'i dynasty (479–502 CE), T'ao served as a secretary and librarian in the imperial court. His abilities were not recognized by the Ch'i court and he was never promoted. Disillusioned, he resigned his post in 492 CE and decided to pursue the Tao. It is ironic that when T'ao Hung-ching aspired to rise in politics, success never came, but when he became a Taoist hermit, his fame spread and his advice was sought by kings and nobles.

When T'ao Hung-ching settled on Mao-shan, a mountain range in today's Kiang-su Province in southeast China, he set about collecting and collating the Shang-ch'ing scriptures. He wrote down the lineage of Shang-ch'ing Taoism, recorded the authority of its transmission, set up a hierarchy of deities, and documented the structure of administration within the celestial realm. In the hands of T'ao Hung-ching, the Taoist pantheon became orderly. Deities and immortals were classified into ranks according to their levels of enlightenment. Their appearances were described in detail, all the way down to the kind of robes they wore and the symbols of authority they carried.

T'ao Hung-ching's knowledge and learning were vast and deep. In addition to his study of Shang-ch'ing teachings, he was interested in physical alchemy and had a laboratory on Mao-shan devoted to the research and making of the elixirs of immortality. The first emperor of the Liang dynasty (following the Ch'i dynasty) was both a friend and patron of T'ao's. T'ao Hung-ching's laboratory was supported by imperial funds, as were his trips to other mountains in search of minerals for making the immortal pill.

T'ao Hung-ching was knowledgeable not only in the Taoist arts: he also edited and wrote treatises on herbal medicine, was adept at divination, military strategy, astronomy, geology, and metallurgy, and his forges on Mao-shan were famous for crafting some of the best swords of the time. T'ao was also a classical scholar, learned in both the Confucian classics and Buddhist scriptures. In literary endeavors, T'ao was prolific: he wrote some eighty treatises on scientific and literary subjects. His works on Taoism, including alchemy and divination, numbered about fifty. And in addition to having expertise in science and scholarship, T'ao Hung-ching was a poet and a skilled practitioner of the martial arts.

Given these wide interests, it is natural that T'ao Hung-ching's breadth was incorporated into his practice of Shang-ch'ing Taoism. In T'ao Hung-ching, Shang-ch'ing Taoism took on new dimensions. His interest in alchemy, medicine, and herbs introduced the use of herbs and minerals into the Shang-ch'ing methods of cultivating health and longevity. Moreover, he incorporated his knowledge of the *I-ching* and the divination arts into the Shang-ch'ing understanding of the human body and the circulation of energy. Internal transformations now followed the rules of transformations laid out in the principles of change, and the circulation of energy and the nourishment of the guardian spirits of the body followed the patterns of celestial movement and changes through the seasons.

By the time of T'ao Hung-ching's death, Shang-ch'ing Taoism had become a spiritual tradition with a sophisticated theory of the human body and the external universe, a developed pantheon of deities and their administrative duties, techniques of longevity with a scientific basis in herbal medicine and mineralogy, a meditation technique based on visualization and internal transformation, and a documentation of spiritual experiences. His form of Shang-ch'ing Taoism became known as the Mao-shan Shang-ch'ing school (a school not to be confused with the Mao-shan sect of sorcery that emerged in the Ming dynasty) and it was taught in learning centers throughout Mao-shan, both during his lifetime and after his death. The Taoist centers on Mao-shan were the first of their kind, and they became a model for the Taoist retreats and monasteries that were to flourish during the Sung, Yüan, Ming, and Ch'ing dynasties.

The Teachings of Shang-ch'ing Taoism

The teachings of Shang-ch'ing Taoism can be grouped under three topics: the internal universe (the human body); the external universe (celestial and terrestrial realms); and unifying the external and internal universe.

THE INTERNAL UNIVERSE

In Shang-ch'ing Taoism, the human body is a universe filled with deities, spirits, and monsters. The Chinese words for deity and spirit are the same *(shen)*. For the sake of clarity, I shall use the word *deity* to refer to the greater spirits and *spirit* to refer to the lesser spirits. Shang-ch'ing Taoism believes that there are spirits and deities who guard the body and protect it from illness; when these guardians leave, the body will weaken and die. Therefore, the practices of Shang-ch'ing Taoism are primarily concerned with keeping these guardians within and not letting them weaken or wander off.

The One. In the Shang-ch'ing internal universe, the highest and most important deity is called the One. It is the Tao inside us; the undifferentiated primordial vapor that keeps us alive. Sometimes it is called the sacred fetus of immortality. Keeping the One inside is holding onto the Tao. Embracing the One is holding and nourishing the sacred fetus, as a mother holds and nourishes an infant.

The Three Ones. The Three Ones are the next highest guardian deities in the body. They are called the San-yüan, or the Three Primal Ones. The San-yüan are the emanations of the undifferentiated oneness of the Tao. In the human body, they are the generative, vital, and spirit energies. These three energies and their guardians reside in the three *tan-t'iens* (fields of elixir).

Spiritual energy is the highest manifestation of the One. It rules all the activities of the mind, including the potentials of the enlightened mind. It and its guardian reside in the upper tan-t'ien in the region between the eyes in a part of the body that is called the Celestial Realm.

Vital energy is energy associated with the breath. It and its guardian reside in the middle tan-t'ien located in the region of the heart in a part of the body called the Terrestrial Realm.

Generative energy is responsible for procreation. It and its guardian reside in the lower tan-t'ien just below the navel. This part of the body is called the Water Realm.

If the levels of the energies are high, the guardians will appear bright, and health and longevity are assured; if the energies are low, the guardians will appear dull, and the body is weak or ill. In Shang-ch'ing practice, keeping the Three Ones in the body corresponds to preserving generative, vital, and spirit energy. However, only the One can be "embraced."

The Five. Next in importance are the spirits that protect the five viscera: the heart, liver, spleen, lungs, and kidneys. If these spirits leave or become weak, the internal organs will not function effectively and bodily functions will not be regulated. Each spirit protecting the organ is associated with a color. When the viscera are strong and healthy, the colors of the guardian spirits will be bright and vivid. When the organs are weak, the colors will lose their brightness and saturation.

The appearance of the guardian deities and spirits in the body is an integral part of visualization in Shang-ch'ing meditation. On the one hand, visualizing the images of the guardians helps to keep them within the body; on the other hand, the visualizations serve as feedback, because their appearances are indicators of the state of health. If the images are not radiant, vivid, and colorful, it means that the body is weak and ill. Many lesser spirits protect each part of the body down to each joint and pore. Health and longevity require all the deities and spirits to be bright and clear.

Monsters also reside in the body. They live in the cavities near the three gates along the spine. Each gate is associated with a tan-t'ien and controls activity in it: the upper gate controls access to the upper tan-t'ien, the middle gate to the middle tan-t'ien, and the lower gate to the lower tan t'ien (fig. 4.1). If the gate is locked, energy will not be gathered in that tan-t'ien. The monsters have the ability to close the gates and affect the level of energy in the tan-t'iens. According to Shang-ch'ing belief, the monsters thrive on our desires and the grains we eat. Therefore, to eradicate the monsters, the Shang-ch'ing

像琚彭尸上　　像瑨彭尸中　　像璚彭尸下

FIGURE 4.1. The three monsters in the body, from *Yi-men ch'ang-sheng pi-shu* (Chen Hsi-yi's Secret Methods of Longevity). These pictures are based on descriptions of the three monsters described in the Shang-ch'ing texts. *Left to right:* The monster of the upper cavity, of the middle cavity, and of the lower cavity. The cavities are situated at the three gates along the spinal column.

Taoists practiced fasting and abstinence from grains. Another way to eradicate the monsters is to still the mind and eliminate craving.

In the Shang-ch'ing scriptures, the monsters are sometimes depicted as attractive and good-looking, sometimes as misshapen and ugly. When an individual does not realize that the monsters are harmful, worldly things and even unethical deeds can appear attractive; however, when the individual realizes that the monsters can shorten life, the entities will become repulsive and ugly. In visualizing the internal universe, the first step to eradicating the monsters is to see them in their undesirable shape, or what is called their "true form." When Shang-ch'ing Taoists speak of "seeing the True Forms," they are referring to the brilliant and radiant form of the guardians and the ugly and repulsive form of the monsters.

There are also pathways in the internal universe that connect various parts of the body. These are the conduits of energy. Major junctions in the pathway are given names and their locations are specified so that the flow of energy can be directed through them. The pathway begins on the top of the head and descends through the forehead into the upper tan-t'ien between the eyes. It continues down the throat into the middle tan-t'ien. From there energy flows into the lower tan-t'ien to nourish the sacred fetus (the seed of immortality). When the fetus is completely formed, the practitioner will attain immortality. The body will become light; it will float up to the sky to join the sun, moon, and stars in the High Pure (Shang-ch'ing) Realm.

THE EXTERNAL UNIVERSE

The Shang-ch'ing external universe is inhabited by many spirits and deities. The most important live in the sun, moon, and stars. To the Shang-ch'ing Taoists, the celestial bodies are the manifestations of the primordial vapor of the Tao, and the essence of the Tao is carried in their light. Thus, to absorb the essence of the sun, moon, and stars is to swallow the energy of the Tao.

According to Shang-ch'ing Taoism, the sun contains the essence of yang energy and the moon is the vessel of yin energy. Absorption of the essences of the sun and moon can help nourish the immortal fetus and strengthen the guardians of the body. To absorb the energy of the sun, the Shang-ch'ing adept visualizes the sun traveling from the mouth to the heart, merging with the internal light in the tan-t'iens, at specific times of the year. When a warmth is felt in the heart, the practitioner recites a short invocation asking the deities to hasten this unity so that the immortal pill can be completed. Another method of absorbing the essence of the sun is to face east three times a day and visualize the large disk of the sun and its rays rising from the heart, up the throat, through the teeth, and then back into the stomach.

To absorb the yin essence of the moon, at midnight the adept visualizes the moon in the top of the head and channels the moonbeams into the stomach; alternatively, the practitioner visualizes the moon in the upper tan-t'ien and directs the strands of white light to enter the throat, and thence to the stomach.

The North Star and the Northern Bushel (Big Dipper) constellation are important celestial bodies. They are home to the deities who control longevity and destiny, and Shang-ch'ing practitioners developed ceremonies, talismans, invocations, and mantras to ask them for protection.

Mist, clouds, and dew also contain the essence of the primordial vapor of the Tao, and Shang-ch'ing adepts are instructed to absorb them by inhaling in a specific manner at dawn when these vapors are present.

The Shang-ch'ing practices of absorbing the yin and yang essences from nature involve elaborate rituals. First, talismans that protect the practitioner and facilitate the practice are drawn. Because these practices are performed in the middle of the night, and often in remote regions, the practitioner must be protected from wild animals and malevolent spirits that may steal the essence that the adept had gathered. Next, the adept performs the rituals of visualization, invoking the deities whose celestial energy he or she will absorb; sometimes this is accompanied by incantations and recitation of petitions. Finally, the body of the practitioner is readied: saliva is swallowed, the teeth are knocked together, and inhaling and exhaling of the breath is done in a specific manner.

Absorption of the essence of the sun, moon, stars, and vapors involves uniting the microcosms of the body and macrocosms of the universe. Once the division between the Tao inside and the Tao outside is dissolved, the practitioner can merge with the underlying origin of all things, draw nourishment from the source of life itself, and attain immortality.

UNIFYING THE EXTERNAL AND INTERNAL UNIVERSES

Ascension, flight, and travel in the celestial realm are ways in which the Shang-ch'ing Taoist achieves a union with the Tao in the external universe. Ascension represents final union, when the practitioner leaves the mortal realm forever to become an immortal in the High Pure Realm. Immortals of the highest caliber ascend to the sky in the physical body and in broad daylight, often in the presence of witnesses. It was said that both Lao-tzu and the Yellow Emperor ascended to immortality in this manner, as did Sun Pu-erh, one of the Seven Taoist Masters of the Complete Reality School of Taoism. (For an account of Sun Pu-erh's ascension, see my *Seven Taoist Masters.*) In the case of immortals of secondary caliber, only the spirit ascends: at death, the immortal spirit within rises to the celestial realm. This is called "shedding the shell." Often, the shell, or body, disappears after the spirit has ascended. Hao T'ai-ku of the Seven Taoist Masters and the famous alchemist Wei Po-yang were reputed to have attained immortality in this manner.

In contrast to ascension, the practitioner's journey to the celestial realm is only a temporary departure from the world of ordinary experience. There are two stages to the celestial journey: rising to the sky, and traveling in the celestial domain.

In the first stage, the practitioner leaves the earth and steps up to the celestial entity. The body becomes light and loses its form, allowing the adept to rise to the celestial entity on the wind and clouds. This process is called *fei-t'ien*, or rising to the sky. The second, traveling stage involves journeying from constellation to constellation.

This is called *fei-hsing*, or flying in the sky. In this stage, the adept is said to be walking the patterns of the stars.

In the Shang-ch'ing practice of celestial travel (figs. 4.2, 4.3), these two stages are not necessarily both performed: sometimes the adept simply steps up to the stars, sun, or moon and stays there to absorb the celestial energy before returning to earth; at other times, the ascent is the beginning of a journey through the constellations. The two parts of the celestial journey are distinct, requiring different incantations, petitions, talismans, and preparatory actions.

The preparations for the celestial journey are elaborate. First, there are certain days of the year when the journey should be taken. Most of them coincide with major seasonal markers such as the equinoxes and the solstices and with the new and full moon. Second, the adept must perform rites of purification before taking the journey;

FIGURE 4.2. Shang-ch'ing adept visualizing the pattern of the Northern Bushel stars, from the *Wu-shang hsüan-yüan san-t'ien yü-t'ang ta-fa* (The Incomparable Mysterious, Original Great Methods of the Jade Hall of the Three Celestial Realms). *Right:* Visualizing the Northern Bushel enveloping the body. *Center:* Keeping the Northern Bushel inside the mouth. *Left:* Climbing the Celestial Ladder to the Northern Bushel constellation.

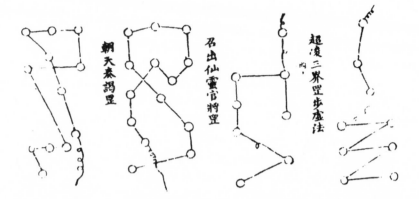

FIGURE 4.3. Dances of flight, from the *Wu-shang Hsüan-yüan san-t'ien yü-t'ang ta-fa* (The Incomparable Mysterious, Original Methods of the Jade Hall of the Three Celestial Realms). *Left:* Audience with the celestial spirits, going beyond the world of spirits and celestial guards. *Center:* The subtle gait for journeying in the three realms (Jade Pure, Great Pure, and High Pure). *Right:* Walking on the wind.

this includes abstaining from meat, grains, and sexual activity. Third, an altar is built and offerings are made to the celestial deities. This is followed by the ritualistic drawing of talismans, and eating them. Fourth, in a secluded and quiet place, the practitioner draws talismans on the ground to protect the area where he or she will leave the body when the spirit flies to the sky. If the body is left unguarded, animals or malevolent spirits may harm it and the spirit will have no shell to enter when it returns from its celestial journey. Finally, there is a series of visualizations (fig. 4.2) of the celestial deities, petitions, incantations, and dancing, followed by specific patterns of inhalation and exhalation, swallowing of saliva, and the knocking of teeth. When the procedures are completed, the adept rises to the celestial realm.

Leaving the earth and stepping up to the celestial bodies is the more elementary form of the two stages of the celestial journey. The spirit needs only to leave the body of the practitioner to be received by the guardian deities of the celestial entity that it is going to. After it has reached its destination, the spirit stays in the embrace and protection of the deity. The journey from one constellation to another, however, is a more difficult task (fig. 4.3). Not only are more steps involved, the journey takes the adept farther and farther away from earth (and the body). This part of the celestial journey is called wandering in the skies. Needless to say, the journey through the celestial realm is a more advanced practice than the initial ascent. Later, the practitioners of internal alchemy would liken similar experiences to a child leaving its mother, first to play near the house, and then leaving its home to travel far and wide.

The Legacy of Shang-ch'ing Taoism

Shang-ch'ing Taoism, especially the form that was associated with T'ao Hung-ching, continued to flourish after the end of the Southern dynasties. Mao-shan became the center of Taoist learning, and generations of Shang-ch'ing adepts were trained in its mountain retreats. Mao-shan's tradition continued to be enriched by some of the most prominent leaders of Taoist thinking, such as Ssu-ma Ch'eng-chen (T'ang dynasty, 618–906 CE). The Mao-shan Shang-ch'ing school of Taoism remained a distinct lineage well into the Sung dynasty (960–1279 CE); thereafter, its beliefs and practices were absorbed into schools of Taoism that emerged in the Ming (1368–1644 CE) and Ch'ing (1644–1911 CE) dynasties.

Today, the beliefs and practices of Shang-ch'ing Taoism can be found in several major systems of Taoism. For example, the notions of the guardian deities within the body and the journey of the spirit to the celestial realm have been adopted and developed by the internal-alchemical sects. Moreover, the *Huang-t'ing ching*'s descriptions of the pathways of internal energy have helped generations of Taoists practice the *ch'i-kung* (work of energy) techniques of the Microcosmic and Macrocosmic Circulation. The Shang-ch'ing maps of the internal universe have also become valuable tools for internal alchemists seeking to transform body and mind for health, longevity, and immortality. The Shang-ch'ing techniques of absorbing the essence of the celestial bodies are practiced today by high-level initiates of some internal-alchemical sects.

The celestial pantheon and the administration of the celestial realm delineated by Shang-ch'ing Taoism are still accepted by many practitioners of a system of Taoism called Ceremonial or Devotional Taoism. In the Ming and Ch'ing dynasties, Shang-ch'ing rituals were adopted by internal-alchemical sects and incorporated into their ceremonies. Today, we can identify many Shang-ch'ing rituals in ceremonies of the Complete Reality School and other sects that emerged after the philosophical synthesis of Buddhism, Taoism, and Confucianism.

The belief that monsters in the body can cause illness was adopted by the Action and Karma School that emerged in the latter part of the Sung dynasty (twelfth century CE) and became integral to that school's belief in reward, retribution, and the need to do good deeds. The notions of Keeping the One, Embracing the One, and Guarding the One have influenced the development of techniques of meditation that focus on stilling the mind, cultivating inner nature, and dissolving desire. And finally, the techniques of swallowing, inhaling and exhaling, and directing the flow of internal circulation, have been incorporated into many forms of ch'i-kung, the art of circulating energy, and Taoist calisthenics that are practiced today.

FURTHER READINGS

Chapter 8 of Kristofer Schipper's *The Taoist Body* offers a brief but lucid introduction to the Shang-ch'ing idea of Keeping the One. The same chapter contains a translation of a small section of the *Huang-t'ing nei-ching yü-ching* and a discussion of that scripture.

Isabelle Robinet's book *Taoist Meditation* is probably the definitive work on Mao-shan Shang-ch'ing Taoism. In this book are detailed discussions of the Mao-shan form of Shang-ch'ing Taoism, an interesting interpretation of *ching*, or scripture, and a handy list of the dates of major events in the history of Shang-ch'ing Taoism. Although titled *Taoist Meditation*, it is *not* a manual on Taoist meditation, not even of the Shang-ch'ing kind. You will not find instructions on how to meditate. Robinet's book is an insightful and scholarly study of Shang-ch'ing practices.

For a clear presentation of the mysticism of Shang-ch'ing Taoism, its philosophical and historical background, and the influence of Buddhism on Taoism, see *Early Chinese Mysticism*, by Livia Kohn.

An account of Lao-tzu's ascension to immortality is given in Livia Kohn's *Taoist Mystical Philosophy*, which is a translation and discussion of the *Hsi-hsing ching* (The Scripture of Western Ascension). Although the text talks about Lao-tzu leaving the central lands to teach in India, ascension as the final act in the attainment of immortality is implied. In addition to translating the text, Kohn also presents an interesting study of the Taoist ideas of ascension, sagehood, and the physical universe.

Kohn's anthology, *The Taoist Experience*, is interesting for those wanting to read more about the Shang-ch'ing practices of flying to the stars and visualizing the guardian deities. See the following sections:

The Gods Within: The Outer Radiance Scripture of the Yellow Court (reading #24, a translation of the *Huang-t'ing wai-ching yü-ching*)

Lights in the Body: Secret Instructions of the Holy Lord on the Scripture of Great Peace (#25)

The True One: Book of the Master Who Embraces Simplicity, Inner Chapters, Chapter Eighteen (#26)

The Three Ones: Scripture of the Three Primordial Realized Ones by the Lord of the Golden Tower (#27)

One in All: Mysterious Pearly Mirror of the Mind (#28)

Trips through the Stars: Three Ways to Go Beyond the Heavenly Pass (#34)

Michael Saso, too, has translated the *Huang-t'ing wai-ching yü-ching*. In a book titled *The Golden Pavilion: Taoist Ways to Peace, Healing, and Long Life*, he includes a translation of a popular commentary on the *Huang-t'ing ching* and his own understanding of the meaning of Shang-ch'ing meditation.

In the midst of the ethnocentric views of older studies and the dry, detached approach of many contemporary scholars, Schipper's, Robinet's, Kohn's, and Saso's approaches to Taoism are refreshing. I hope that the recent appearance of the works of these authors is a sign that the Western scholastic community is beginning not merely to look at Taoism as an object for intellectual dissection but also to recognize it as a meaningful spiritual experience for practitioners.

5

The Development of Alchemical Taoism

(200–1200 CE)

In the alchemist's crucible, ordinary metals are transformed into gold when their impurities are purged by the fire of the furnace. In Taoist alchemy, it is not metals that are refined, but the body and mind of the alchemist. Renewed by the harmonious vapors of yin and yang and transformed by fire and water, the alchemist emerges from the cauldron reconnected to the primordial life-energy of the Tao.

Taoist alchemy is sometimes called physiological alchemy, because its goal is to transform the physiological structure and functions of the body. There are two forms of physiological alchemy: external alchemy and internal alchemy. In external alchemy, minerals and herbs are used to concoct a pill or elixir that, when ingested, can make the alchemist immortal; the methods of external alchemy are therefore concerned with such practices as building a furnace, gathering minerals and herbs, and compounding substances. In internal alchemy, all the ingredients of immortality are found inside the body, and it is these substances that are refined and transformed; the methods of internal alchemy are therefore concerned with cultivating the energy of life in the body without the aid of external substances.

Although the methods of external and internal alchemy are different, the early alchemists saw no conflict between the two. Most of the early alchemists practiced calisthenics, meditation, and sexual yoga while they were engaged in the research and manufacturing of elixirs. Because the term *nei-tan* (internal pill) began to appear only in the Taoist writings of the T'ang dynasty (618–906 CE), many people are misled into believing that before the seventh century CE, Taoist alchemists were preoccupied with ingesting minerals. This was not so. The early alchemists, seeing no conflict between the methods of ingesting of minerals and transforming the body and mind from within, had no need to distinguish between external and internal techniques. It was only when the two methods were regarded as incompatible (especially after the T'ang dynasty) that it became necessary to distinguish between them.

Today, the term internal alchemy is used to describe any Taoist practice whose goal is to transform mind and body for health and longevity. Many modern practitioners of internal alchemy use herbs and special foods to supplement their practice of ch'i-kung and meditation. Thus, internal alchemy as practiced today is actually closer in spirit to the early form of physiological alchemy in the third century CE. It incorporates both external and internal methods.

The Beginnings of Alchemy:
The Age of Wei Po-yang and Ko Hung (Eastern
Han, Wei, and Chin Dynasties 200–589 CE)

Taoism's concern with health and longevity dates back to the writings of Lao-tzu and Chuang-tzu. Throughout the Warring States Period, Taoism's emphasis on health and caring for the body increased, and by the end of that period (in 221 BCE) there was a class of people who claimed to be experts in the arts of longevity and immortality. They were the fang-shih (the masters of the formulae, discussed in chapter 3). One group of fang-shih specialized in the use of talismanic magic for healing and became the predecessors of the Celestial Teachers or Central Orthodox Taoism. Another group of fang-shih, who specialized in the techniques of prolonging life, ingested minerals, practiced calisthenics, sexual alchemy, and yoga-like methods of internal hygiene, and became the pioneers of both external and internal alchemy.

The belief in immortality was very strong during the Han dynasty, and the fang-shih's search for the elixirs, or pills, of immortality was supported by the emperors and the nobility. While the fang-shih themselves were adepts in both external and internal methods of alchemy, including both "sudden" and "gradual" techniques, the emperors and the upper class were most interested in fast-acting formulas. As a result, experimentation with minerals and herbs was favored over the disciplined practice of calisthenics and meditation.

Not all alchemists had rich patrons: some were hermits who worked in their own laboratories. Wei Po-yang, of the Eastern Han (25–220 CE) was such a person, having a laboratory in the mountains. Legend tells us that Wei Po-yang experimented with making the elixir of immortality and, when he was confident that he had succeeded, gave one of the pills to his dog. The dog fell over and appeared dead. Wei Po-yang himself swallowed a pill and fell over, unconscious. One of Wei Po-yang's apprentices, an untrusting one, left, but a faithful apprentice swallowed the last pill; he, too, fell unconscious. Not too long afterward, Wei Po-yang got up, felt a lightness in his body, and floated up to the sky. The faithful apprentice and the dog also recovered and flew up behind their master. Wei Po-yang (fig. 5.1) not only attained immortality but left an alchemical treatise titled the *Tsan-tung-chi* (The Triplex Unity), which is considered by Taoists as the ancestor of all the texts of alchemy, external and internal.

The Teachings of the *Tsan-tung-chi* (*The Triplex Unity*)

The *Tsan-tung-chi*'s view of the universe is similar to that of classical Taoism. It regards the Tao as the origin of all things and the primordial energy of the Tao as the source of life. As nature renews itself by following the principles of the Tao, mortals, too, can renew themselves and attain immortality by living in accordance with these principles.

FIGURE 5.1. Wei Po-yang with apprentice, alchemical cauldron, and dog.

The most important principle in the process of creation and renewal is the copulation of yin and yang. The concrete manifestation of yin and yang is water and fire; thus, knowing how to use fire and water and when to apply heat and when to cool are crucial to cultivating energy and renewing life. Life is renewed when impurities in the body are purged. Similarly, a pill or elixir of immortality is created when the appropriate substances are refined and compounded. Tempered by heat and purified by the rising vapor of water exposed to fire, the alchemist is said to be reborn in the cauldron and embraced by the Breath of the Tao.

Success in the alchemical endeavor depends on the quality of the furnace, the bellows, and the cauldron (fig. 5.2). A good furnace is needed to provide fires that are hot enough for tempering the ingredients; efficient bellows are required to produce accurate temperatures at different stages of refining; and a leak-proof cauldron is

FIGURE 5.2. The alchemical furnace and cauldrons, from the *Hsiu-chen li-chien miao-t'u* (The Subtle Illustrations of Experiences on Cultivating the Real). At top is a furnace with a cauldron and sword on top. The two animals, a phoenix and a dragon, are copulating. From their union, the Golden Elixir emerges. The lower sketch shows examples of two furnaces. Between the furnaces are three alchemical substances (*left to right*): mercury, the elixir, and lead.

needed to contain the substances after they have been purified. In external alchemy, these items refer to laboratory equipment, but in internal alchemy, furnace, bellows, and cauldron have physiological equivalents.

The furnace generates yang fire, or vital energy, and it is driven by the yin power of water or generative energy. (see chapter 8 for a discussion of yin and yang.) Using the bellows is applying the breath to fan the inner fire to produce the heat necessary for transforming vital energy into vapor (*ch'i*). The cauldron is the location in the body where energy is refined and collected. When the impurities are burned off, the golden pill, or the elixir of immortality, emerges. In Taoist alchemy, the elixir is also called the sacred fetus, because, like a fetus in a womb, to mature it has to be incubated for a period of time. Thus, when the *Tsan-tung-chi* speaks of water and fire, heating and cooling, building the furnace, positioning the cauldron, and applying the bellows, it is simultaneously describing the processes of external and internal alchemy.

The early alchemists did not neglect the importance of stilling the mind and dissolving desire. Parts of the *Tsan-tung-chi* describe meditation-like techniques. For example, it states, "Nourish yourself internally. In peace, stillness, and complete emptiness, the hidden light of the origin will glow to illuminate the entire body."

The *Tsan-tung-chi* also contains references suggesting that sexual techniques might have been used, together with nonsexual methods, in the gathering and transformation of internal energy. Consider the following statements: "When ch'ien [sky, or male] moves, it becomes erect. The vapor spreads as the generative energy flows. When k'un [earth, or female] is still, it contracts, becoming the furnace in the lodge of the Tao. Apply firmness, then withdraw. Transform it into softness to provide stimulation."

It is therefore not surprising that the *Tsan-tung-chi* is considered by Taoists to be the ancestor of all alchemical texts. Internal and external alchemy, sexual and nonsexual techniques, are all presented together in this alchemical classic, suggesting that the early alchemists saw no conflict in these methods of seeking immortality.

The Teachings of Ko Hung's P'ao-p'u-tzu (The Sage Who Embraces Simplicity)

Another great figure of early Taoist alchemy was Ko Hung. Ko lived in the latter part of the Chin dynasty, around the end of the fourth century CE, and was a member of a powerful and established family of southeast China. Members of the Ko family played important parts in the development of Taoism in the fourth and fifth centuries CE: one of them, Ko Hsüan, was the custodian of the Ling-pao scriptures of the Celestial Teachers. The Ko family also had marital ties with the Hsü family of the Shang-ch'ing lineage. These relationships probably accounted for the eclectic nature of Ko Hung's own practice and beliefs.

Ko Hung's writings are collected in a book titled the *P'ao-p'u-tzu* (The Sage Who Embraces Simplicity). The *P'ao-p'u-tzu* is very different from Wei Po-yang's *Tsan-tung-chi*. Whereas the *Tsan-tung-chi* is entirely concerned with alchemy, the *P'ao-p'u-tzu* is almost like an encyclopedia. In it are formulas, lists of ingredients, procedures for making the external pill, advice on stilling the mind and minimizing desire, methods of calisthenics and breath control, and ideas about holding the One. *P'ao-p'u-tzu* also describes methods for getting rid of internal monsters that are characteristic of Shang-ch'ing Taoism, the use of talismans and other protective measures for traveling in the mountains to look for herbs and minerals, stories of immortals, discussions of ethical action, reward, and retribution, and miscellaneous advice on Taoist practice. The amazing thing is that Ko Hung did not see these practices as inconsistent or conflicting.

Although an eclectic, Ko Hung still regarded external alchemy as the royal road to immortality. For him, the key to making the pill of immortality was in collecting the right ingredients and preparing them in the correct way. Ingredients should be collected only on specific days and in designated areas in the mountains. Moreover, collectors need to protect themselves by taking talismans with them, chanting the appropriate incantations, and dancing the steps of Yü.

Despite the emphasis on ingesting minerals, the *P'ao-p'u-tzu* is very clear about the role of ethics in the arts of immortality. Physical techniques, external and internal, must be accompanied by the correct mental attitude to be effective in prolonging life. Thus, for Ko Hung, stilling the mind, minimizing desire, regulating the emotions, and doing good deeds are all integral to cultivating longevity.

In his practice of alchemy, Ko Hung may not be a purist like Wei Po-yang, but he is still an alchemist, because he experimented with minerals and herbs, advocated the cultivation of mind, and used physical techniques to transform the body. Like Wei Po-yang before him, he saw no conflict between ingesting external substances and using internal techniques to transform body and mind.

The Separation of Internal and External Alchemy
(T'ang Dynasty, 618–960 CE)

Toward the end of the Southern dynasties (circa 580 CE), the Taoist alchemists were having doubts about ingesting compounds made from lead, mercury, cinnabar, and sulphates. Many alchemists and their patrons died eating elixirs concocted from poisonous materials. The lack of confidence in producing an immortal pill was seen in the use of prisoners on death row as guinea pigs in the alchemical experiments. The failure to produce a pill of immortality called for a reexamination of the techniques of external alchemy and a reevaluation of the theoretical foundations of the entire endeavor. All this was to affect the development of alchemy in the T'ang dynasty.

With the T'ang dynasty, China entered an era of political stability and prosperity. Some of the greatest poetry, art, and calligraphy of China came from this era. Trade routes and diplomatic relations were opened, east to Japan and west to Central Asia, India, and Europe. The T'ang emperors were strong believers in the pills of immortality. More emperors died of poisoning from ingesting minerals in the T'ang than in any other dynasty.

In the early T'ang, all the conditions were ripe for external alchemy to make a comeback after its decline toward the end of the Southern dynasties. The emperors and the nobility longed for immortality; the Taoist alchemists were ready to reevaluate their research and theories; and Taoism was embraced by all social classes. Elixirs of immortality became an integral part of the social life of the T'ang dynasty. Poets like Li Po and Po Chu-i celebrated the arts of immortality, and the research and practice of external alchemy reached new heights of development.

The imperial patronage of external alchemy created a new group of Taoist alchemists: those who worked solely in the research and fabrication of the elixir of immortality. Before the T'ang dynasty,

Taoists who experimented with the external pill also practiced other techniques of longevity. Some (like Ko Hung), were eclectics who practiced external alchemy, herbal medicine, talismanic magic, calisthenics, breath control, and meditation; others (like T'ao Hung-ching) were adepts at Shang-ch'ing methods of longevity, using minerals and herbs as supplements. Some (like the legendary Wei Po-yang—page 68), practiced a mixture of external alchemy, internal alchemy, and sexual yoga. It was only in the T'ang dynasty that we begin to see an increasing number of Taoists who were solely involved with external alchemy.

The renewed enthusiasm for external alchemy produced several new ideas. In the T'ang dynasty, alchemists acknowledged that there are two kinds of elixirs. The first kind occurs naturally and is found in minerals and stones that have absorbed the yin and yang vapors of the universe. When correct amounts of sunshine and moonlight have been absorbed over a period of four thousand three hundred and twenty years, substances like lead and mercury will be transformed into cinnabar, and will eventually crystallize into a pill with a golden color. The person who ingests this pill will become immortal. Needless to say, pills that occur under these natural conditions are very rare; thus, alchemists were forced to find ways to manufacture the pills under artificial conditions. The rationale was that if the yang heat and yin cooling could be simulated in laboratory conditions, it might be possible to create the immortal elixir under controlled conditions. Much of the research of external alchemy of the T'ang dynasty was therefore concerned with building a furnace and cauldron that was patterned after the natural furnace and cauldron of sky and earth.

In fabricating the immortal pill, increasing and reducing the heat of the furnace must follow the movement of the sun, moon, and stars. If the alchemical process is to succeed, the firing process should also follow the sequence of the waxing and waning of the yang fire of the sun and the yin essence of the moon. The furnace must therefore be lighted in the eleventh month and its heat must be regulated at critical times throughout the year. When these details are observed, the alchemist will succeed in creating laboratory conditions that simulate the natural conditions.

Finally, ingredients must be selected and mixed with the same precision as herbal medicine. Twenty-seven substances are listed in an authoritative text of the time. These substances include lead, mercury, zinc, nickel, sodium sulphate, rock salt, mercuric sulphide, silver, cinnabar, various forms of malachite, and arsenious oxides. Even a glance will reveal that most of these substances are poisonous; indeed, alchemists admitted that if incorrect quantities were taken, death could result.

Many poisonings did occur. People who swallowed the pills of immortality suffered slow poisoning that led to the failure of the liver and spleen. Other fatal effects included breakdown of the nervous system and various forms of mental disorder. After three hundred years of failure in research and experimentation, external alchemy declined.

Toward the latter part of the T'ang dynasty, the Taoists began to question whether immortality was indeed possible. This led to a rethinking of the meaning of immortality. One definition of immortality was influenced by Buddhism: immortality was the liberation from the endless cycles of reincarnation. Another definition equated immortality with living a long and healthy life. The practitioners of the arts of immortality gradually turned to meditation, massage, calisthenics, and yoga-like postures for cultivating life. By the end of the T'ang dynasty, the heyday of external alchemy was over.

During the final decades of its rule, the T'ang dynasty was beset with court intrigues, peasant uprisings, insubordinate provincial governors, and the constant threat of invasion from neighboring tribes. Eventually, a powerful provincial governor led an army into the capital, dethroned the emperor, and established a new dynasty—his own.

For the next fifty years, China was again plunged into political chaos. Five dynasties came and went as one military government replaced another. The violence that surrounded the rise and fall of these short-lived dynasties surpassed even that of the Southern and Northern dynasties. Moreover, these dynasties controlled only a small portion of what was formerly held by the T'ang empire. Many areas were annexed by powerful provincial governors who ruled like petty kings. These semiautonomous regions were called the Ten Kingdoms.

During the political chaos of the Five Dynasties and Ten Kingdoms, many intellectuals abandoned politics and became recluses. Most of them were trained in the Confucian tradition. The most famous of these Confucian-trained Taoists were Lü Tung-pin, Chen Tuan (Chen Hsi-yi), and Wang Ch'ung-yang. These scholars retained Confucian values even as they embraced Taoism. The kind of Taoism that interested them was not the talismanic magic of the Celestial Teachers or the external alchemists' obsession with a pill of immortality, but a form of Taoism that focused on cultivating virtue, health, quietude, and living a simple and harmonious life.

The Height of Development of Internal Alchemy:
The Age of Chang Po-tuan (Northern and Southern
Sung Dynasties 960–1368 CE)

The Sung dynasty (960–1279 CE) was the golden era of internal alchemy. During this period, the theory and practice of internal alchemy reached a sophistication unmatched in any other period of Chinese history.

Lü Tung-pin is generally acknowledged as the grand patriarch of internal alchemy. Born toward the end of the T'ang dynasty and living through the era of the Five Dynasties and Ten Kingdoms into the early Sung, Lü was disillusioned by the political conditions of his time. He abandoned his political aspirations and followed an immortal named Chung-li Ch'uan into the mountains to learn the arts of internal alchemy.

Lü Tung-pin transmitted his teachings to several students who in turn became founders of their own schools of the arts of longevity. One of them was Chen Hsi-yi, who was most famous for his innovative techniques of ch'i-kung. Chen Hsi-yi's form of internal alchemy integrated the cosmology of the *I-ching*, the Confucian ideas of cultivating virtue, and physical techniques of circulating energy.

Another student of Lü Tung-pin was Wang Ch'ung-yang, who founded the Complete Reality School and was one of the first Taoists to integrate Taoism, Buddhism, and Confucianism explicitly. We shall look at the Complete Reality School in more detail in chapter 6, when we examine the philosophical synthesis of these three schools of thought.

But if anyone is to be recognized as foremost theorist and practitioner of internal alchemy in the Sung dynasty, it is Chang Po-tuan. Chang (987–1082 CE) lived in the early part of the Sung dynasty and received the teachings of Lü Tung-pin through Liu Hai-ch'an. Chang's writings are filled with metaphors of alchemy: he spoke of the furnace and cauldron, the firing process, the copulation of yin and yang, and the crystallization of the golden pill by compounding lead and mercury. When his book the *Wu-jen p'ien* (Understanding Reality) was published, Chang Po-tuan was hailed as the successor to Wei Po-yang. However, there is a difference between these two alchemists: for Wei Po-yang, there was the possibility of making an elixir from substances external to the body; for Chang Po-tuan, all the ingredients and equipment necessary for the alchemical processes are inside the body.

In the internal alchemy of Chang Po-tuan, lead and mercury are the essence of yin and yang energies in the body, the furnace is the heat generated in the lower tan-t'ien (fig. 5.3), the cauldron is where the internal energy is refined, pumping the bellows refers to regulating the breath and controlling the heat of the lower tan-t'ien, the immortal fetus is the bundle of refined energy that is the seed of longevity and immortality, and the ten-month incubation of the fetus in the womb refers to the length of time required for the internal pill to mature.

Chang Po-tuan's internal alchemy was part of a revolution in Taoist thinking that occurred in the Sung dynasty. Out of this revolution emerged a form of Taoism that was influenced by Zen Buddhism and Confucianism. It advocated the dual cultivation of body and mind and combined methods of emptying the mind with physical techniques for circulating internal energy.

FIGURE 5.3. The furnace and cauldron in the body of the internal alchemist, from *Nei-wai-kung t'u-shuo* (Illustrations of Internal and External Methods of Cultivation), collected by Hsiao T'ien-shih. The drawing is titled "Picture of Light Radiating in All Directions." The three-legged cauldron symbolizes both the furnace and cauldron of the lower tan-t'ien; the crescent moon is the middle tan-t'ien; and the disk on the head is the ni-wan (mud ball) cavity. The practitioner is holding the orbs of the Red Raven and the Jade Rabbit, which are the essence of yang and yin, respectively. The writing (top), translated, reads, "Cavities: the openings of the three cavities; inside the cavities are subtleties; when the subtle cavities are visible, this is called light radiating in all directions."

Of the internal alchemists of the Sung dynasty, Wang Ch'ung-yang was the one most influenced by Confucianism. Virtue, honor, and other Confucian values formed an important part of his teachings. Chang Po-tuan, by contrast, was less influenced by Confucian codes of behavior. More pragmatic in his approach to the techniques of longevity, he considered sexual techniques viable in the early stages of cultivating the body. Wang Ch'ung-yang, to the contrary, did not consider sexual alchemy to be a legitimate technique.

After Chang Po-tuan's death, his students founded the southern branch of the Complete Reality School. An opposing northern branch was founded by Wang Ch'ung-yang's student Ch'iu Ch'ang-ch'un. Toward the end of the Sung dynasty, internal alchemists like

Chang San-feng, the originator of t'ai-chi ch'uan, began to incorporate the practice of internal martial arts into internal alchemy. Other
practitioners combined meditation and calisthenics, and some even
incorporated the Shang-ch'ing methods of absorbing the essence of
the sun, moon, and stars in their practice of cultivating health and
longevity. Others reintroduced the use of herbs (but not minerals)
to supplement the internal methods. These internal alchemists,
however, had one thing in common: they all acknowledged that internal alchemy involved both physical and psychological transformation. In this respect, all were proponents of the dual cultivation of
body and mind.

Further Readings

Those interested in the history of external alchemy, the ingestion
of minerals, and the manufacturing of the pills of immortality, will
find material in vol. 5, part 3, of Joseph Needham's *Science and Civilization in China*. That volume also contains a good discussion of
the contributions of Wei Po-yang and Ko Hung to the development
of the science of physical alchemy.

For a history of internal alchemy, see Needham's *Science and Civilization in China*, vol. 5, part 5. Needham is interested more in the
scientific ramifications of internal alchemy than in its practice as a
spiritual discipline. It is interesting to compare his approach to the
Taoist arts of health and longevity with those of Maspero, Robinet,
Kohn, and others who focus more on the spiritual value of internal
alchemy.

To get a feel for the early writings of alchemy, look at James Ware's
selected translation of Ko Hung's *P'ao-p'u-tzu Nei-p'ien* (Inner Chapters of the Sage Who Embraces Simplicity). Although Ware uses anti-
quated words that may sometimes mislead the reader (he equates
shen with God where it would be better understood as spirit), it is
still a good source of information on the early alchemical literature.

There is a complete translation of Chang Po-tuan's *Wu-jen p'ien*
in Thomas Cleary's *Understanding Reality*. Cleary has also included

the Outer Chapters that Chang wrote later for nonadepts. There is less technical terminology in the Outer Chapters: the discussions are concerned more with the mental than the physical side of internal alchemy. Cleary has also included a commentary by Ch'ing dynasty author Liu I-ming. Liu's commentary should not be taken as the definitive interpretation of Chang's original work; in fact, Liu I-ming tends to psychologize the physical phenomena described by Chang Po-tuan. Liu I-ming's form of Taoism represents an approach that considers internal alchemy as primarily mental phenomena. (More about this form of Taoism in chapter 6). Liu's view of internal alchemy is very different from Chang Po-tuan's, and his commentary on the *Wu-jen p'ien* is more like a reworking or "demythologizing" of Chang's text than an effort to clarify it. Cleary separates Chang's original text from Liu's commentary by setting the original text in boldface type and the commentary in roman.

Another famous work of Chang Po-tuan is a short treatise titled *Chin-tan ssu-po tzu*. This is translated by Thomas Cleary in *The Inner Teachings of Taoism* as "Four Hundred Words on the Golden Elixir." Again a commentary by Liu I-ming is included.

Isabelle Robinet has a short chapter titled "Original Contributions of Nei-tan to Taoism and Chinese Thought" in a book edited by Livia Kohn, *Taoist Meditation and Longevity Techniques*. Robinet's work is a brief but good account of the development of internal alchemy in the T'ang and early Sung dynasties.

Good summaries of the history of Taoism that we have looked at in chapters 3, 4, and 5 can be found in books 5 and 7 of Maspero's *Taoism and Chinese Religion*.

6

The Synthesis of Taoism Buddhism, and Confucianism (1000 CE–present)

By the end of the tenth century CE, the dream of discovering a pill of immortality by compounding minerals seemed to be over. Three hundred years of reevaluating the theory and practice of external alchemy had not produced positive results, and the numerous poisonings and deaths had convinced the Taoist community that it was time to find another way to attain longevity.

The political chaos of the Five Dynasties and Ten Kingdoms (907–960 CE) made hermits out of many Confucian scholars. They embraced the quintessence of Taoism and admired the mental discipline of Zen Buddhism, but they did not want to abandon Confucian values. These scholars initiated a synthesis of Taoism, Buddhism, and Confucianism that focused on the dual cultivation of body and mind. This synthesis would characterize much of the Taoist arts of longevity that are practiced today.

The Philosophical Synthesis
(Northern Sung Dynasty 960–1126 CE)

The first synthesis of Taoism, Buddhism, and Confucianism was primarily philosophical: it integrated a form of Taoism that was already sympathetic to cultivating inner peace and stillness with Zen

Buddhism's theory of original mind and Confucianism's idea of the original nature of goodness. Its foremost proponent was Wang Ch'ung-yang.

Wang Ch'ung-yang (Wang Che) had a classical Confucian education, but the violent and militaristic rule of the emperors of the Five Dynasties had no use for Confucian values and benevolent politics. At age forty, Wang Che gave up his hopes for a career in the civil service, apprenticed himself to the Taoist immortals Lü Tung-pin and Chung-li Ch'uan to learn the arts of longevity, and adopted the Taoist name of Wang Ch'ung-yang.

History and legend tell us that Wang Ch'ung-yang explored various forms of Buddhism, including Zen and T'ien-tai, before he became a student of the Taoist arts. Even after he had completed his training in Taoism, he continued to have a high regard for both Zen Buddhism and Confucianism. He believed that the integration of the Zen experience of emptiness, the ethics of Confucianism, and the Taoist techniques of health and longevity could offer a complete understanding of the ultimate reality of things. Thus, he named his form of Taoism the Complete Reality (Ch'üan-chen) School.

Wang Ch'ung-yang's school adopted Confucianism's *K'ao-ching* (Classic of Filial Piety) and Buddhism's *Heart Sutra* into its repertoire of scriptures. Of the Taoist texts, the *Tao-te ching* and the *Ch'ing-ching ching* (Cultivating Stillness) were especially important.

Complete Reality Taoism is not an eclectic system of thought. Its integration of Taoism, Zen Buddhism, and Confucianism initiated a unique approach to Taoism that is characterized by the dual cultivation of body and mind. Taoism formed the foundation of the synthesis: Confucianism and Zen Buddhism were integrated to complement it; however, of all the forms of Taoism that emerged during the Sung dynasty, Wang Ch'ung-yang's had the most Confucian and Zen Buddhist flavor.

In Wang Ch'ung-yang's system of thought, the Tao, the formless and undifferentiated energy, is the underlying reality of all things. To merge with the Tao is to draw energy from this source of life. This is longevity. However, the ultimate reality of the Tao can be experienced only by original mind, which is empty of thoughts, attachments, and desire. In Complete Reality Taoism, original mind is also the original spirit *(yüan-shen)*, or immortal fetus. According to Wang Ch'ung-yang, everyone has the spark of the Tao inside them, but craving and mindless thinking have prevented this spark from developing. The goal of Taoist practice is to return to the original mind by removing the barriers that have kept us from it. As in Zen Buddhism, spiritual training in the Complete Reality School begins with the eradication of desire and emptying the mind of thoughts. This allows us to cultivate stillness and experience the Tao.

The Confucian influence on Wang Ch'ung-yang's thinking is strong. In addition to incorporating values such as virtue, benevolence, and honor into spiritual training, Wang Ch'ung-yang equates original mind with the Confucian notion of the original nature of goodness. For him, the original mind is not only empty of desire but also has a tendency toward goodness; thus, doing charitable deeds is an important part of Complete Reality Taoism. Despite the Confucian and Buddhist influences, however, Wang Ch'ung-yang's Complete Reality School is essentially Taoist: it recognizes that spiritual training involves the transformation of both body and mind and that this transformation is alchemical.

DIVISION OF THE COMPLETE REALITY SCHOOL

Not all of Wang Ch'ung-yang's students agreed with his approach to cultivating body and mind; moreover, variations in interpretation of the master's thought, even by his closest students, the Seven Taoist Masters, gave rise to different sects within the Complete Reality School.

The most famous division within the school was the formation of the southern branch, by Chang Po-tuan, and the northern branch, by Wang Ch'ung-yang's closest student, Ch'iu Ch'ang-ch'un (fig. 6.1). Chang Po-tuan did not study directly under Wang, but his

FIGURE 6.1. Ch'iu Ch'ang-ch'un, one of the Seven Masters of the Complete Reality School. Picture courtesy of the White Cloud Monastery in Beijing.

teacher, Liu Hai-ch'an, was a student of Lü Tung-pin; thus, Chang's teacher was a fellow student of Wang Ch'ung-yang's.

Differences already existed between Wang Ch'ung-yang's form of Taoism and that of Liu Hai-ch'an. Thus, the division of the Complete Reality School actually occurred in the generation before Chang Po-tuan. These divergent forms of Complete Reality Taoism were formed right from the beginning, when Liu Hai-ch'an and Wang Ch'ung-yang both learned from Lü Tung-pin. When the two systems of teachings were transmitted to Chang Po-tuan and Ch'iu Ch'ang-ch'un, the two branches of Complete Reality Taoism were officially recognized. Taoist historians now identify Ch'iu Ch'ang-ch'un's northern branch as the Lung-men (Dragon Gate) sect and Chang Po-tuan's southern branch as the Tzu-yang (Purple Yang) sect.

Several major differences exist between the two branches of Complete Reality Taoism. First, Wang Ch'ung-yang placed more importance on cultivating the mind and taught that mind must be cultivated before body. Chang Po-tuan, on the other hand, advocated cultivating the body before mind and placed more emphasis on strengthening the body. Wang Ch'ung-yang's Complete Reality Taoism used Zen-like meditation methods to build the foundation of spiritual development: emptying the mind of thoughts, minimizing desire, and becoming nonattached to external situations are all part of cultivating the mind. Chang Po-tuan's southern branch, by contrast, focused on techniques of gathering, refining, and circulating internal energy to cultivate health and longevity.

For Wang Ch'ung-yang, the physical techniques introduced in the latter part of the training functioned to teach the practitioner how to apply the physical transformations that were brought about by cultivating the mind; whereas, for Chang Po-tuan, refining the body was a prerequisite for the forms of meditation practiced in the advanced stages of training. Moreover, where Wang Chung-yang's form of Complete Reality Taoism would not use sexual techniques for gathering energy, Chang Po-tuan's sect considered sexual yoga a viable method of replenishing energy in the early stages of training, especially for older people.

By the end of the Northern Sung (circa 1100 CE), the Complete Reality School, especially the Lung-men sect, had become a powerful religious organization. Monastic and highly disciplined, it had an efficient administration, owned land, and had a network of monasteries. The invasion of the Chin tribe and the Sung dynasty's loss of its northern lands did not hinder the momentum of the Lung-men sect. In fact, when the Sung ruling family fled south from the northern invaders, the Lung-men sect won the respect and patronage of the new rulers and flourished in the Chin kingdom. It continued to be favored by the Mongols after Kublai Khan conquered the Chin tribe.

In the south, where the Sung dynasty clung to its dwindling territory, the picture was very different. The southern branch of Complete Reality Taoism began to decline, and political and social conditions favored a form of Taoism that synthesized the popular beliefs of devotional Buddhism, religious Taoism, and the ethics of Confucianism. This synthesis gave rise to the Action and Karma School of Taoism, and in the south made ethics and devotion the focus of Taoist practice.

The Religious Synthesis: Southern Sung Dynasty (1127–1279 CE) and Ming Dynasty (1368–1644 CE)

The fall of the Northern Sung in 1126 CE brought a flood of refugees to the regions of China south of the Yang-tze. Not only did these refugees lose their lands and fortune, they also lost their faith in the imperial government's ability to protect them from the invaders. The Southern Sung dynasty was always threatened with invasion from the north; its emperors were weak, and the officials corrupt. An attempt to regain its lost territory after the Mongol conquest of the Chin tribe brought the Southern Sung in direct conflict with Kublai Khan's expanding empire. The days of the Southern Sung were spent retreating from the invasion of the Mongols and in 1279 it was finally conquered by Kublai.

Throughout the last hundred years of the Southern Sung, as people fled from invading armies, food was scarce and relief from the central government, appropriated by corrupt officials, was sold at enormous prices. When the common citizens of the Southern Sung could not find protection from their government, they turned to the deities for guidance. What fulfilled their spiritual needs was not the individual enlightenment of Zen Buddhism, nor the arts of longevity of the Taoist internal alchemists, nor even the religious ceremonies of the Celestial Teachers: it was a popular religion that integrated religious Taoism, devotional Buddhism, and commonsense Confucian ethics. This was Action and Karma Taoism—a movement that taught that ethical action was rewarded and unethical action invited karmic retribution. Its patron deities included Taoist immortals, Buddhist bodhisattvas, and Confucian sages. This popular religious movement was inspired by the teachings of the *T'ai-shang kan-ying p'ien* (Lao-tzu's Treatise on the Response of the Tao), a book written by a Taoist scholar named Li Ying-chang.

Aurora Public Library
(905)-727-9494
www.aurorapl.ca

The synthesis of Taoism, Buddhism, and Confucianism in popular religion was not so much a conscious intent on the part of Li Ying-chang when he wrote the *T'ai-shang kan-ying p'ien;* rather, this treatise provided the impetus and sparked a movement that created its own momentum. Between the end of the Sung dynasty and the late Ming dynasty, moral tales were developed around the *Kan-ying p'ien,* and it was in these stories that traditional Confucian values, Buddhist ideas of reincarnation and karma, and the Taoist deities' power over health and longevity were woven together.

The Southern Sung fell in 1279 CE and was replaced by the Yüan dynasty of the Mongols. Although it was the Lung-men branch of the Complete Reality School that was favored by the Yüan emperors, Action and Karma Taoism, the popular movement, was firmly established among the common people.

POPULAR RELIGION IN THE MING

Mongol rule over a unified China was brief. Ninety years after their conquest of the Southern Sung, Kublai Khan's Yüan dynasty ended. A popular uprising drove the Mongols out of central China and ushered in the Ming dynasty (1368–1644 CE).

The Ming dynasty emperors were sympathetic to popular religion. They participated in state-sponsored ceremonies, appointed the Celestial Teachers to preside over the rituals, and were strong believers in Taoist magic and sorcery.

The rise of popular religion changed not only the face of Taoism but also affected Buddhism. Zen Buddhism's focus on individual enlightenment and disciplined practice lost its appeal, to be replaced by a form of devotional Buddhism that emphasized chanting the names of the buddhas, praying to the bodhisattvas, and believing in reincarnation and karmic retribution. Enlightenment, or becoming immortalized as a buddha, became equated with the acquisition of magical abilities, rather than attaining stillness and experiencing the reality of the Tao. Thus, in the Ming dynasty, an enlightened person was considered to be an individual with power.

Popular religion in the Ming dynasty was facilitated by the development of the novel. Some of the literature, like *Seven Taoist Masters*, combined philosophy and spiritual teachings with the legends of Taoist sages. Other writings, like the *Feng-shen yen-yi* (Investiture of the Gods) and *Hsi-yu chi* (Journey to the West), blended Taoist and Buddhist spiritual values with fantasy. By the end of the Ming dynasty, there was a collection of stories built around Li Ying-chang's teachings in the *T'ai-shang kan-ying p'ien*, which incorporated the Buddhist ideas of reincarnation, Taoist beliefs in immortals, and the Confucian values of dedication, filial piety, and honor.

The religious synthesis of Taoism, Buddhism, and Confucianism was so thorough that by the time of the Ch'ing dynasty (1644–1911 CE), the popular religion of the Chinese had a pantheon of deities consisting of Taoist immortals, Buddhist bodhisattvas, and Confucian sages. Taoist immortals were given Buddhist names and bodhisattvas became incarnations of Taoist immortals. Today, in popular Taoism, Lü Tung-pin, the Taoist immortal, is regarded as an incarnation of Manjushri Buddha, and Lao-tzu is sometimes identified as the Tathagata (Suchness) Buddha.

*Variations of the Synthesis and the Rise of Sects
in Taoism (Ming Dynasty 1368–1644 CE)*

The flowering of popular religion in the Ming dynasty encouraged the development of sects in Taoism. Official religious ceremonies were conducted by the Celestial Teachers, but there was no state-sponsored religion. The Ming emperors admired individuals who had magical or supernatural powers; thus, in the Ming we see the investiture of many Taoists as *chen-jen*, or realized beings. Some were distinguished Taoist thinkers (e.g., Wang Ch'ung-yang and Chang Po-tuan), some were leaders of Taoist sects (e.g., the seven disciples of Wang Ch'ung-yang), and some were hermits (e.g., Chang San-feng).

More Taoist sects were formed in the Ming dynasty than in any other period of Chinese history. Disagreement over theory and practice might have motivated the formation of sects, but it was the social and political climate that encouraged their existence. The

Ming emperors and the common citizens were probably not interested in how Chang San-feng's methods of cultivating body and mind differed from those of the Lung-men sect: what mattered to them was that these individuals had magical abilities and power. Sects were therefore free to develop, and their rise and fall were tied to the power and charisma of their leaders.

The most famous of the chen-jen of the Ming dynasty was Chang San-feng (fig. 6.2). Most people know him as the originator of t'ai-chi ch'uan, the set of slow-moving exercises for cultivating health and circulating internal energy, but Chang San-feng was also an expert in herbal medicine and wrote treatises on internal alchemy. His form of internal alchemy emphasized cultivating the body and favored techniques of moving over nonmoving meditation. Chang San-feng was respected and honored by several Ming emperors, and the Wu-tang-shan sect established by his students even today has wide influence in Hupei and Shensi Provinces in central China.

In the late Ming, a division within the Lung-men sect created the Wu-Liu sect, named after Wu Chung-hsü and Liu Hua-yang.

FIGURE 6.2. Chang San-feng, patriarch of the Wu-tang-shan sect and originator of t'ai-chi ch'uan. The caption reads, "Chang the Immortal, who understands the subtleties and reveals the mysteries."

Originally a high-level initiate of the Lung-men sect, Wu Chung-hsü left the sect because he disagreed with the mainstream Lung-men doctrines. Wu's form of internal alchemy integrated Zen Buddhism, Hua-yen Buddhism, and the Taoist arts of longevity, but excluded the Confucian elements and ceremonial rituals of the Complete Reality School. In the Ch'ing dynasty, Wu Chung-hsü's successor, Liu Hua-yang, took Wu's teachings, combined them with the Shang-ch'ing ideas of spirit travel, and wrote the *Hui-ming ching* (The Treatise on Cultivating Life).

The popularity of magic and sorcery in the Ming dynasty gave rise to several sects that combined talismanic magic with cultivating body and mind. Out of this strange union emerged the Mao-shan sect (not to be confused with the Shang-ch'ing Mao-shan Taoism of T'ao Hung-ching—see page 52), which used a combination of sorcery, talismanic magic, and ch'i-kung techniques to cultivate an "indestructible body." This sect became extremely powerful and influential in the Ch'ing dynasty, and even today Mao-shan sorcerers are still feared and respected.

There was also the Eastern sect—so called because it flourished in southeast China—which used a combination of sexual alchemy, calisthenics, breath control, and quiet sitting to cultivate health and longevity. Proponents of this sect claimed to be influenced by the form of Complete Reality Taoism taught by Chang Po-tuan.

The Ming dynasty was indeed the era of sectarian Taoism. Since there is no such thing as heresy in Chinese religion, disagreements led to division, and division led to the formation of a new sect. Some sects (for example, the Lung-men sect) were monastic and celibate; there were also sects (for example, the Celestial Teachers) with a priestly clergy that was allowed to marry. The Wu-Liu sect, which separated from the Lung-men sect, did not allow the use of sexual yoga but was opposed to enforced celibacy and monastic life. For the Mao-shan sorcerers, who were neither monks nor priests, celibacy was recommended to help in training in the magical arts. Then there was Action and Karma Taoism, which emerged from the synthesis of Taoist, Buddhist, and Confucian popular beliefs. This movement became a form of lay Taoism, its leaders coming from all walks of life.

By the end of the Ming dynasty, there were so many Taoist sects that it was difficult to keep track of all of them. Some sects lasted for only one generation, disappearing when their founders died; others continued for several generations. When the Ming was replaced by the Ch'ing dynasty in 1644, another form of Taoism emerged. This kind of Taoism is sometimes called contemplative Taoism, for it re-vived the practice of cultivating the mind and considered internal alchemy to be a purely psychological phenomenon.

A New Synthesis of Confucianism, Zen Buddhism, and Taoist Internal Alchemy (Ch'ing Dynasty 1644–1911 CE)

During the last fifty years of the Ming dynasty, the emperors fre-quently relied on magic, prayers, and petitions to solve the problems of the country. Priests replaced ministers as confidants of the emper-ors, and the advice of many skilled administrators was dismissed. Some Taoists and Buddhists took advantage of the emperors' trust in them and became extremely powerful. Court politics were domi-nated by antagonism between the civil servants and the religious advisers. Factions conspired against each other and the administra-tion of the country was neglected.

Other problems also contributed to the end of the Ming dynasty. By 1600 CE, the Manchu tribe was emerging as a powerful force in northeast China. The Manchu conquered the smaller tribes in the region between Korea and Russia and were poised to invade central China. Internally, within the Ming empire, the nobility was divided, and the eunuchs rose to power by allying themselves with ambitious and worldly Taoist and Buddhist priests. Corruption in the provincial government brought discontent, and discontent led to peasant upris-ings. When the Ming government turned down a trade treaty with the Portuguese, its fate was sealed. Trade goods, muskets, and can-nons from the Western nations went to the Manchus. With superiority in firepower, the Manchu conquest of the already crumbling Ming empire was sure and swift.

The Ch'ing dynasty (1644–1911 CE) ushered in an era of "critical reflection" of everything from the past. The "past" was the Ming dynasty, and most of Ch'ing intellectual activity consisted of criticizing the literary, artistic, and spiritual trends of the Ming dynasty.

Magical practices in Taoism were especially under attack, for several reasons: the intellectual atmosphere encouraged criticism of the popular and religious Taoism of the Ming dynasty; the prevailing intellectual trend was suspicious of anything that was nonrational (magic, sorcery, belief in deities and spirits, and even aspects of internal alchemy were all targets of criticism); and many intellectuals blamed religious Taoism and the belief in magic for the fall of the Ming dynasty and the humiliation of being conquered by "foreign" invaders.

This intellectual atmosphere produced two kinds of Taoism: the intellectual and contemplative Taoism represented by Liu I-ming, and a new synthesis of Buddhism and internal alchemy found in the Wu-Liu sect led by Liu Hua-yang.

LIU I-MING

Liu I-ming (1734–1821 CE) was a Confucian scholar who turned to Taoism in middle life. Originally initiated into the Lung-men sect of the Complete Reality School, Liu soon found that he disagreed with that sect's monasticism and its increasing emphasis on liturgy and ritual. Leaving the Lung-men sect, he apprenticed himself to an internal alchemist in Kansu Province, learned the arts of longevity, and became a hermit.

Liu I-ming was adept at many branches of Taoist knowledge. He wrote treatises on medicine and internal alchemy as well as commentaries on the *I-ching*. The most famous of his writings included commentaries on Chang Po-tuan's *Wu-jen p'ien*, the *Tsan-tung-chi*, and several treatises on advice on cultivating mind and body.

Liu I-ming's form of Taoism could be described as contemplative Taoism. It emphasized stilling the mind, understanding original nature, and living a life of harmony and simplicity. The most important features of Liu I-ming's ideas were their distinct Confucian influence and Liu's unique approach to internal alchemy. The Confucian influence probably came from Liu's own experience: he started his career as a Confucian scholar and civil administrator and became a Taoist recluse only after retirement.

Liu's form of internal alchemy is unique in its interpretation of the alchemical process. For Liu I-ming, internal alchemy is psychological, and much of the alchemical work is concerned with transforming the mind. To realize the Tao is to recover original nature, and the recovery of original nature involves developing true knowledge. Since true knowledge is often silenced by conscious knowledge, stilling the mind becomes central in allowing true knowledge to develop. Terminology such as *fire, water, sweet nectar, yellow sprouts, lead, mercury, dragon, tiger, furnace,* and *cauldron* all refers to psychological, not physical phenomena. Thus, in Liu's form of internal alchemy, the male tiger represents innate knowledge of goodness in the original mind; the female dragon is the clear consciousness of an uncluttered mind; sweet nectar becomes purity of mind, and yellow sprouts symbolize the stillness of mind. The furnace symbolizes the flexibility of earth, and the cauldron, the firmness of sky. The term *building the furnace and positioning the cauldron* refers to stabilizing and balancing firmness and flexibility, rather than refining the internal energies in the three tan-t'iens.

With the psychologizing of internal alchemy, the dual cultivation of body and mind becomes the cultivation of original nature, and physical health and longevity are the by-products of a tranquil mind. This form of internal alchemy is very different from that of Chang Po-tuan and Wei Po-yang, for whom the alchemical processes are both physical and mental.

While Liu I-ming's form of Taoism was integrating Taoist internal alchemy with the Confucian ideas of cultivating original nature, moderation, and balance, another form of Taoism was emerging from the synthesis of Taoist internal alchemy and Buddhism. This was Liu

Hua-yang's Wu-Liu sect, and his ideas are presented in his famous book, the *Hui-ming ching.*

LIU HUA-YANG

Liu Hua-yang (1736–1846? CE) learned the arts of longevity from a student of Wu Chung-hsü. Wu Chung-hsü was sympathetic to methods of Zen meditation and incorporated them into his theory and practice of internal alchemy. Liu Hua-yang took Wu Chung-hsü's approach to cultivating body and mind and developed a form of Taoism that combined what he thought was the best of Taoist internal alchemy and Buddhism.

In Liu Hua-yang's system of internal alchemy, immortality and attainment of Buddhahood are different names for the same spiritual experience. A Buddhist who embraced Taoism in his middle years, Liu Hua-yang claimed that Taoist alchemy alone could cultivate life but not original mind, and Buddhism alone could cultivate original mind but not health and longevity. Thus, his approach used both Taoist internal alchemical techniques and Zen and Hua-yen Buddhist meditation to attain the highest level of spiritual experience.

According to Liu Hua-yang, everyone possesses the essence of life, which is the energy of the Tao inside the body. Desire, negative attitude, and emotional attachment cause this life force to leak from the body, resulting in the loss of health and immortality. If the mind is still and if craving is curbed, the leakage will be stopped, and the life force will circulate through the body. With continued cultivation, the spiritual fetus, or original spirit, which is the seed of immortality, will grow within. This fetus is the consciousness of the original mind, as well as the energy that nourishes the body. After a period of incubation, the spiritual fetus emerges from the body to create a spirit-body that can travel to other realms of existence. Eventually, the spirit is mature enough to be independent of the shell that bore it. When the shell dies, the spirit, in the form of energy, is liberated, to merge with the energy of the universe.

During the Ch'ing dynasty and the republican years (1911–1949

CE), many sects came and went. Some sects had small followings and did not survive beyond the lifetime of their founders. But some survived the social chaos, the wars, and the political changes to form the five major systems of Taoism that are practiced today. These "schools" of Taoism are Magical Taoism, Divinational Taoism, Ceremonial Taoism, Internal-Alchemical Taoism, and Action and Karma Taoism, and we shall look at the teachings of each of these schools in Part Two.

FURTHER READINGS

My *Seven Taoist Masters* tells the story of Wang Ch'ung-yang and his seven disciples and the founding of the northern school of Complete Reality Taoism. This provides a good introduction to the teachings of that school of Taoism: the stories are delightful, and the book presents valuable insights into what it means to pursue spiritual training in Taoism.

For a further exploration of the synthesis of Taoism, Buddhism, and Confucianism, and to see how this synthesis influenced internal alchemy in the more recent history of Taoism, read my translation of *Cultivating Stillness*.

Chung-ho chi, translated by Thomas Cleary as *The Book of Balance and Harmony*, is an internal-alchemical classic. Influenced by the synthesis of Taoism, Buddhism, and Confucianism, it was written by Li Tao-shun, a master of the Complete Reality School. Although influenced by Buddhism and Confucianism, Li's form of internal alchemy places equal emphasis on cultivating body and mind. It is clear that the phenomena described by Li in his book are both physical and mental. Cleary's lucid and readable translation unfortunately does not include the illustrations that accompany the original text collected in the Taoist canon.

The contemplative form of Taoism is best illustrated in Thomas Cleary's translations *Awakening to the Tao* and *Back to Beginnings*.

To get a feeling for how a classic of internal alchemy is "psychologized," read Liu I-ming's commentary on Chang Po-tuan's *Wu-jen p'ien*. Both Chang's original text and Liu's commentary can be found in Thomas Cleary's *Understanding Reality*.

The synthesis of Taoism, Buddhism, and Confucianism in the Action and Karma School of Taoism and in popular religion is discussed in detail in my translation of the *T'ai-shang kan-ying p'ien*, titled *Lao-tzu's Treatise on the Response of the Tao*. This book includes both a translation of this representative text of Action and Karma Taoism and stories inspired by it.

An anthology of readings translated by Thomas Cleary as *Vitality, Energy, Spirit* contains representative writings of Taoists influenced by the philosophical synthesis of Taoism, Buddhism, and Confucianism. Relevant sections are "Ancestor Lü," "The Founding of the Southern and Northern Schools," "Extracts From Contemplative Literature," "Chang San-feng," and "Liu I-ming."

PART TWO

Systems of Taoism

7
Magical Taoism
The Way of Power

O F A L L T H E S Y S T E M S of Taoism, Magical Taoism is probably the oldest. Its beliefs have not changed much since prehistoric times, and its practitioners today perform the same tasks as the shamans and sorcerers did of old. These tasks include calling for rain, fending off disasters, offering protection, divining, healing, driving off malevolent spirits, exorcism, traveling to the underworld to help dead souls, and acting as mediums for deities, spirits, and the dead.

Magical Taoism is the Way of Power. It believes that there are forces in the universe, natural and supernatural, that can be harnessed and used. Two kinds of power are recognized by the practitioners of Magical Taoism: those that come from nature, and those that come from spirits and deities. Typically, an individual who draws power from nature is a magician, whereas a person who draws power from deities and spirits (including animals and plants) is a sorcerer. In some cultures, the arts of magic and sorcery are exclusive, but in Magical Taoism, the practitioners are usually both magicians and sorcerers.

Basic Beliefs of Magical Taoism

1. The world is filled with power. Spirits, deities, elements (wind, rain, thunder, lightning, and so on), animals, plants, rocks . . . all these have power in them.

99

2. With the correct methods, power can be manipulated, channeled, directed, and used by the practitioner. However, the personal power of the magician or sorcerer is required to summon and control the powers in the universe.

3. The power in the natural elements is neutral and the practitioner can manipulate and control it without entering into a personal relationship with it. A Taoist magician can call down thunder, rain, or snow if he or she has knowledge of the correct methods and enough personal power. However, the extent to which the magician can control the elements will depend on the amount of personal power.

4. Power from deities and spirits is not neutral. Some spirits are benevolent and some are malevolent. Moreover, the power often takes on the personality of the deity or spirit. This kind of power is difficult to control because it has a will of its own. For example, if a deity with a stubborn nature is invoked, the sorcerer will have an especially difficult task in getting it to come and asking it to leave. Like controlling the natural forces, the extent to which the sorcerer can direct the deity or spirit will depend on the strength of the sorcerer's personal power.

5. There are several ways in which sorcerers can obtain power from a deity or spirit. First, they can draw on the power of the deity or spirit to enhance their own power. This is the safest form of sorcery, since power is under the sorcerer's conscious control. Second, the sorcerer can petition the deity or spirit to appear as a helper. In this condition, the sorcerer may cooperate with the summoned spirit or allow the spirit or deity to unleash its power. The sorcerer has less control in this situation, because once the spirit or deity has been summoned, it controls its own power. However, the sorcerer can still cast spells to dismiss the spirit. Finally, the sorcerer can offer himself as a medium for the deity or spirit to enter, thus providing a body in which the spirit can manifest its power. This is the most dangerous form of sorcery; it is also the most powerful. The personal power of the sorcerer is bonded with the power of the spirit or deity to form a

single force, but if the spirit gets out of control and overwhelms the sorcerer, the sorcerer will not be able to dismiss or contain it.

6. Objects can carry power. Objects can be endowed with the personal power of the magician or sorcerer, or they can carry the power of a deity or spirit. Not all objects can be empowered, and some are better carriers of power than others. Mirrors, bells, swords, gourds, fans, umbrellas, and lanterns are the best carriers of power. Some objects, like talismans (scripts of power) and amulets, embody power in themselves, because of the presence of the magical script; however, the magic needs to be activated by the appropriate methods. Some objects will carry power once they have been endowed and activated. An example is a talisman of protection posted on a door. Other objects require direction and control and are useless if the magician or sorcerer is absent.

Principal Practices of Magical Taoism

RAINMAKING

The magic of rainmaking can be traced to the shamans of prehistoric times, and it is still practiced by many religious and spiritual traditions. When I was about eight or nine years old, in Hong Kong, there was a drought, and all the religious groups held rainmaking ceremonies. Not only the Taoists, but the Buddhists, Catholics, and Mormons—all were praying or petitioning for rain.

There are two approaches to rainmaking in Magical Taoism. In the first approach, elements like clouds and rain are summoned. A magician with strong personal power can create clouds and rain out of a clear sky, whereas an individual with less power may be able only to call in the clouds and rain that are already in the area. In the second approach, a petition is made to a deity or spirit, asking for rain.

The preparations and ceremonial procedures for rainmaking are similar regardless of whether an element is summoned or a deity is petitioned. I shall describe a typical procedure used in many Taoist rainmaking rituals.

Before the ceremony is conducted, preparations are made. First, the leader of the rainmaking ceremony and seven helpers must purify themselves. The purification rite consists of abstaining from meat, wine, sex, and stimulants for three days before the ceremony. During these days of purification, the Taoist magician writes the talismans that summon the elements or the petitions that are to be sent to the deities. An individual who is in mourning or a woman who is in her menstruation cycle may not participate in a rainmaking ceremony.

While the leader of the ceremony is purifying himself—the leader can be either male or female—an altar is built on a mound, or plat-form. The front of the altar must face south, and sandalwood incense is burned in the four corners of the mound to purify the ceremonial ground. Only individuals who have been through the purification rites may build and arrange the altar. On the altar is placed a tortoise shell, a piece of marble, a bowl of chicken's blood (to serve as red ink), a new brush-pen, five sheets of clean, yellow paper, and a needle that has not been used. A large bucket and five branches are placed in front of the altar. The five branches are used to gather water from the five directions of the universe (north, south, east, west, and center) and direct it into the bucket.

On the appointed day, the leader of the ceremony and the helpers take a ritual bath. The ceremony begins at the hour of *tzu* (11:00 PM). The leader ascends the mound, followed by the seven helpers. Two helpers represent the female and male spirits of the dragon, and the five represent the spirits of thunder from the five directions. The leader begins the ceremony by cleansing the ground. He or she takes a talisman designed for purification purposes, burns it, and collects the ashes in the water. Sometimes, the leader scatters the water while walking around the mound, covering the four directions and then returning to the altar in the center. At other times, he puts the water in his mouth and spits it out as he walks around the mound.

After the cleansing, the attendants take their places. The repre-sentative of the female dragon stands to the left of the leader and the representative of the male dragon stands to the right. Four of the five thunder spirits are positioned in the four directions, the fifth, in the center, standing behind the leader.

When everyone is in position, the ceremony continues. If the magician is summoning natural elements, incantations will be uttered; if a deity is to be petitioned, invocations will be chanted. The nature of the invocation will differ depending on the sect conducting the ceremony; for example, the Celestial Teachers sect will send a petition to the founder of their sect, Chang Tao-ling. Some sects may include Yü's dance of power and walk the pattern of the seven stars of the Northern Bushel. The leader of the ceremony then takes the brush, dips it into the chicken's blood, and draws talismans designed to call down rain. He then takes the talismans, burns them, and collects the ashes in seven cups of water. The cups are given to the seven attendants to drink. The talismanic water allows the rain-spirits to enter the bodies of the seven helpers. Next, the leader takes the needle, dips it in chicken's blood, and goes to each helper to "open their eyes." *Opening the eyes* means activating the rain-spirits that have entered the seven helpers. Then incantations or invocations are made by the leader of the ceremony, by which the rain-spirits are directed from the five directions to the ceremonial grounds. The leader ends the ceremony by thanking the deities and the elements.

The ceremony may be repeated for three, five, or seven days, if necessary. During the days of the ceremony, the leader and the seven helpers observe the same rules of purification as those during preparation for the ceremony.

PROTECTION

Protecting people from disasters, illness, and malevolent spirits forms a large part of the practices of Magical Taoism. A person can be protected by the wearing of amulets, by having talismans of protection drawn on one's body, and by placing talismsans over the doorway or window of one's bedroom. Talismans of protection painted on the body are the most powerful, because they protect the person wherever he or she goes. Amulets can protect the individual from everyday mishaps, and they are worn by many Chinese children. When I was a child, I wore one all the time. Talismans placed over a window or on a bedroom door will protect only when the person is in that room.

Houses can be protected by placing the appropriate talisman of protection on the front door or over the doorway of the house. If there is a shrine in the house, the talismans are framed in a glass case and placed beside the deity who is enshrined. Some talismans are powerful enough to protect not only the household but also the household's livestock.

Other objects that can protect a household are mirrors and miniature weapons. A mirror hung over a doorway is designed to reflect away anything that is harmful. Any round mirror can be used, but a mirror with a *pa-k'ua* pattern on its rim is preferred (fig. 7.1), because

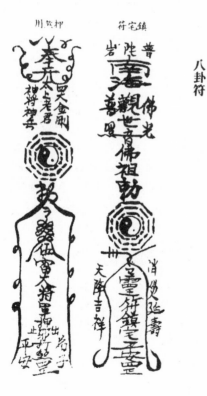

FIGURE 7.1. Kun-lun talismans of protection. These talismans are called pa-k'ua talismans. They invoke the power of the pa-k'ua—the trigrams surrounding the *t'ai-chi* (the yin-yang symbol) in the two talismans. The talisman on the right is the kind used to protect a house, and the one on the left is used to ward off destructive forces.

the pa-k'ua on the object increases its power. Sometimes, miniature weapons (for example, a pair of swords or a spear) are hung over the doorway to fight off malevolent or mischievous spirits that are trying to enter the house. These weapons have enhanced power if they are wielded by warrior deities. A picture of a warrior deity wielding a weapon is a very powerful protection object (fig. 7.2).

All talismans and objects of protection must be activated by a magician or sorcerer with the appropriate ceremony. One can get already activated talismans and objects in temples or one can invite a Taoist magician to draw and activate them in one's house.

BLESSING

The most popular kind of blessing is a petition for health and longevity. These petitions are generally made to the North Pole Star and the celestial deities of the Northern Bushel. Petitions for bless-

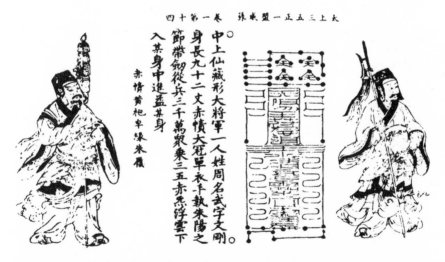

FIGURE 7.2. Celestial Teachers talisman invoking warrior deities, from the *T'ai-shang san-wu cheng-i meng-wei lu* (The Central Orthodox Register of Talismans of the Great One, the Three (Primal Ones), and the Five (Emperors). The warriors are described as commanding thirty million celestial soldiers. The talisman invokes them to enter the body of the individual to protect him.

ings are usually accompanied by a ritual and chanting. The Taoist sorcerer can send petitions for herself, or for another person. In each case, an altar is specially built, and the carrier of the petition must undergo the rituals of purification similar to those of rainmaking. The first and fifteenth days of the lunar month are the best for this ceremony, because those are the days when the celestial deities of the Northern Bushel make a brief visit to the mortal realm.

The altar is usually built on a mound or a platform facing the north. It is preferable to perform the ceremony on a cloudless night when the Northern Bushel is visible. On the altar are an oil lamp, two candlesticks, a special lantern, called the Seven Star Lantern, and small cauldrons for offering incense. Flags of power with the pattern and names of the deities of the Northern Bushel drawn on them are positioned in a circular design surrounding the altar. The most important object on the altar is the Seven Star Lantern. The Seven Star Lantern (also called the Lantern of Longevity) is shaped like a tree, and seven cups of oil are mounted on the branches. Sometimes the lantern consists of seven cups arranged in the pattern of the Northern Bushel.

The ceremony begins at the hour of tzu (11:00 PM). At the appointed time, the carrier of the petition purifies the ceremonial ground and the altar and lights the seven lamps of the Seven Star Lantern. During the ceremony, it is important that the seven lamps do not go out; otherwise, misfortune can result. In some ceremonies, the leader dances Yü's Steps of the Seven Stars; in others, the carrier of the petition traces the talismanic pattern of the seven stars with a wooden sword.

The main part of the ceremony consists of reading the petition, which is written on yellow paper. The petition typically begins with invoking the Northern Bushel deities by their sacred names. This is followed by the petition itself and the name and date of birth of the person asking for health and longevity. Then the petition is burned, the rising smoke carrying the message to the deities.

SANDWRITING DIVINATION

A kind of divination unique to Magical Taoism is sandwriting. It involves asking deities and spirits to send their messages or reveal the future through the sorcerer. Acting as a medium, the sorcerer enters a trance and writes the messages in sand.

Sorcerers must be specially empowered before they can act as a medium in sandwriting divination. An authorized medium—male or female—petitions the deities to allow the initiate to perform the divination. A talisman that endows the initiate with this power is burned and its ashes are collected in a cup of water. After the initiate drinks the talismanic water, she is authorized to do sandwriting divination.

The equipment of sandwriting divination consists of a box measuring approximately four feet square that is filled with fine, white sand. The sand is carefully smoothed before divination takes place. Most mediums hold a stick that acts as a pen, but I have also seen quite elaborate sandboxes that have one end of the writing stick suspended over the box and the other end mechanically attached to a handle. The diviner grasps the handle to move the stick and write the words.

The divination begins with the medium chanting incantations and drawing talismans to ask the deity to descend into her body. The medium then falls into a trance and moves the stick through the sand to write the words. Helpers stand by to record what is written and smooth out the sand so that the writing will not be disrupted.

Practitioners of sandwriting divination tell me that while they are in a trance they have no control over the writing stick: the stick seems to take on a power of its own and all they can do is to hang onto it; moreover, the mediums do not remember what was written during the trance. Having attended several sandwriting divination sessions, I have to admit that something out of the ordinary happens in these situations. On each occasion, the diviner closed his eyes and the stick moved rapidly over the sand. Beads of sweat poured from the medium; helpers smoothed out the sand with wooden blocks as soon as the words were recorded.

Sometimes the writing appears in archaic script—something that the diviners do not know how to write in their normal mode of consciousness. I am told that, traditionally, illiteracy was one of the requirements for being a sandwriting diviner. This ensures that the messages from the deities are genuine.

The message delivered in sandwriting divination is sometimes cryptic, and an interpreter is often needed to decipher the message. Generally, the interpreter is someone other than the diviner, because the two tasks require different skill and disposition. One might say that the interpreter needs to have knowledge and intuition, and the medium needs to have power to hold the deity or the spirit within.

GUIDING, SEARCHING, AND RESCUING
THE SOULS OF THE DEAD

A common practice of Magical Taoism is guiding the soul of a dead person to the underworld. This practice is built around the belief that, when a person dies, the soul is left to wander if it is not guided to the appropriate destination in the underworld. Between the realm of the living and the dead is a boundary region inhabited by ghouls, zombies, and malevolent spirits, who prey on the dead souls. If a dead soul loses its way in this region and does not reach the underworld within forty-nine days, it may turn into a ghoul, zombie, or an undead creature and prey on other dead souls passing through the boundary realm.

To locate the lost soul, the sorcerer uses a lantern, named the Kung-ming Lantern, after a famous Taoist magician and sorcerer of the Three Kingdoms. The Kung-ming Lantern is essentially a hot-air balloon with talismans written on it. After the sorcerer has made the appropriate incantations and activated the talismans, the balloon is released. The balloon's landing place is the location where the sorcerer should enter the boundary realm: sometimes, the sorcerer enters a trance to track the flight of the balloon; in other cases, the sorcerer and the attendants physically follow the balloon to its land-ing place, and there conduct the rituals for entering the underworld.

Before entering the boundary region between the mortal realm and the underworld, the Taoist sorcerer must first protect himself. Talismans of protection are drawn on his body and clothing. In case of an encounter with malevolent spirits or undead, the sorcerer must be prepared to fight them, so a sword with scripts of power written on the blade is carried. The sorcerer then conducts a ritual that takes his spirit to the realm between the living and the dead. Flags of power and protection surround the spot where the sorcerer will leave the body, to ensure that malevolent spirits will not attack it while the spirit is away.

There are various ways of entering into the boundary realm and the underworld. The most colorful one that I have seen involves the use of an umbrella: the sorcerer first utters incantations and draws talismans of protection; then he takes the umbrella, opens it, and jumps off a ledge. Landing, he sits in the trance that will take his spirit to the underworld.

If a soul is attacked or captured by malevolent spirits, the sorcerer will need to fight the spirits to rescue the soul. An arsenal of tech-niques is available to the sorcerer. These techniques will be de-scribed in the next section.

FIGHTING MALEVOLENT SPIRITS

Sorcerers sometimes need to fight malevolent spirits when they rescue a dead soul or when the malevolent spirits are harming inno-cent people. There are four strategies in fighting malevolent spirits: driving them away, containing them, binding them, and dissolving them.

Driving a malevolent spirit away is a temporary solution, because the spirit may return. This strategy is generally used by the sorcerer to buy time, so that he can work out a more effective solution. Ma-levolent spirits can be driven off by talismans of warding, mirrors, talismanic flags of power, talismanic swords, and fire.

A more effective way of overcoming a malevolent spirit is to contain it or bind it, but the spirit must first be captured. Several power objects can be used to capture the spirit. Sometimes, the object that captures the spirit can be used to contain it; for example, a gourd, or a jar with a lid, or even a bag can be used by the sorcerer to both capture and contain the malevolent spirit. At other times, the spirit is captured first and then transported to another location to be contained; in this case, the technique of binding is used. The equipment used to bind the spirit is usually a net made of vine, jute, or hemp. Materials are not as important as the power of the sorcerer. In the hands of a powerful sorcerer, a net made of any material can be effective. I have seen sorcerers use nylon ropes, fishing nets, and chains. After the malevolent spirit is bound, it is transported to a cave, or a hollow, where it is contained. Sometimes, the entrance of the cave or the hollow will be sealed with rocks; at other times, talismans of containment are written around the cave entrance or the hollow to contain the spirit.

The most powerful strategy for fighting a malevolent spirit is to dissolve it. Dissolution obliterates the spirit in such a way that it will never again materialize. There are three commonly used methods. In the first method, a sword is used to pierce the spirit, and the sword must be enchanted with talismans (fig. 7.3). Before the sword is used, the sorcerer must smear his or her blood on the blade to endow it with personal power.

The second method involves drawing talismans of dissolution and dancing a gait of power. The talismanic pattern is traced in the air with the tip of a sword while the sorcerer is performing the dance of power. (See fig. 7.4.)

The third method—Tibetan in origin—is a series of mudras, gestures made with the hands. Figures 7.5 and 7.6 show the mudras used for dissolving malevolent spirits. In this technique, the sorcerer first makes nine hand-signs in sequence, accompanying each with a word of power. The words, translated, are "come," "warriors," "fighting," "ones," "ready," "formation," "line-up," "take position," and "in front" (fig. 7.5). A final command, "destroy," accompanied

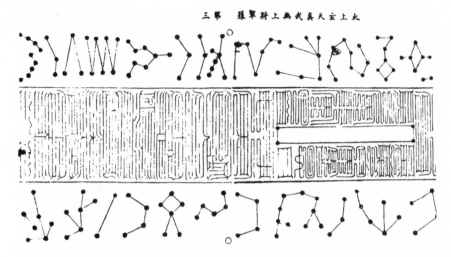

三郎　隗軍辨上無武真天玄上太

FIGURE 7.3. Talisman used to endow a sword with the power to pierce and ward off evil spirits, from the *T'ai-shang hsüan-t'ien chen-wu wu-shang chang-chün lu* (The Register of Talismans of the Great One of the Mysterious Heaven, the Incomparable General). The talismanic script is depicted in the center of the illustration. The patterns at top and bottom are symbols of the constellations, used to invoke the power of the celestial armies.

by a sword mudra, (fig. 7.6) is then given. Power from the deities, all the good spirits, and the sorcerer are concentrated and directed at the malevolent spirit to wipe it out of existence.

If the malevolent spirits are powerful, the sorcerer will be forced to engage in a series of battles before the spirit can be dissolved, captured, or even driven away. In such a case, elements are summoned, and deities and spirits are invoked. Warrior deities are generally preferred, but sometimes when the malevolent spirits are cunning, deities and spirits with superior cunning are called.

EXORCISM

Exorcism is another form of combat against supernatural forces, but it differs from fighting malevolent spirits because in exorcism the sorcerer's opponent is not necessarily malevolent. The goal of

FIGURE 7.4. Ling-pao talismans and dances of power for fighting evil spirits and malevolent ghosts, from *Ling-pao wu-liang tu-jen shang-ching ta-fa* (The Limitless Highest Scripture and Great Method of Deliverance). The talisman and pattern of steps to the right of center are used to destroy malevolent spirits and ghosts; the set to the left of center is used to capture and bind them. In both dances of power, the practitioner begins the steps of the dance from the bottom of the star pattern.

exorcism in Magical Taoism is not to destroy the ghost but to prevent it from doing mischief in the future. This can take the form of educating, placating, or rehabilitation.

Many ghosts are mischievous or disgruntled because their former manifestation was killed wrongfully or mistreated. Ghosts of murdered people and soldiers who died in war are especially discontented. They may haunt a place or possess a person to vent their anger.

In exorcising a ghost from a location, the sorcerer prepares an altar at the haunted site. On the altar are talismans of exorcism (fig. 7.7), a sword made of copper coins, and a bowl of chicken's blood. Sometimes, dog urine is also used. The sorcerer begins the incantations that will draw the ghost or spirit out from its hiding place. Next, the sorcerer captures the ghost by throwing the coin-sword, flaming

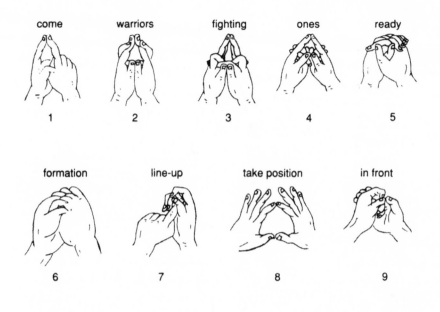

come   warriors   fighting   ones   ready

1   2   3   4   5

formation   line-up   take position   in front

6   7   8   9

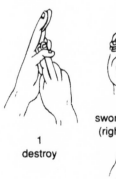

1
destroy

2a
sword mudra
(right hand)

2b
sword mudra
(left hand)

FIGURES 7.5. and 7.6. Mudras
(hand gestures) used to destroy evil
spirits, as described on page 110.

FIGURE 7.7. Kun-lun talisman of exorcism. The talisman invokes the power of the thunder spirit and the patron deity of exorcism. The triangular symbol with a horizontal line at its apex (*bottom right*) is used to enhance the power of the talisman.

talismans, chicken's blood, or dog urine at it—actions that freeze the ghost while the sorcerer speaks words telling it never to haunt the realm of the living. Sometimes, offerings are made to placate the ghost. The offerings typically consist of "banknotes for the dead"— paper printed with silver and gold ink and folded into the shape of ingots. Sometimes, colorful papers folded into the shape of clothing are also offered. The offerings are then burnt and sent to the underworld. If a ghost is especially recalcitrant, the sorcerer may have to fight it, capture it, and then guide it down to the underworld.

In exorcising a ghost from a person, the sorcerer prepares a talisman of exorcism and places it on the head of the individual who is possessed. Appropriate incantations are chanted to lure the ghost out of the individual. The ghost is then captured, rehabilitated, and sent to the underworld.

FIGHTING OTHER SORCERERS AND MAGICIANS

Black sorcerers and magicians can harm people by inflicting them with illness, or even killing them. To combat such unethical practitioners, the Taoist magician or sorcerer will fight an opponent by using similar skills and power.

In duels of sorcery and magic, practitioners of Magical Taoism call on everything they can muster: elements, animals, plants, spirits, and deities. They also use all available objects of power in the same manner as they would fight malevolent spirits. One of the strategies is effective against a human opponent but not against spirits: illusion or mind control. However, illusions are only effective when the opponent is susceptible; therefore, mind control is not effective against powerful sorcerers and magicians.

HEALING

Taoist magicians and sorcerers are also healers, and talismanic magic is the most commonly used method of healing. A talisman that invokes the power of the deities to heal a certain ailment is burned and the ashes are mixed with water. The talismanic water is either swallowed by the patient or sprinkled on the body. Figure 7.8 shows examples of talismans used to counter different kinds of illness.

Sects in Magical Taoism

There are three major sects in Magical Taoism: the Mao-shan sect, the Celestial Teachers sect, and the Kun-lun sect.

The members of the Mao-shan sect are sorcerers par excellence. As mentioned in Part One, this sect is not to be confused with the Shang-ch'ing Mao-shan Taoists, who are mystics. Mao-shan sorcerers prefer to draw power from spirits and lesser deities, and are especially skilled in exorcism, fighting malevolent spirits and other sorcerers, offering protection, warding off disasters, and guiding, searching, and rescuing dead souls. Mao-shan sorcerers use talismans and objects of

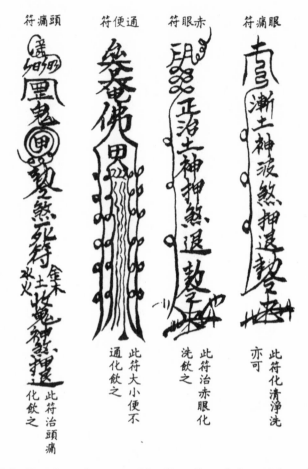

FIGURE 7.8. Kun-lun talismans of healing. From left to right: talisman for curing headaches, talisman for curing constipation and bladder problems, talisman for curing eye infections, talisman for curing pain in the eyes.

power such as mirrors, bells, and coin-swords. They are especially adept at calling deities and spirits to enter their bodies to enhance their personal power. Practitioners from other sects will invoke only certain deities, but Mao-shan sorcerers are pragmatic, and will muster anything that will help them. Today, the practitioners of the Mao-shan sect are found in Taiwan, Hong Kong, remote regions of southern China, and Chinese communities in southeast Asia. Of all the sects of Magical Taoism, the Mao-shan sect is the most secretive. Admittance to the sect is extremely selective. Apprentices are accepted only on the recommendation of trusted friends of the master.

The Celestial Teachers sect was founded by Chang Tao-ling, the popularizer of the use of talismanic magic. Today, the Celestial Teachers sect still uses talismans to call for rain, to ward off disaster, drive away malevolent spirits, offer blessings and protection, heal the sick, and guide dead souls into the underworld. However, unlike the Mao-shan sorcerers, the priests of Celestial Teachers Taoism invoke only deities and their founder Chang Tao-ling in their incantations. Their talismans are said to be revealed by the deities to Chang Tao-ling himself. There are certain deities or spirits that the Celestial Teachers will not invoke. These include the spirits of the underworld, animal spirits, and plant spirits.

The Kun-lun sect, the third major sect of Magical Taoism, originated in western China in the region of the Kun-lun Mountains and is strongly influenced by Tantric magic from Tibet. Several features distinguish the Kun-lun sect from the other sects of Magical Taoism. First, their practitioners invoke both Taoist and Buddhist deities in their talismans. Second, they use mudras (as shown in figures 7.5 and 7.6; Tibetan in origin, the mudras are adopted not only by the Kun-lun sect but also by Buddhist sects who practice magic). Third, the Kun-lun practitioners are called *fa-shih* (masters of the laws), after the manner of Buddhism, and not *Tao-shih* (masters of the Tao). Today, the Kun-lun sect is popular in southern China, Hong Kong, Taiwan, and southeast Asia. The Kun-lun fa-shih are especially in demand for bestowing blessings, giving protection, and warding off malevolent spirits.

Further Words on Magical Taoism

Magical Taoism is the Way of Power. It manipulates, controls, and channels power from the natural elements, the spirits, and deities. Power is not something to trifle with. This chapter is designed to introduce the reader to the basic beliefs and practices of Magical Taoism. I have deliberately left details out of the procedures so that this chapter cannot be used as a manual for the practices described. If you wish to learn Magical Taoism, you need to talk to someone who is familiar with this system of Taoism before committing yourself to any sect or program of training. Magical Taoism is not a path that you can dabble with and then abandon.

FURTHER READINGS

Livia Kohn has translated two Taoist treatises on magical talismans. Both can be found in reading #14 of her book *The Taoist Experience*, titled "Protective Measures."

8

Divinational Taoism
The Way of Seeing

DIVINATION IS A WAY of seeing the patterns of change in the universe. Change is a part of the Tao, and to see change is to see the movement of the Tao in all things. In Taoist thinking, divination is not simply predicting the future and relying on these predictions to live. Rather, it is a way of appreciating the flux and the permanence of the Tao and directly perceiving the interdependency of all things.

A Brief History of Divinational Taoism

All practitioners of divination claim Fu Hsi (fig. 8.1) as the patriarch and patron of their art. Fu Hsi was a legendary shaman-king in the prehistoric times of China and was reputed to have discovered the Ho-t'u (the pattern of the River Ho), one of the most important building blocks of the divinational arts. The Ho-t'u is a prototype of the Earlier Heaven *pa-k'ua* (trigram) and it describes the underlying structure of the nature of things.

Another shaman-king, Yü (the man we met in chapter 1, who danced the steps of the Northern Bushel), discovered the pattern of the Later Heaven pa-k'ua. After turning back the floodwaters, Yü saw a giant tortoise emerge from the River Lo, and on its back was the pattern of the Later Heaven pa-k'ua. The Later Heaven pa-k'ua is called

119

像氏羲伏

FIGURE 8.1. Fu Hsi, patron of the divinational arts of China.

the Lo-shu, and it describes the nature of change in the universe.

At the end of the Shang dynasty (1766–1121 BCE), the Ho-t'u and Lo-shu were revised by King Wen, who defeated the corrupt tyrant of Shang and founded the Chou dynasty. It was said that King Wen used his system of divination based on the Ho-t'u and Lo-shu to predict not only the death of his son but his own capture and eventual triumph over the last emperor of Shang. King Wen's efforts in systematizing the Ho-t'u and Lo-shu resulted in the *Chou-i* (The I-ching of the Chou Dynasty). In this system of divination, the Ho-t'u and Lo-shu were expanded from the eight trigrams to sixty-four hexagrams. The *I-ching* that we have today consists of fragments of the *Chou-i* collected by Confucius in the sixth century BCE. Two other I-chings, one called the *Lin-shan i*, written by Yü's descendants, and the *Kuei-chuang i*, written by the first emperor of the Shang dynasty and his shaman advisor I

Wen, are lost. We know of their existence only from references made by the historians of the Han dynasty.

Between the end of the Chou dynasty and the end of the Han dynasty, the arts of divination gradually took shape and became what they are today. The most important factor in making the divinational arts into a branch of knowledge is the emergence of a group of people called the fang-shih (previously described in chapter 3).

The fang-shih were divided into those who healed the sick with talismanic magic and those who specialized in divination and the arts of longevity. One of the most colorful predecessors of the fang-shih was named Kuei-ku Tzu, or Master of Ghost Valley. Kuei-ku Tzu was not only adept at divination, but also a master of military strategy and diplomacy. Most of the advisers of the Warring States feudal lords were students of Kuei-ku Tzu. However, in the history of China, and Taoism, Kuei-ku Tzu was best known as a theorist of the yin-yang school of thought. The theorists of the Yin-yang School emphasized the cosmology of the *I-ching* and the notion of change as the underlying factor behind the nature of events. The close association between the yin-yang theorists and the divinational arts is shown by the inclusion of the treatises of *k'an-yu* (or *feng-shui*, a form of terrestrial divination) and celestial divination in the section on the Five Elements and the Yin-yang School of Thought in the Han dynasty histories.

Another group of fang-shih, whose patron was Liu An, the lord of Huai-nan, contributed their learning to a book now known as the *Huai-nan-tzu.* In the *Huai-nan-tzu* we find the teachings of the fang-shih on government and politics, military strategy and technology, the arts of longevity and immortality, cosmology, and the theory of change.

The divinational arts reached their height of development in the T'ang and Sung dynasties. During the T'ang, feng-shui, or geomancy, a form of terrestrial divination based on observing landforms and the flow of energy in them, became a systematic science. The foremost theorist and practitioner of feng-shui in the T'ang dynasty was Yang K'un-sun—acknowledged today by feng-shui practitioners as the father of geomancy.

The divination arts today would not be where they are without the contribution of Chen Hsi-yi and Shao K'ang-chieh of the Sung dynasty. Both men were Taoist hermits; both shunned imperial gifts and positions of power.

CHEN HSI-YI AND SHAO K'ANG-CHIEH

Chen Hsi-yi is credited with being the author of the Wu-chi Diagram. This diagram is one of the most important intellectual developments in the history of ideas in China; it not only revolutionized the understanding of change for the divinational arts but made the *I-ching* and the study of change a focus in Taoist thinking. The Wu-chi Diagram describes how the universe came into being and how it changes. A discussion of the Wu-chi Diagram can be found later in this chapter, in the subsection "Taoist Cosmology."

According to the *Hua-shan chi* (Chronicles of Hua-shan), the Wu-chi Diagram was carved on the face of a cliff on Hua-shan (the Grand Mountains) in Shensi Province. This diagram has inspired both Taoists and Neo-Confucianists. Taoist legends say that the Wu-chi Diagram was first revealed to Ho-shang Kung, the Sage of the River. Inspired by it, Wei Po-yang wrote the *Tsan-tung-chi*. The teachings of the Wu-chi Diagram were then revealed to Chung-li Ch'uan, one of the Eight Immortals, who taught them to Lü Tung-pin. When Lü lived as a hermit on Hua-shan, he transmitted the teachings to Chen Hsi-yi; Chen Hsi-yi taught Wu-hsiu; and Wu-hsiu had two students—one of them, the father of Neo-Confucianism, Chou Tun-i, and the other, Li T'ing-chi. Shao K'ang-chieh was Li T'ing-chi's student.

The Wu-chi Diagram and its cosmology were not the only contributions that Chen Hsi-yi made to Divinational Taoism: Chen was also the originator of a system of celestial divination known as Tzu-wei Tu-su (System of the Ruling Star Tzu-wei and the Numerics of the Bushel Stars). This is one of the most popular and sophisticated systems of celestial divination practiced today.

Shao K'ang-chieh, or Shao Yung, is considered to be the successor of Chen Hsi-yi. Shao took the theory of change to new limits and combined it with a mathematics of transformation based on numbers. The study of the pa-k'ua and the five elements became a science: cycles and changes could be "calculated," and the numerical principles could be "seen" by observing things in the universe.

Shao K'ang-chieh is best known for his book *Wang-chi ching* (Treatise on the Supreme Limitless Principle), a monumental work on the structure of the universe, the nature of change, the interpretation of the historical events in China, and a record of observations of celestial events. Like Chen Hsi-yi, Shao K'ang-chieh was not only a theoretician: he practiced the arts of divination and was adept at celestial and terrestrial divination and the reading of omens. It was said that he predicted several disasters that beset the Sung dynasty, including some drastic political changes instituted by the minister Wang An-shih.

DIVINATION IN THE MING AND TODAY

When the Sung dynasty fell, in 1279 CE, it was replaced by the Yüan dynasty of the Mongols. Less than a hundred years later, the Yüan was replaced by the Ming dynasty. It was said that in overthrowing the Mongols, the founder of the Ming dynasty, Chu Yüan-chang, had the assistance of a Taoist magician and diviner, Liu Po-hun, who was an expert in not only magic and divination but also military strategy and logistics. He could predict the movement of enemy forces and anticipate their maneuvers, allowing Chu Yüan-chang's peasant army to win decisive battles. When Chu began to murder his former associates and advisers, Liu's divinational skills saved him.

Today, the practitioners of the divinational arts include both Taoists and non-Taoists. Although some practitioners work in temples and monasteries, the practice of Divinational Taoism does not conflict with sect affiliation. Divinational Taoism is practiced by the Celestial Teachers sect, the Mao-shan sorcerers, and the internal-alchemists of the Lung-men and the Wu-tang-shan sects. However, many practitioners of the divinational arts are not affiliated with any Taoist sect. These are the "kui-shih," lay people who embrace Taoist beliefs and practice divination as a Taoist art. There are also professional diviners who are neither associated with a Taoist sect nor embrace Taoist beliefs. However, divination is a Taoist art, whether its Taoist origins are acknowledged or not.

Principal Ideas of Divinational Taoism

TAOIST COSMOLOGY: WU-CHI AND T'AI-CHI

In the Taoist view of the universe, all things originate from the Tao and return to the Tao. Change is that which sets in motion the coming and going of things, and divination is a way of seeing the patterns of change.

The Wu-chi Diagram describes the process—this coming into existence and the return to the Tao. Creation and dissolution occur all the time. If we understand the underlying nature of the change, we will know what has occurred in the past and what will come in the future.

In the Wu-chi Diagram (fig. 8.2), the circle at the top is the symbol of *wu-chi* (the Limitless), or the Tao. It is the state of stillness in which things are undifferentiated from the origin and the source of life. The idea of wu-chi can be traced back to chapter 28 of the *Tao-te ching*, where "the return to the wu-chi" is first mentioned. The *Chuang-tzu* also mentions "enter the Nameless Gate" and "wander in the expanse of wu-chi." Thus, wu-chi is the Taoist conception of the origin or source of all things.

The symbol below the wu-chi is the t'ai-chi, or the Great Ultimate. Today we are more familiar with the t'ai-chi as a swirling pattern (also shown in figure 8.2, for comparison). The form that appears in the Wu-chi Diagram is an older symbol, and I think it tells us more about the nature of t'ai-chi than its newer representation. Where wu-chi is stillness, t'ai-chi is change. The concentric circles are half yin and half yang. Each circle describes a "moment" of change, and each moment of change is the transition from yin to

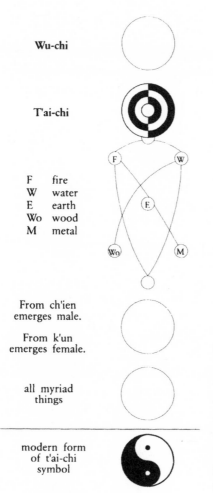

Wu-chi

T'ai-chi

F   fire
W water
E   earth
Wo wood
M metal

From ch'ien
emerges male.

From k'un
emerges female.

all myriad
things

modern form
of t'ai-chi
symbol

FIGURE 8.2. The Wu-chi Diagram. A modern rendition of the t'ai-chi symbol is shown at the bottom for comparison with the older form—the circle next to the top of the diagram. See page 124 for further explanation.

yang (creation) and yang to yin (dissolution and return). The three concentric circles describe the interplay of yin and yang in their three manifestations. The innermost circle is ancient yang and ancient yin; the next circle is greater yang and greater yin; the outermost circle is lesser yang and lesser yin. Taoists describe the t'ai-chi as "yang embracing yin." Run your eye across the older t'ai-chi from left to right and you will notice that, in the left half of the picture, you get an overall pattern of white-black-white (yang-yin-yang); in the right half, you get black-white-black (yin-yang-yin). This is the same in the modern t'ai-chi symbol, if your eye moves top to bottom on a line through the white and black dots. For Taoists like Chen Hsi-yi and Shao K'ang-chieh, wu-chi, or stillness, is the origin of things, and t'ai-chi is change, or movement, which initiates creation.

To move on from the t'ai-chi to the next layers of symbols in the Wu-chi Diagram, we must understand how ancient yang and ancient yin, greater yang and greater yin, and lesser yang and lesser yin interact to generate the eight pa-k'ua or trigrams. This process is described in the adjacent table. From the father and mother trigrams of the pa-k'ua, *ch'ien* and *k'un*, all the myriad things of the universe are created. (See table 8.1.)

THE NATURE OF THE UNIVERSE: YIN AND YANG, PA-K'UA, NINE PALACES, AND FIVE ELEMENTS

Yin and yang, the pa-k'ua, and the five elements are the building blocks of all things.

Yin and *yang* translated literally mean shade and light. Originally used to describe the absence and presence of sunlight on mountain slopes, it was adopted by the *I-ching* to refer to female and male and other pairs of complementary opposites. Thus, yin became associated with stillness, tranquility, softness, flexibility, female, and receptivity; and yang became associated with movement, activity, hardness, strength, male, and initiative.

The *pa-k'ua*, or eight trigrams, are *ch'ien* (sky), *k'un* (earth), *k'an* (water), *li* (fire), *chen* (thunder), *sun* (wind), *ken* (mountain), and *tui* (lake). The five elements—metal, wood, water, fire, and earth—are associated with the four cardinal directions—west, east, north, and south—and the center respectively. (See fig. 8.3.)

The eight trigrams themselves can be subdivided into sixty-four hexagrams. Figure 8.4 shows how the sixty-four hexagrams are generated from the eight trigrams. Today, many divination techniques, especially those that utilize the *I-ching*, are based on the interpretation of the meaning of the hexagrams.

The pa-k'ua has two forms: Earlier Heaven and Later Heaven. The

TABLE 8.1. The creation of the pa-k'ua from the interaction of yang and yin. In Taoism, the process by which movement and stillness, yang and yin, interact to create the pa-k'ua from wu-chi (the Tao) is called the Sacred Path.

Wu-chi	{ in movement generates yang in wang-chi { in stillness generates yin in wang-chi
Wang-chi	{ in movement generates yang in t'ai-chi { in stillness generates yin in t'ai-chi
T'ai-chi	{ in movement generates the ancient yang { in stillness generates the ancient yin
Ancient yang Ancient yin	in movement generates the greater yang in stillness generates the greater yin
Ancient yang Ancient yin	in stillness generates the lesser yin in movement generates the lesser yang
Greater yang Greater yin	in movement generates ch'ien in stillness generates k'un
Greater yang Greater yin	in stillness generates tui in movement generates ken
Lesser yang Lesser yin	in stillness generates k'an in movement generates li
Lesser yang Lesser yin	in movement generates chen in stillness generates sun

Earlier Heaven pa-k'ua describes the nature of things and the Later Heaven pa-kua describes the nature of transformation. Earlier Heaven literally means "before the existence of the celestial realm"; Later Heaven means "after the existence of the celestial realm." In Taoist cosmology, *before the celestial realm* refers to the state of undifferentiation, before sky and earth were separated; *after the existence of the celestial realm* refers to the state of existence when sky and earth have become separate entities. In figure 8.3 you will notice that in the Later Heaven pa-k'ua, the locations of the trigrams are

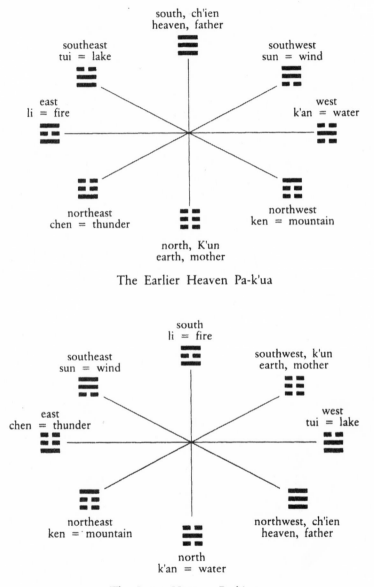

south, ch'ien
heaven, father

southeast
tui = lake

southwest
sun = wind

east
li = fire

west
k'an = water

northeast
chen = thunder

northwest
ken = mountain

north, K'un
earth, mother

The Earlier Heaven Pa-k'ua

south
li = fire

southeast
sun = wind

southwest, k'un
earth, mother

east
chen = thunder

west
tui = lake

northeast
ken = mountain

northwest, ch'ien
heaven, father

north
k'an = water

The Later Heaven Pa-k'ua

FIGURE 8.3. The Earlier Heaven and Later Heaven pa-k'ua compared.

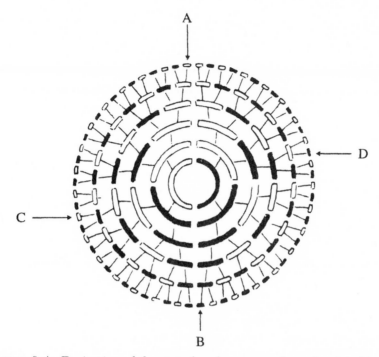

FIGURE 8.4. Derivation of the sixty-four hexagrams from the t'ai-chi. White bars indicate yang components and dark bars indicate yin components. Each yin and yang component divides to give another pair of yin and yang. Thus, the yin and yang in t'ai-chi (the innermost ring) divide to give the four directions (second ring from center). Moving outward, the next ring is formed by the result of eight from each of the four directions dividing into two parts, and so on from eight to sixteen, from sixteen to thirty-two, and from thirty-two to sixty-four. The six rings form the six components of the hexagrams. To find out the composition of a hexagram, trace a line from a component in the outermost ring toward the center. For example, the hexagram ch'ien (heaven) is made of six yang components. You can identify the ch'ien hexagram by tracing the line from position A to the center. You will see that this line connects all the yang components. Similarly, try this with the hexagram k'un (earth), which is made of six yin components at position B. Notice that k'un is directly opposite to ch'ien. The hexagram li (fire), which is yang/yin/yang/yang/yin/yang, can be found at position C, and k'an (water), which is yin/yang/yin/yin/yang/yin, can be found at Position D.

different from those of the Earlier Heaven pa-k'ua. Li (fire), not ch'ien (sky), occupies the position of south in the Later Heaven pa-k'ua, and k'an (water), not k'un (earth), occupies the position of north. To understand how the Later Heaven pa-k'ua is used to describe changes, we must turn to another idea that is central to Divinational Taoism: the Nine Palaces.

The Nine Palaces is the pa-k'ua set in motion. With the Nine Palaces, the trigrams of the pa-k'ua are no longer tied to a direction. Their positions will move according to the cycles of the year, month, day, and season.

The Nine Palaces are the eight directions and the center. Each palace is designated by a pair of number and color. They are one-white, two-black, three-jade, four-green, five-yellow, six-white, seven-red, eight-white, and nine-purple. Each number-color combination is called a star, and each star is associated with a trigram in the pa-k'ua. Thus, one-white is *k'an* (water), two-black is *k'un* (earth), three-jade is *chen* (thunder), four-green is *sun* (wind), five-yellow is the center (*chung-kung*), six-white is *ch'ien* (sky), seven-red is *tui* (lake), eight-white is *ken* (mountain), and nine-purple is *li* (fire). The numbers in the following grid illustrate the "root structure" of the Nine Palaces:

$$4 \quad 9 \quad 2$$
$$3 \quad 5 \quad 7$$
$$8 \quad 1 \quad 6$$

The root arrangement is also known as the Magic Circle, because the numbers are so arranged that the rows, columns, and diagonals all add up to fifteen. In the root structure of the Nine Palaces, five is always located in the center. The root structure of the Nine Palaces is also the Later Heaven pa-k'ua.

The Nine Palaces represent the pattern of energy moving in the universe. Some energies are destructive and some are beneficial. Many systems of divination rely extensively on the principles of the

Nine Palaces to find out where and when the beneficial and destructive energies will occur.

The five elements are related to each other in a cycle of creation and a cycle of destruction. An understanding of these cycles is important in seeing and predicting changes in the universe. In the cycle of creation, metal in the veins of the earth nourishes the underground waters; water gives life to vegetation and creates wood; wood feeds fire and fire creates ashes forming earth. The cycle is completed when metals are formed in the veins of the earth. The cycle of destruction begins with metal cutting and destroying wood; wood dominates earth as the roots of the trees dig into the ground; earth has mastery over water and prevents the flow of rivers and seas; water destroys fire and finally fire melts metals.

In Divinational Taoism, the cycles of creation and destruction describe the nature of change. They occur naturally, and are neither good nor bad. Only when human activity interferes with the natural process of change will there be disasters. When disasters are imminent, it is up to human effort to change the conditions so that the disasters can be averted.

THE NOTION OF TIME: THE CHINESE CALENDAR

The Chinese calendar plays an important part in the divinational arts. The notion of time in the Chinese calendar is cyclical. Events and change follow cycles, and to know the order of the cycles is to understand how changes occur.

There are four major cycles in the Chinese calendar: the Sexagenary Cycle of sixty years; the Three Eras, with sixty years to an era; the Nine Cycles, with twenty years to a cycle; and the twenty-four seasonal markers, with two markers for each of the twelve months of the year.

The sixty years of the Sexagenary Cycle are obtained by pairing the Ten Celestial Stems and the Twelve Terrestrial Branches. The Celestial Stems are *chia, i, ping, ting, wu, chi, keng, hsin, jen, kuei.* The Twelve Terrestrial Branches are: *tzu, ch'ou, yin, mao, ch'en, ssu, wu, wei, shen, yu, hsü, hai.* Each year in the Chinese calendar is identified by the combination of a stem and a branch. Lining up the Ten Celestial Stems and Twelve Terrestrial Branches until the first pair is repeated will result in sixty pairs, making the sixty years of the Sexagenary Cycle (see table 8.2).

The Sexagenary Cycle is used in all the divinational arts of China. It is also the basis of the Chinese calendar.

The twelve animals, attached each to a year in a twelve-year cycle, are more of a popular amusement than serious divination. The twelve-animal system's reckoning of time is less accurate than the sixty-year cycle. By way of illustration, let us consider the year 1997 in the Western calendar. In the animal scheme, 1997 is the year of the bull, and in the Sexagenary Cycle it is *ting-ch'ou*. The year 2009 will be the year of the bull again, but in the sixty-year cycle it will be *chi-ch'ou*. Since the flow of energy in ting-ch'ou and chi-ch'ou is different, to use the animal scheme in divination would be to lose this difference.

Each Sexagenary Cycle is called an era. Each era begins with the year *chia-tzu* and ends with *kuei-hai*. There are three eras: upper, middle, and lower, and again, different patterns of energy accom-

TABLE 8.2. The Ten Celestial Stems and Twelve Terrestrial Branches paired to yield the sixty years of the Sexagenary Cycle.

Stem-Branch	*Stem-Branch*	*Stem-Branch*	*Stem-Branch*	*Stem-Branch*
chia-tzu	ping-tzu	wu-tzu	keng-tzu	jen-tzu
i-ch'ou	ting-ch'ou	chi-ch'ou	hsin-ch'ou	kuei-ch'ou
ping-yin	wu-yin	keng-yin	jen-yin	chia-yin
ting-mao	chi-mao	hsin-mao	kuei-mao	i-mao
wu-ch'en	keng-ch'en	jen-ch'en	chia-ch'en	ping-ch'en
chi-ssu	hsin-ssu	kuei-ssu	i-ssu	ting-ssu
keng-wu	jen-wu	chia-wu	ping-wu	wu-wu
hsin-wei	kuei-wei	i-wei	ting-wei	chi-wei
jen-shen	chia-shen	ping-shen	wu-shen	keng-shen
kuei-yu	i-yu	ting-yu	chi-yu	hsin-yu
chia-hsü	ping-hsü	wu-hsü	keng-hsü	jen-hsü
i-hai	ting-hai	chi-hai	hsin-hai	kuei-hai

pany each era. The three eras are subdivided into nine twenty-year segments; thus, in one hundred and eighty years there are three sixty-year periods (the Three Eras) and nine twenty-year segments (the Nine Cycles).

THE NOTION OF CHANGE

All things are subject to change. Because everything is interrelated, change in one thing will lead to change in others. Moreover, change is not predetermined. At every point in time, a number of possible events can occur depending on what happened before. Divinational Taoism does not see a person locked into a destiny that cannot be changed. If we understand the nature of change, we can alter the possibilities by our own actions.

Destiny may be revealed in omens, in celestial and terrestrial phenomena, and in facial features, but it is not guaranteed that what is predicted will happen. In fact, Divinational Taoism does not teach that people should resign themselves to fate; rather, knowing the possibilities of what may happen, we can take action to avert disaster. Taoists call this "changing Earlier Heaven destiny (what is given) by Later Heaven efforts (what we do)."

Divination is a sophisticated art. It is not simply casting sticks and looking up the interpretation in a book. Divination is a way of seeing changes in the universe that is deeply rooted in Taoist philosophy and cosmology. To understand the notion of change is not only to see the patterns of nature, but also to know how our actions can affect the course of events. Seeing the changes and living in harmony with them are the essence of Divinational Taoism.

Forms of Divination

The arts of divination consist of celestial divination, terrestrial divination, event divination, the divination of human destiny, and the interpretation of omens. Celestial divination is based on observing and interpreting the position of stars—being, in this respect, similar to Western astrology; terrestrial divination is based on observing and interpreting features in the landscape; event divination is based on observing seasonal, daily, and hourly movements of energy in nature; divination of human destiny is based on observing human features and traits and includes the arts of physiognomy and palmistry; and the reading of omens is based on observing phenomena in nature.

Of all the forms of divination practiced today, celestial divination and terrestrial divination are the ones most clearly influenced by Taoist thought. In this exploration of Divinational Taoism we shall focus on these two forms of divination.

Celestial Divination: Tzu-wei Tu-su

Celestial divination is based on the assumption that phenomena in the macrocosm of the sky have their parallels in the microcosm of humanity. This comes from the fundamental principle in Taoism that sky, earth, humanity, and all things follow similar laws of existence and change.

There are several systems of celestial divination and it is beyond the scope of this book to discuss all of them. I have therefore chosen Tzu-wei Tu-su, a system of divination originated by the Taoist sage Chen Hsi-yi, to illustrate some aspects of celestial divination.

Tzu-wei Tu-su translated means System of the Ruling Star Tzu-wei and the Numerics of the Bushel Stars. It uses the pattern of the stars occurring at an individual's moment of birth to predict personal destiny. Tzu-wei is the name of the star of destiny, and tu-su means "numerics of the Bushel Stars." The Bushel Stars are the stars that make up the Northern Bushel (Big Dipper) and another constellation in Chinese astronomy called the Southern Bushel.

Briefly, this is how Tzu-wei Tu-su works. The positions of the stars are mapped into twelve celestial palaces named after the Twelve Terrestrial Branches. The arrangement of the celestial palaces is determined by the lunar month in which the individual was born. (Fig. 8.5.)

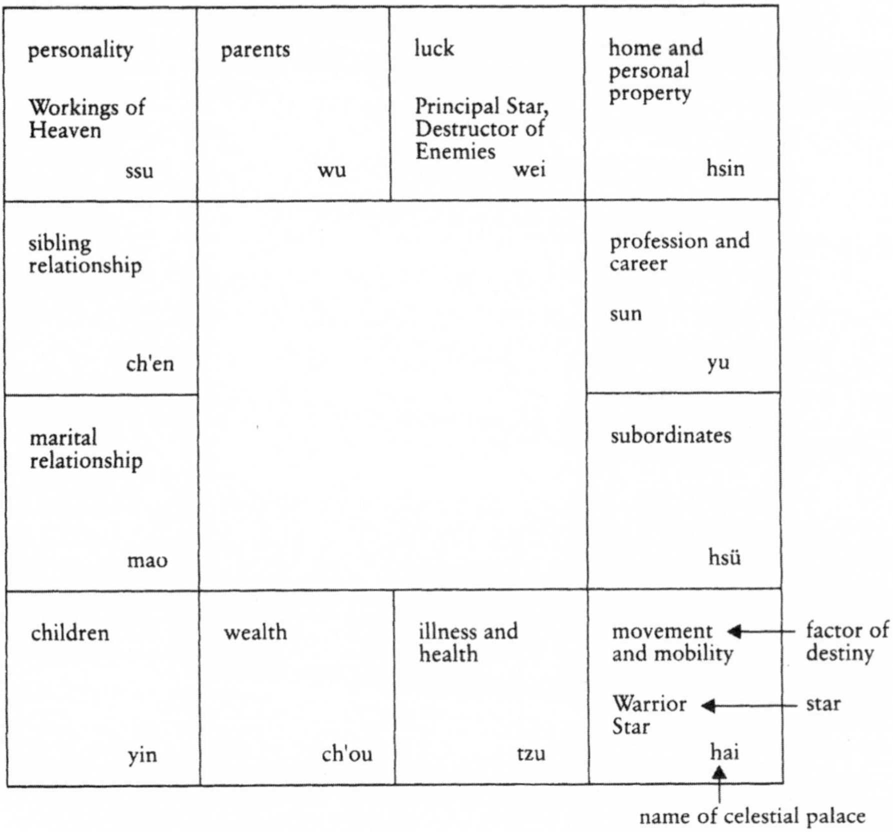

personality **Workings of Heaven** ssu	parents wu	luck Principal Star, Destructor of Enemies wei	home and personal property hsin
sibling relationship ch'en			profession and career sun yu
marital relationship mao			subordinates hsü
children yin	wealth ch'ou	illness and health tzu	movement ← and mobility factor of destiny Warrior ← star Star hai

name of celestial palace

FIGURE 8.5. Celestial palaces, factors of destiny, and principal stars in a sample astrological chart of Tzu-wei Tu-su celestial divination. More than one star can occupy a celestial palace. In the example, both the Principal Star and a star named Destructor of Enemies are in the celestial palace wei.

Twelve factors of destiny are then mapped onto the celestial palaces. The positions of the factors of destiny are determined by the individual's hour of birth. The factors of destiny, in their order, are personality, sibling relationship, marital relationship, children, wealth, illness and health, movement and mobility, subordinates, profession and career, home and personal property, luck, and parents.

Next, the positions of the stars in the celestial palaces are determined. These stars include Tzu-wei (the Ruling Star of Destiny), the seven stars of the Northern Bushel, the stars of the Southern Bushel, the Left and Right Guardian Stars, and various stars of importance and brightness identified in traditional Chinese astronomy. In Tzu-wei Tu-su, the positions of more than fifty stars are used to predict an individual's destiny, but because this book is not about Tzu-wei Tu-su, I shall not go into the details.

Once the positions of the stars are determined, the meaning of their positions and interactions can be interpreted. I shall briefly describe some examples of how the positions of the stars in the celestial palaces affect the twelve factors of destiny. Let us work with the sample chart in figure 8.5. The most important star is Tzu-wei, the Ruling or Principal Star. It has the power to ward off disaster, protect the individual from illness, and enhance the beneficial effects of any factor of destiny that it is positioned with. In the example, Tzu-wei is in the palace of wei, where the factor of luck is located. This means that the individual will always have luck in whatever he or she does. Unexpected benefits will occur and the person will have a knack of avoiding disasters.

Another important star is the Workings of the Celestial Realm, or Heaven; it belongs to the Southern Bushel constellation and is the star that governs harmony. An individual with this star situated with the factor of personality (as in the example) will be kind, gentle, and harmonious. It is also star of wisdom and spiritual development. Thus, if this star were to be positioned with the factor of profession or career, the individual would have deep spiritual interests and develop his or her potential best in spiritual matters.

The sun is also an important star in Tzu-wei Tu-su divination; it governs prosperity, power, and fame. Situated (as in the example) with the factor of profession and career, the star will grant the individual fame, honor, and respect in the chosen career.

Another important star is the Warrior Star; it is a star of the Northern Bushel constellation and it governs wealth. Were it to have been situated with the factor of personality, the individual would be enterprising and would accumulate great wealth from success in business. Situated (as in the example) with the factor of movement and mobility, the individual will be promoted rapidly or rise from poverty to wealth within a brief period of time.

Some stars have negative effects; for example, the star named Destructor of Enemies. If this star is positioned with a benevolent star like Tzu-wei (as in the example), the beneficial effects of the Tzu-wei will be diminished. (In this case, the individual's luck will be diminished severely. If the Destructor of Enemies were to be positioned with the wealth factor, the individual would always be poor or would lose money in investments.) Not only do the stars interact with each other when they are in the same palace, but they can also affect the stars in the palace directly opposite them.

Because Tzu-wei Tu-su involves the interpretation of at least fifty stars and their interactions, it is said to be the most complete system of celestial divination. Simpler systems of celestial divination use only the five planets and the sun and moon, but diviners today agree that Tzu-wei Tu-su produces the most accurate reading of an individual's destiny.

Terrestrial Divination: Feng-shui

Unlike celestial divination, which is based on reading the pattern of stars, terrestrial divination interprets the pattern of the land. In Taoism, terrestrial divination is synonymous with feng-shui, which is translated as "wind and water." As a system of divination, feng-shui has a longer history than celestial divination, and what is practiced today is the product of centuries of development of the art.

In the center of the philosophy and practice of feng-shui is the idea that the land is alive and filled with energy. Depending on the forms taken by the land, energy in a region can be beneficial or destructive. Energy in a region affects people who live there. Beneficial energy can enhance health, longevity, harmony, wealth, and success; destructive energy can bring ill-health and disaster. Energy in a region also changes with the year and seasons. The movement of energy in a particular year or month can be calculated, using the principles of the pa-k'ua, five elements, and the Nine Palaces. When a dwelling or a grave is built on a particular site, the energy of the site is gathered into the edifice. Energy gathered in a dwelling will affect not only the inhabitants of the dwelling but immediate family members who live elsewhere. Energy gathered in a grave will affect the descendants of the individual who is buried there. The practice of feng-shui is therefore concerned with the selection of locations. In the case of building a dwelling, this is called yang-domain feng-shui; in the case of a grave, it is known as yin-domain feng-shui.

The most important factor in selecting an appropriate site, whether for living or for burial, is protection. A site is said to be protected if the ground behind it is higher than the ground in front. Another important factor in selecting a site is the presence of beneficial landforms and the absence of destructive landforms. Smooth, round shapes carry beneficial energy; rough, sharp objects carry destructive energy. Thus, a house opposite a craggy cliff or across from irregularly-shaped skyscrapers will be buffeted by destructive energy.

Roads, rivers, and valleys are pathways along which energy flows. Energy that flows down steep roads, gorges, or slopes is destructive; energy that meanders is beneficial. The most undesirable places to build a house or erect a grave are the end of a T-junction and in the fork of a Y-junction in a road. At a T-junction, energy rushes straight at the house, as waves crash against the shore. In a Y-junction, the dwelling is squeezed between two roads.

Not only is the surrounding environment important: the flow of energy within a house also affects the fortunes and well-being of the inhabitants. Several factors—for example, the floor plan and other architectural details—contribute to whether energy flowing in the dwelling is positive or negative.

To work out the positions and movement of benevolent and destructive energy, the practitioner of feng-shui uses a geomantic compass (fig. 8.6). This device is a twenty-four point compass with markings that describe the kind of energy, yin or yang, flowing in that direction. The geomantic compass is used to determine the direction a building is to face, or how it faces. This information, together with the year when the dwelling is being built, or was built, is used to construct a geomantic chart that shows the positions of benevolent and malevolent energies in the house.

The arrangement of the geomantic chart is based on the principle of the Nine Palaces. The chart is a grid with nine squares and a sample is shown in figure 8.7, at A. Each square has three numbers: the large number in each square is called the Earth Base. These are the numbers of the Nine Palaces. Their positions in the grid are based on the year of construction. The smaller numbers on the upper right-hand corner of each square are called the Facing Stars and ones

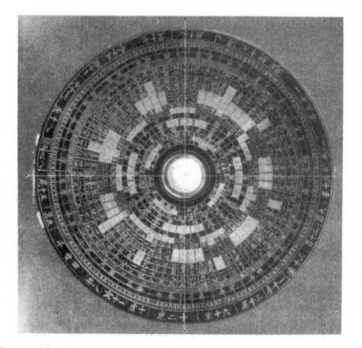

FIGURE 8.6. Geomantic compass used by feng-shui practitioners.

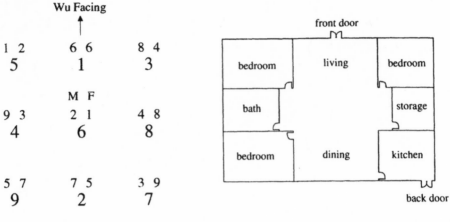

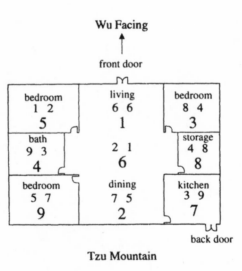

FIGURE 8.7. Sample geomantic chart superimposed on the floor plan of a building. See text for explanation.

on the upper left-hand corner are called the Mountain Stars. These two sets of numbers are obtained from the geomantic compass.

When superimposed onto the floor plan of a house (fig. 8.7, at C), the geomantic chart provides a map of the flow of energy in the building. The numbers one, six, and eight—whether large or small—are associated with beneficial energy, whereas the numbers two and five are associated with malevolent energy. Three, four, and seven can be neutral, destructive, or beneficial depending on other factors. Nine is associated with a powerful energy that can be malevolent or benevolent but not neutral.

Needless to say, it is not desirable to have a bedroom located in an area occupied by a two or a five, especially if these numbers are the Earth Base or the Facing Star, or even more especially, both. The interpretation of a geomantic chart is a complex process that involves evaluating the effects of the combination of the numbers in each square given the usage of the space. For example, some combinations are bad for bedrooms but are all right for storage; others are especially good for a study or office but neutral for a kitchen.

The goal of feng-shui, or terrestrial divination, is to discover how energy flows in the land and to live in harmony with it. The oldest form of divination in Taoist practice, it cultivates a sensitivity to the land and advocates a philosophy of living with nature, rather than against it.

Other Forms of Divination

This section will deal with several other systems of divination. One is event divination, based on understanding the movement of beneficial and malevolent forces through each day, month, year, and season; another is the reading of omens—a form of divination, steeped in both shamanic and Taoist beliefs, in which patterns of cloud, mist, lightning, thunder, flight of birds, and natural phenomena are signs that can tell us what will happen. Unlike Tzu-wei Tu-su and feng-shui, this form of divination relies more on intuition than calculation. The Taoist sage and scholar Shao K'ang-chieh was said to have been an expert in reading omens. Today, only a handful of diviners are knowledgeable in this art.

A third system is the reading of human features to predict the destiny of individuals. One branch of this is physiognomy, the reading of facial features. It involves seeing the pattern of "clouds" or colorations on an individual's face and interpreting features in the eyes, nose, ears, mouth, lips, forehead, cheeks, and chin. Another branch, palmistry, examines the destiny of an individual by looking at the pattern of lines on the palm. These two systems of divination are less influenced by Taoist beliefs and are not as old as Tzu-wei Tu-su and feng-shui. Most likely they entered China from India and were absorbed into Chinese culture in more recent times.

A further system of divination is the casting of joss sticks with hexagrams written on them. Focusing on an inquiry or question, the petitioner shakes a jar containing the joss sticks until one stick falls out. The meaning of the hexagram on the stick is interpreted by looking up its reference in a book. The most popular reference books used by people in Hong Kong and other Asian communities are the *Chou-i*, or *I-ching*, *Lü-tsu chien-chieh* (Immortal Lü Tung-pin's Book of Divination), and *Kuan-yin chien-chieh* (Bodhisattva Kuan-yin's Book of Divination). Although popular with the Chinese people and Westerners who use the *I-ching* to interpret patterns of coins, tea leaves, and so on, this kind of divination is not recognized by the Taoist community as part of Divinational Taoism.

Further Words on Divinational Taoism

There are no sects in Divinational Taoism. As mentioned earlier, divination is practiced by individuals who may or may not belong to a Taoist sect (see page 123). Training in Divinational Taoism is a serious endeavor that requires discipline and commitment. Many teachers accept only apprentices who are willing to commit to several years of tutelage.

Some master practitioners specialize in one system of divination, such as celestial divination or feng-shui. Others may practice a combination of physiognomy, palmistry, and celestial, terrestrial, and event divination. Training is usually restricted to learning one method at a time, and the period of apprenticeship can vary from three to ten years. Knowledge of Chinese is required, because most classics and manuals of divination are still untranslated. The most important reference, the *Wan-nien li* (Cross-reference of the Chinese and Western Calendar), is available only in Chinese. However, it is now possible to learn the basics of feng-shui from a book (see the "Further Readings" section, where I recommend my *Feng-shui: The Ancient Wisdom of Harmonious Living for Modern Times*).

If you would like to study the Taoist divinational arts, first select the system you want to learn and then find a teacher who is willing to accept you as an apprentice. Whichever system you choose, your early attempts will be difficult: it is necessary to become grounded in the general principles that underlie all forms of divination. In some cases, like feng-shui, you can get an introduction to the subject matter from a book or a weekend course; however, if you wish to study the divinational arts seriously, you need to obtain personal instruction. Having learned three systems of divination and written a book on one, I find that apprenticeship is still the only way to learn Divinational Taoism.

FURTHER READINGS

An account of the fang-shih and their activities between the third century BCE (the Han dynasty) and the sixth century CE (the Six Dynasties) can be found in *Doctors, Diviners, and Magicians of Ancient China: Biographies of Fang-shih*, edited and translated by Kenneth DeWoskin. This is a collection of stories of fang-shih from the histories of the Eastern Han, the Three Kingdoms, and the Chin dynasties.

For selected translations of Shao K'ang-chieh's *Wang-chi ching*, see chapter 29 of *A Source Book in Chinese Philosophy*, edited by Wing-tsit Chan,

A more detailed rendering of the theory of numbers embodied in the cosmology of the *I-ching* can be found in *I Ching Mandalas*, translated by Thomas Cleary.

The Taoist I Ching, a collection of interpretations of the hexagrams by Taoist and Taoist-influenced Confucians, is a translation by Thomas Cleary. This book is not an instruction manual on divination: it is necessary to know how to cast the hexagrams before you can use this book to interpret your results. However, this is also a good reference on how Taoists interpret the meaning of the hexagrams. If you wish to compare approaches, you might also want to look at *The Buddhist I Ching*, which is a Buddhist interpretation of the hexagrams, and *I Ching: The Tao of Organization*, a Neo-Confucianist interpretation of the hexagrams. Both books are edited and translated by Thomas Cleary.

A collection of essays on the philosophy of the *I-ching* and the meaning of hexagrams can be found in Helmut Wilhelm's *Heaven, Earth, and Man in the Book of Changes*.

The history, theory, and practice of feng-shui can be found in my book *Feng-shui: The Ancient Wisdom of Harmonious Living for Modern Times*. This presents more details on the history and theory of feng-shui and is also an instruction manual.

9

Ceremonial Taoism
The Way of Devotion

CEREMONIAL TAOISM IS the Way of Devotion. By honoring the sacred powers with ceremonies, humanity renews and strengthens its bonds with the deities, and in return for the devotion given to them, the sacred powers grant protection and blessings, and deliver the people from suffering and disaster.

The Main Features of Ceremonial Taoism

The principal features of the Way of Devotion, or Ceremonial Taoism, are:

1. At the core, the belief that there are sacred powers, in the form of deities and spirits, that direct human destiny.

2. Deities will grant blessings, protection, and deliverance if they are respected and honored; therefore, devotion and dedication are central to the practice of Ceremonial Taoism.

3. Devotion is expressed in the performance of ceremonies and celebrations of the sacred festivals, and ceremonies consist of rituals, offerings, chanting of liturgies, and the reading of sacred scriptures.

4. The belief that a two-way interaction exists between the devotee and the sacred powers. Ceremonies are performed to renew and strengthen the bond between humanity and deities so that a cooperative effort can be made to bring harmony to all realms of existence.

5. Because ceremonies are sacred to the deities, they are performed by people who have dedicated their lives to this purpose—people who are the masters of rituals and who intercede on behalf of the common believer. Thus, in Ceremonial Taoism, the believers are not necessarily the practitioners: the lay person who believes in the deities is not trained or authorized to perform the rituals.

The Taoist Deities

Taoist religion is pantheistic and pluralistic. Deities, spirits, and immortals are ranked according to their power and level of enlightenment. Usually, the ranks are identified by titles given to the deities; thus, the highest deities are called T'ien-tsun, or Celestial Lords, followed by Ti (Emperor) and Hou (Empress), then Wang (King), Hsien (Immortal), and finally Shen (spirit). Because Taoist religion has incorporated folk beliefs and local cults, its deities also include the nature spirits of prehistoric times, sages and folk heroes, deities of other religions, and founders of sects who have been invested with immortality.

The deities of Taoism are a large and varied group. Some have been embellished with colorful personalities as legends have grown around them. Although some deities and spirits are portrayed as mischievous and playful in folktales and drama (for example, the Eight Immortals and the Monkey King), Taoist ceremonies are themselves serious affairs. There is a vast difference between the world of legend and the world of ritual. Play and humor are appropriate only under certain circumstances. When the deities are presented in religious festivals, they are stately and serious.

The vast Taoist pantheon is divided into Earlier Heaven deities and Later Heaven deities. Earlier Heaven deities are deities who have existed since the beginning of time (before the separation of sky and earth, or creation of the celestial and terrestrial domains); Later Heaven deities are mortals who have become immortal. However, it is not correct to assume that all the greater deities are Earlier Heaven deities, because some formerly-mortal immortals, like Lü Tung-pin and the Kuan Emperor, occupy the highest levels of the pantheon. Since religious Taoism has incorporated both shamanism and folk beliefs, some nature spirits of the prehistoric times are also included in the hierarchy. Most notable are the spirits of the wind, rain, and thunder, who, although they are Earlier Heaven deities, are not as powerful as the Later Heaven deities like Lü Tung-pin.

THE GREAT DEITIES

The following Great Deities are listed in the order of importance recognized by Taoist religious communities. First come the Earlier Heaven deities:

T'ai-shang Lao-chün (fig. 9.1) is Lao-tzu deified. He is recognized by all Taoists as the patriarch of the Taoist religion. The name T'ai-

FIGURE 9.1. T'ai-shang Lao-chün, the highest deity in the Taoist religion.

shang Lao-chün was first used in the Ling-pao scriptures of the third century CE and was quickly adopted by orthodox religious Taoism. T'ai-shang Lao-chün, the highest deity in the Taoist pantheon, is the embodiment of the Tao and the incarnation of the primordial origin, the undifferentiated vapor, and the source of life. Thus, he is sometimes called the Emperor of the Undifferentiated Realm (Hun-yüan Huang-ti).

The Three Pure Ones (San-ch'ing) are the three emanations of the T'ai-shang Lao-chün. They are the Celestial Lords of the Three Pure Realms: Jade Pure (Yü-ch'ing), Great Pure (T'ai-ch'ing), and High Pure (Shang-ch'ing). The Jade Pure Realm is the domain of the Celestial Lord of the Limitless (Wu-chi T'ien-tsun) or Celestial Lord of the Ancient Beginning (Yüan-shih T'ien-tsun); the Great Pure Realm is the domain of the Celestial Lord of the Sacred Spirit (Ling-pao T'ien-tsun); the High Pure Realm is the domain of the Celestial Lord of Virtue (Tao-te T'ien-tsun). In the hierarchy of Taoist deities, the Three Pure Ones (fig. 9.2) are the deities next highest to T'ai-shang Lao-chün.

The Three Pure Realms represent three levels of Taoist immortality and enlightenment. The Jade Pure Realm is the Realm of Wu-chi. It is the highest level of immortality, and to rise to this realm is to attain complete union with the Tao. The Great Pure Realm is the next level of immortality. It is the Realm of T'ai-chi, and to rise to this realm is to exist in a state where subject and object are differentiated but are integral parts of the Tao. The third realm, the High Pure, is the Realm of Pa-k'ua, and to attain this level of immortality is to live a long life on earth in harmony with nature and humanity.

The Three Pure Ones have a special meaning for practitioners of internal alchemy. They represent the pristine and original pure state of the three internal energies. All people are endowed with these energies in their mother's womb. The Jade Pure is original spiritual energy (shen); the Great Pure is original vital or breath energy (ch'i); and the High Pure is original generative energy (ching). The three pristine energies emerge when the yin and yang energies of the female and male copulate. The goal of internal alchemy is to refine

FIGURE 9.2. The Three Pure Ones on an altar of a temple affiliated with the Hsien-t'ien Tao sect. In the center is the Jade Pure (Yü-ch'ing). To the right is Great Pure (T'ai-ch'ing), and to the left is the High Pure (Shang-ch'ing).

and transform internal energies into the pristine form given to us when we were conceived.

The Jade Emperor (Yü-ti) is the ruler of the celestial realm. Some Taoist sects identify the Jade Emperor (fig. 9.3) as an incarnation of the Celestial Lord of the Great Pure Realm (Ling-pao T'ien-tsun), giving him the titles Great Celestial Lord Jade Emperor (Yü-huang Ta-t'ien-tsun) and High Emperor of the Mysterious Realm of the Sacred Spirit (Hsüan-ling K'ao-shang Ti).

The Jade Emperor is the governor of human destiny. His celestial abode is the star Tzu-wei and he sits there to judge humanity. He grants health, longevity, and prosperity to those who have accumulated good deeds and punishes those who have done unethical deeds by taking away health and longevity.

FIGURE 9.3. The Jade Emperor (Yü-ti). On his right is his subordinate, Wen-chang Ti-chün.

The Mother Empress of the West (Hsi-wang Mu) is the Celestial Empress of the Western Realms of Paradise. She is said to reside in a palace in the peaks of the Kun-lun Mountains, a range of mountains in western China. The keeper of the doorway to the celestial realm and the bestower of longevity and immortality, the Mother Empress of the West keeps a garden where the tree of the immortal peaches is grown (fig. 9.4). Men and women alike must meet her standards before they are granted the status of immortal. It is said that she alone has the power to open and close the gates of life to mortals. Thus, the Mother Empress of the West is revered especially by practitioners of internal alchemy and the arts of immortality.

The Mother of the Bushel of Stars (Tou-mu)—a very interesting deity—is Hindu in origin. The Chinese romanization of her Sanskrit name is Mo-li-chih. She is the healer and giver of the Great Medicine (the elixir of immortality) and is the patron of healers and prac-

FIGURE 9.4. The Mother Empress of the West (Hsi Wang-mu). Her attendant is holding a tray of immortal peaches.

titioners of the arts of immortality. She is usually depicted as having eight arms (fig. 9.5), holding the orbs of the sun and moon, a bow and a spear, a bell and a seal, and, clasped as a mudra, the gesture of compassion. The sun and moon symbolize Tou-mu as the mother of all the celestial bodies; the bow and spear symbolize her power over illness; the bell symbolizes her compassion and the seal her power over death. The mudra of compassion symbolizes her power to heal the sick.

Internal alchemists invoke Tou-mu to help them in completing the Great Medicine, or the Golden Elixir, for she is the director of the movement of the stars and the mover of internal energy in the body.

The Celestial Lord of the Great Beginning (T'ai-i T'ien-tsun) is a subordinate of the Jade Emperor. He presides over the realm of the dead. T'ai-i T'ien-tsun (fig. 9.6) is recognized as the deity who taught

FIGURE 9.5. Statue of the Mother of the Bushel of Stars (Tou-mu) at the White Cloud Monastery, Beijing.

humanity the ceremonies of the Festival of Chung-yüan (Middle Season, or Festival of the Officer of the Terrestrial Realm). He is the symbol of compassion and his compassion extends to all souls, both living and dead. Thus, his festival is also known as the Festival of All Souls.

The Seven Star Lords of the Northern Bushel are deities who live in the seven stars of the Northern Bushel (Big Dipper) constellation. They are subordinates of the Jade Emperor and they carry messages of his verdicts regarding an individual's destiny.

In Taoist belief, each individual is born under the guardianship of one of the seven stars. This guardian, or birth star, is responsible for the individual's health and longevity. If a person's health is good, the guardian star will be bright; if the health is poor, the guardian star will be dim. On the first and fifteenth days of each lunar month and on the first seven days of the ninth lunar month, the deities of the Northern Bushel descend to the mortal realm to proclaim the judgment of the Jade Emperor to humankind. The Seven Star Lords also

FIGURE 9.6. The Celestial Lord of the Great Beginning (T'ai-i T'ien-tsun). Painting from the Hsüan Yüan Hsüeh Institute of Hong Kong.

report to the Jade Emperor the good and bad deeds of those in their charge. Based on the reports, the Jade Emperor will reward or punish, according to individual merit. Because human health and longevity depend on their reports to the Jade Emperor, the Seven Star Lords of the Northern Bushel are considered to be the masters of health and longevity.

The Seven Star Lords are attended by the Left and Right Guardians. These stars, which are themselves celestial deities, reside in constellations to the left and right of the Northern Bushel. The Seven Star Lords and the Two Guardians are sometimes called the Nine Kings of the Northern Bushel.

For internal alchemists, the stars of the Northern Bushel have a special meaning. In a cosmology in which the North Pole Star represents the unmoving and permanent underlying reality of the Tao, the seven stars of the Northern Bushel represent the moving and changing aspect of the Tao. The Northern Bushel constellation is associated with the element water, and it symbolizes the generative energy in the body. The direction north and the element water being associated with yin, the Northern Bushel constellation therefore also symbolizes the essence of yin energy.

The Southern Bushel Stars, on the other hand, are associated with prosperity. There are six stars in this group and each is accompanied by a young attendant. It is said that the lords of the Southern Bushel are fiery and quick-tempered, and their actions are swift and uncompromising.

For internal alchemists, the Southern Bushel is associated with the element fire and the essence of yang energy. The Southern Bushel constellation represents the fire of vital or breath energy of the middle t'an-tien in the region of the solar plexus.

The Officers of the Celestial, Terrestrial, and Water Realms (San-kuan) are agents who carry out the verdicts of the Jade Emperor. When rewards are given, the Officer of the Celestial Realm grants prosperity, the Officer of the Terrestrial Realm forgives wrongdoings, and the Officer of Water delivers humanity from disaster. When punishment is enforced, the Three Officers withdraw their gifts and create disasters in the three realms of sky, earth, and water. Thus, the Officer of the Celestial Realm causes droughts, the Office of the Terrestrial Realm creates earthquakes, and the Officer of Water causes floods.

In addition to carrying out the verdicts of the Jade Emperor, the Three Officers are also lords of three feasts that mark the beginning, the middle, and the end of the year. The Officer of the Celestial Realm presides over the Beginning Season (shang-yüan), the Officer of the Terrestrial presides over the Middle Season (chung-yüan), and the Officer of Water presides over the Last Season (hsia-yüan). These feasts are held on the fifteenth day of the first lunar month, the fifteenth of the seventh lunar month, and the fifteenth of the tenth lunar month, respectively.

The Patron of the Arts and Literature (Wen-chang Ti-chün) is the immediate subordinate of the Jade Emperor. In the celestial domain, he resides in a group of stars adjacent to the Northern Bushel. Originally charged by the Jade Emperor with rewarding honorable scholars and punishing unscrupulous ones, Wen-chang Ti-chün's duties have been expanded, and he is now also the announcer of the Jade Emperor's judgments.

The Lords of the Five Mountains (Wu-yüeh Ti-chün) are the guardians of the five sacred mountains of China: Hua-shan in the west, T'ai-shan in the east, Heng-shan, in Hunan, in the south, Heng-shan, in Shansi, in the north, and Sung-shan, in the center. Each lord is also the guardian of the direction that he is associated with and the keeper of the element of that direction. Thus, the lord of the west wears a white robe and is the keeper of the element metal; the lord of the east wears a green or blue robe and is the keeper of the element wood; the lord of the south wears a red robe and is the keeper of the element fire; the lord of the north wears a black robe and is the keeper of the element water; the lord of the center wears a yellow robe and is the keeper of the element earth.

The Lords of the Five Mountains are also the keepers of the gates to the underworld, located in the depths of the mountains. Thus, these deities are often invoked in ceremonies that involve a journey to the underworld.

The next deities to be listed are Later Heaven deities. Typically, they are sages and heroes who have been granted the status of Immortal or Celestial Emperor or Empress because of their deeds in both the mortal and immortal realms.

Immortal Lü Tung-pin is probably the most popular immortal in Chinese culture. Regarded as the patriarch of many Taoist sects, he symbolizes the wisdom that cuts through the illusion of the material world. Lü Tung-pin was a historical figure. He lived in the T'ang dynasty. Legends tell us that when he was on his way to the capital to take the qualifying examinations for service in the government, he met the immortal Chung-li Ch'uan, who gave him a pillow to sleep on. That night, Lü had dreams that showed him the futility of politics, fame, and power. He dreamed that after a brief success in court politics, he was drawn into intrigues that brought him exile and death far from his home. The next day, Lü realized the illusions of fame, fortune, and temporal power, and followed Chung-li Ch'uan into the mountains to learn the arts of immortality.

In icons, Immortal Lü is often shown with a whisk or a sword (fig. 9.7). The sword cuts through the illusion of impermanence and the whisk sweeps away the dust that covers the reality of the Tao. There are many legends of Immortal Lü returning to the mortal realm to heal the sick, deliver people from suffering, and help others to attain immortality.

Immortal Lü is especially honored by internal-alchemical sects.

FIGURE 9.7. Immortal Lü Tung-pin.

Many founders of internal-alchemical sects, such as Wang Ch'ung-yang, Liu Hai-ch'an, and Chen Hsi-yi, were taught by Lü Tung-pin.

Emperor Kuan (Kuan-ti) is another historical figure who was elevated to the status of deity. A general of Shu of the Three Kingdoms, Kuan Yü was skilled in the military arts and was uncompromising in his integrity and sense of honor. Killed in the war against Ts'ao-ts'ao the unscrupulous minister, Kuan Yü stood for everything that was virtuous, honest, and honorable in the eyes of the Chinese people. Initially a folk hero, he was elevated to the status of deity when he was made the patron of the military arts, and given the name Kuan-ti, or Emperor Kuan. In his role as General of the Celestial Armies, Emperor Kuan accumulated many heroic deeds fighting demons and monsters. His accomplishments were acknowledged by the Great Deities, and in a series of promotions he was given the titles Kuan the Sacred Emperor (Kuan Hsing-ti) and Emperor of the Golden Tower (Chin-ch'üeh Ti-chün). Some sects believe that he eventually became the Jade Emperor. Today, the Emperor Kuan is revered as the patron of the military arts, the keeper of virtue, and the embodiment of all that is upright and honorable.

THE LESSER DEITIES

The Kitchen Lord (Tsao-chün) is the keeper of the fires of the kitchen and the watcher of the household. Usually enshrined in a home, the Kitchen Lord is responsible for keeping the cooking fires going (in Chinese custom, a saying meaning having enough food to feed the family). Originally a spirit from the popular cults, the Kitchen Lord was accepted into the Taoist pantheon and given the duty of reporting the deeds of each household member to the Jade Emperor. This he does at the end of the year, when he ascends to the Celestial Palace to present a list of the good and bad deeds of each member of the household; thus, it is a common practice for many Chinese to make offerings to the Kitchen Lord, asking him to put in a good word for them.

The Rain, Wind, and Thunder Spirits (fig. 9.8), Yü-shih, Feng-po, and Lei-mu, are ancient deities that date back to prehistoric times.

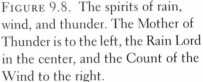

FIGURE 9.8. The spirits of rain, wind, and thunder. The Mother of Thunder is to the left, the Rain Lord in the center, and the Count of the Wind to the right.

Their formal names are Master of Rain, Count of the Wind, and Mother of Thunder. Usually invoked in rainmaking ceremonies, they also appear in high ceremonies in the company of greater deities such as T'ai-i T'ien-tsun, the Emperor Kuan, and Immortal Lü.

The Earth Father (Tu-t'i) is the guardian of a locality. A spirit from the ancient times, he was absorbed into the Taoist pantheon. Today he is revered as the protector of sacred grounds, especially temples and shrines, and a messenger of the deities. At the close of many Taoist ceremonies, the Earth Father is asked to carry the petitions to the deities and he is thanked for keeping mischief out of the ceremonial grounds.

OTHER DEITIES

There are many other deities in the Taoist pantheon and it is beyond the scope of this book to discuss all of them. I have described only the deities who have major festivals and ceremonies devoted to them and whose ceremonies are performed by major Taoist sects. Some deities, especially immortals, are special to certain sects. For example, the Celestial Teachers sect considers their founder Chang Tao-ling a great immortal and has major ceremonies dedicated to him; the Lung-men sect enshrines its founders, Wang Ch'ung-yang and Ch'iu Ch'ang-ch'un, in its temples.

Many local heroes, sages, and miracle workers have large followings in specific geographical regions. One example is a miracle worker named Huang Ta-hsien (Huang, the Great Immortal) who is extremely popular in Hong Kong and the southern regions of Kwantung Province.

Some Taoist sects have incorporated incarnations of the Buddha and the bodhisattvas into their hierarchy of deities. The most popular of these figures are Kuan-yin, the Bodhisattva of Compassion, the Tathagata Buddha, Amitabha Buddha, and Manjushri Buddha. However, when Buddhist deities are enshrined in Taoist temples, they are given Taoist names and are considered to be incarnations of Taoist deities. The Tathagata Buddha, for example, is considered to be the incarnation of the T'ai-shang Lao-chün; Manjushri is recognized by some Taoist sects as the incarnation of Immortal Lü Tung-pin; Amitabha Buddha has been named Wu-liang-shuo Fo (the Enlightened One of Unending Longevity); and Kuan-yin is sometimes considered to be an incarnation of the Mother Empress of the West.

The Administrative Structure of the Taoist Celestial Realm

In the Taoist Celestial Realm, every deity, immortal, and spirit has a specific duty. In the Taoist pantheon are administrators, warriors, and teachers. Within the category of administrators are judges, heralds, officers, bureaucrats, clerks, and messengers; in the category of warriors are generals, captains, soldiers of different ranks, and guards; in the category of teachers are avatars, patrons, and instructors. Specific dress, regalia, and titles identify each type of deity.

Taoist deities are divided into ranks. As mentioned earlier, T'ai-shang Lao-chün is the highest deity of all, but the T'ai-shang Lao-chün is not an administrator; rather, he is the source of wisdom, knowledge, and life. He is the creator and mover of events in celestial and terrestrial realms, and the underworld. Thus, the deities are under his rule. Immediately below him are the Three Pure Ones, who oversee the three realms of existence, but they, too, are not really administrators: their tasks are not concerned with the daily operations of keeping records and managing the three realms. As the T'ai-shang Lao-chün is the power behind creation and dissolution, the Three Pure Ones are the agents that make them happen.

The highest level of administration is headed by the Jade Emperor and the Mother Empress of the West. These two are about the same rank in the Taoist pantheon. As the Director of Destiny, the Jade Emperor passes judgment on mortals and decides their fate. As the keeper of the doorway to immortality, the Mother Empress of the West decides who attains immortality.

Below the Jade Emperor is a large group of administrators and bureaucrats. The Wen-chang Ti-chün, the patron of the arts and literature, announces the verdicts of the Jade Emperor. As we have already seen, the messages are then carried to humanity by the Star Lords of the Northern Bushel, and rewards and punishment are effected by the Three Officers of the Celestial, Terrestrial, and Water Realms. In addition, the Wen-chang Ti-chün also keeps a record of the deeds of each individual, filing reports sent by the Seven Star Lords and the Kitchen Lord.

The Jade Emperor and his subordinate administrators also attend to the petitions of mortals. Requests for blessings and protection, pleas for forgiveness, and messages of repentance are sent to the Jade Emperor via the Three Officers.

The clerks of the celestial realm keep records of shrines, temples, and monasteries. When a new shrine, temple, or monastery is opened, messages are sent by the abbot to the celestial realm, informing the deities that a new sacred space has been inaugurated. The message is addressed to the patron deities of the temple or shrine and delivered via celestial messengers. The names of ordained priests are also entered into registers and kept by the celestial clerks. When a priest is ordained or a monk is initiated into an order, the name of the individual is written in a formal message and sent to the celestial realm. In this way, the deities keep track of who is authorized to perform ceremonies and who is worthy of receiving the transmission of the sacred scriptures.

The realm of the underworld is administered by celestial beings. This is quite different from the system in Buddhism, whereby the underworld is administered by beings who dwell there. In some sects of Taoism, the T'ai-i T'ien-tsun is the chief administrator of all matters in the underworld. These include keeping the records of those who have died, those who are destined to be reincarnated, and those who need to be rehabilitated before reincarnation. The Taoist notion of the underworld, despite the influence of popular devotional Buddhism, is not a hell. It is not a place of punishment but a place of learning and rehabilitation. Dead souls who begrudge their fate and still cling to the mortal world are taught to accept the cycle of life and death and cease haunting the mortal realm. The duty of the T'ai-i T'ien-tsun is to educate dead souls so that they may receive a speedy reincarnation.

Other celestial deities who are responsible for affairs of the underworld are the Lords of the Five Mountains. The gates to the underworld are said to be located deep inside these sacred mountains and the Five Lords are the keepers of the gates. When a priest needs to enter the underworld to teach dead souls or to rescue them, petitions must be sent to the Five Lords to open the gates of the underworld so that the Taoist priest can pass through. Moreover, when an individual dies, he or she must pass through the same gates to the underworld; thus, the Five Lords are petitioned to open the gates to let the dead souls pass to the underworld.

The most important administrators have personal messengers. These messengers and attendants are typically depicted as children. The Lords of the Five Mountains each have an attendant, each dressed in the same color as the lord; the Star Lords of the Northern and Southern Bushels have personal attendants; the Mother Empress of the West is attended by a group of young women; and the T'ai-i T'ien-tsun is often accompanied by a boy who carries his banner.

The warriors of the celestial realm are led by captains, who are commanded by generals. The Emperor Kuan, the Celestial King Li Ch'ing who holds the Celestial Tower, and Yüeh Fei, a Sung dynasty general who was deified, are three of the highest commanders. The spirits of thunder, rain, and wind are captains of celestial warriors, as are many star lords. There are also the rank and file fighters and guards who defend the gateways to the celestial realm.

At the top of the Taoist pantheon of teachers are the avatars—beings who choose to mingle among humanity and take on the appearance of mortals to inspire, instruct, and advise. They are the embodiment of wisdom, instructors of techniques, and transmitters of knowledge. Immortal Lü Tung-pin is such a teacher. The next level of teachers is that of the patrons of the various branches of spiritual knowledge and practice. Tou-mu, the patron deity of healers and internal alchemists, and Fu Hsi, the patron of the divinational arts, are examples of this kind of teacher. Then there are the instructors of specific techniques, whose responsibility it is to impart knowledge and expertise. The immortals Chung-li Ch'uan and Chang Tzu-yang (Po-tuan) are instructors of internal alchemy and techniques of immortality; the immortal Huang-shih Kung is an instructor of terrestrial divination.

The hierarchy of deities in the Taoist pantheon is not rigid: there are promotions and demotions, because the accomplishments of the deities are evaluated constantly. Popularity in the mortal realm is an indicator of a deity's achievement. If a temple or shrine dedicated to a certain deity is frequented by many people asking for a blessing, protection, advice, or forgiveness, the deity is said to have gained the trust of mortals and be worthy of promotion.

Taoist Festivals and Ceremonies

Devotion is expressed in the observance of the sacred festivals and in the performance of ceremony.

There are several kinds of festivals in Ceremonial Taoism. The highest festivals are called *chai-chiao*, or Great Services. Great Services typically last for many days. They can be occasions of celebration, mourning, sending petitions, or repenting. For example, the Festival of the Officer of the Terrestrial Realm is a service that focuses on repentance; the Festival of the Northern Bushel Stars is a combination of celebration and repentance; and major rainmaking ceremonies are services of petitioning (fig. 9.9.)

The Ritual Gathering *(fa-hui)* is another kind of Taoist festival. The Ritual Gathering is not as elaborate as the Great Service, but it is a major festival and can last for several days. The festivals of the Officer of the Celestial Realm and the Officer of the Water Realm are often celebrated as Ritual Gatherings. Depending on their scope, ceremonies of rainmaking or disaster-averting can be performed either as a Great Service or as a Ritual Gathering.

FIGURE 9.9. Photograph taken at a ceremony sending a petition to the deities. Taken at White Cloud Monastery, Beijing.

Another type of Taoist festival is the feast day of a deity, called a *tan*. The rituals performed on these days are entirely devoted to the deity honored in the feast. All the Great Deities have feast days (see table 9.1), and in some temples and shrines, the feast day of the patron deity of the temple is celebrated with as much fanfare as those of the Great Deities. Almost all Taoist religious communities celebrate feast days that honor the T'ai-shang Lao-chün (with the Three Pure Ones), the Jade Emperor, the Mother Empress of the West, and Immortal Lü Tung-pin. The festival for Tou-mu, the Mother of the Stars, is part of the Great Service of the Northern Bushel Stars.

Yet another kind of Taoist festival is the Service Day, when a liturgy is chanted. Typically, on the first and fifteenth day of each lunar month, a liturgy dedicated to a deity or a group of deities is chanted. The most popular liturgies are the scriptures of the Northern Bushel Stars and Southern Bushel Stars. Some temples chant liturgies dedicated to their patron deity.

Other services are performed for private individuals. These include funeral rites and birthday blessings. Funeral rites are usually performed on the day of burial, but the more elaborate ones include rituals and chanting performed on the seventh, twenty-first, and forty-ninth day after a death. These rituals are designed to guide the deceased into the underworld. People wishing to be blessed on their birthdays are typically given a blessing that involves a petition to the Northern or Southern Bushel Star Lords for health, longevity, and prosperity.

Sects in Ceremonial Taoism

The most prominent sect of Ceremonial Taoism is the Celestial Teachers' Way (T'ien-shih Tao), or the Cheng-i Meng-wei (Central Orthodox) sect. Founded by Chang Tao-ling in the Eastern Han and developed by the great liturgists Liu Hsiu-ching and K'ou Ch'ien-chih of the fifth century CE, this sect has the most elaborate and colorful ceremonies. Today in Taiwan, where the sixty-fourth generation of the patriarch of the Celestial Teachers resides, the sect performs many ceremonies that are cosponsored by the government.

TABLE 9.1. The twelve-month cycle of festivals of Taoist deities, which are celebrated by most temples. Some of the festivals also honor Chinese cultural figures; these are listed where appropriate.

1st Lunar Month

1st day. T'ai-shang Lao-chün (Lao-tzu, the Ancient One).
The Patriarch of Taoism and the embodiment of the Tao; the source and origin of all things.

8th day. Yüan-shih T'ien-tsun, or Wu-chi T'ien-tsun (Yü-ch'ing, or Jade Pure One).
The first of the three embodiments of Lao-tzu incarnated from the One Primordial Breath of the Origin. Also known as the Jade Pure One. He is the Lord of the Beginning, a state of existence when everything was part of the undifferentiated wholeness of the Tao and the symbol of spirit energy.

9th day. Yü-ti (the Jade Emperor).
The Jade Emperor is one of the highest deities in the Taoist Pantheon. The Jade Emperor has power over the destiny of all living beings and gives reward and punishment to individuals.

15th day. T'ien-kuan (the Officer of the Celestial Realm).
The Officer of the Celestial Realm grants prosperity and happiness. He is a subordinate officer of the Jade Emperor. He is also known as the Lord of the Beginning Season (shang-yüan). The Festival of Lanterns is also part of this celebration.

2nd Lunar Month

2nd day. Tu-t'i (the Earth Father).
The Earth Father guards a locality from mischievous spirits and acts as messenger for the deities.

3rd day. Wen-chang Ti-chün.
Patron of the arts and literature and subordinate of the Jade Emperor. Keeps a register of achievements of scholars and announces the verdicts of the Jade Emperor.

6th day. Tung-yüeh Ti-chün (the Emperor of the Eastern Mountain).
A chief administrator of the Jade Emperor. He performs scribal duties and records the birth and death of mortals. His element is wood and his color

is green (or blue). He is also the guardian of the gate to the underworld in T'ai-shan, the Eastern Mountain.

15th day. Tao-te T'ien-tsun (Shang-ch'ing or High Pure One).
Third Embodiment of Lao-tzu. The ruler of the realm of pa-k'ua.

3rd Lunar Month

15th day. Chiu-t'ien Hsüan-nü (the Mysterious Lady of the Nine Celestial Domains).
She controls the catalogs of the Nine Celestial Domains, assembles the lists of the gods, and directs the registers of human destiny. Also one of the patrons of the divinational arts.

18th day. Chung-yüeh Ti-chün (the Emperor of the Central Mountain).
Same duties as Emperor of Eastern Mountain except that he guards the central gate to the underworld, located in Sung-shan, the Central Mountain. His element is earth and his color is yellow.

4th Lunar Month

14th day. Immortal Lü Tung-pin.
Also known as the Lord of Pure Yang. The patriarch of all internal-alchemical sects, and deliverer of humanity from illusion and suffering.

18th day. Tzu-wei Shing-chün (Star Lord of the Star of Purple Light).
The Lord of the North Star, ruler of all stars.

5th Lunar Month

5th day. Ch'ü-Yüan.
Sage, poet, and patriot of the Ch'u of the Spring and Autumn Period. Author of the *Ch'u-tzu* (Songs from the Land of Ch'u). The life and death of Ch'ü Yüan are remembered by Dragon Boat races and this feast day is known as the Dragon Boat Festival.

6th Lunar Month

1st day. Wen-ku and Wu-ku Stars (the Lords of the Scholar and Warrior Stars of the Northern Bushel).
Rulers of destiny and the patron of scholars and warriors.

23rd day. Ling-pao T'ien-tsun (T'ai-ch'ing or Great Pure One).
The second of the embodiments of Lao-tzu and ruler of the domain of T'ai-chi.

7th Lunar Month

7th day. Hsi Wang-mu (Mother Empress of the West).
Keeper of the gateway to immortality. Recommends and confers immortality.

15th day. T'i-kuan (Officer of Earth).
Also known as the Ruler of the Middle Season (chung-yüan). Subordinate of the Jade Emperor, he is responsible for pardoning wrongdoings.

8th Lunar Month

3rd day. Tsao-chün (the Kitchen Lord).
The Kitchen Lord is responsible for watching and recording the deeds of people in their homes. He is the keeper and guardian of the stove and the flame. The Kitchen Lord ascends to the celestial realm to report to the Jade Emperor twice a year. Length of life of individuals is evaluated each time a report is made.

10th day. Pei-yüeh Ti-chün (the Emperor of the Northern Mountain).
Same duties as the Emperor of the East, except that he is guardian of the gate to the underworld in the Heng-shan (Shansi), the Northern Mountain. His color is black and his element is water.

9th Lunar Month

1st through 9th day. Descent of the Northern Bushel Star Lords to Earth.
On each of these days, a star from the Northern Bushel Constellation visits the mortal realm to grant happiness, longevity, and prosperity to persons born under their guardianship. Each person is said to be born under one of the Star Lords. If a person has accumulated good deeds, the guardian star will grant life and prosperity.

1st. Descent of the North Star Lord.
The North Star rules over the Seven Stars and grants reward and retribution. An incarnation of the Jade Emperor.

9th day. Tou-mu (the Mother of the Bushel of Stars).
She is the origin of the stars. Her two eldest children are the North and South Pole Stars. The patron of medicine, internal alchemy, and all healing arts.

10th Lunar Month

14th day. Fu Hsi.
Patron of all the divinational arts.

15th day. Shui-kuan (the Officer of Water).
Also known as the Lord of the Last Season (hsia-yüan). He is responsible for protecting people from misfortune.

11th Lunar Month

6th day. Hsi-yüeh Ti-chün (the Emperor of the Western Mountain).
Same duties as the other Emperors of the Mountains as keeper of the gate to the underworld in Hua-shan, the Western Mountain. His color is white and his element is metal.

11th day. T'ai-i T'ien-tsun (Celestial Lord T'ai-i).
He is responsible for delivering both living and dead from suffering and has the power to summon the dead souls and spirits of the underworld. He is said to have transmitted the liturgical Festival of Chung-yüan (All Souls Festival) to humanity.

12th Lunar Month

16th day. Nan-yüeh Ti-chün (the Emperor of the Southern Mountain).
Same duties as the other Emperors of the Mountains as guardian of the gate to the underworld located in Heng-shan (in Hunan) in the south. His color is red and his element is fire.

24th day. Kitchen Lord ascends to the celestial realm.
At the end of the year, the Kitchen Lord reports our deeds to the Jade Emperor.

Training in the Celestial Teachers primarily involves learning the rites, rituals, and liturgies of ceremonies. The student begins training by being initiated into the sect, and when training is completed, the initiate is ordained into the priesthood. The sect is not a monastic order, however: its priests are allowed to marry and lead a family life.

I had the chance to watch Celestial Teachers festivals in Taiwan. The ceremonies are extremely complex and a single ritual can last hours. The leaders, musicians, and chanters perform the rituals from memory, which, even for one ceremony, entails memorizing long lists of names of deities, procedures, and hundreds of pages of liturgy. The performance of the ceremonies must be flawless because any mistake will break the bond between humanity and the sacred powers.

Many internal-alchemical sects incorporate ceremony into their practice. These include the Lung-men (Dragon Gate) sect of the Complete Reality School, and the Hsien-t'ien Tao (Earlier Heaven Way) sect, which claims its lineage through the Patriarch Celestial Dragon of Hua-shan. However, these sects are not really devotional sects: they follow the path of Internal Alchemy, the Way of Transformation.

For internal alchemists, ceremony is a method of cultivating internal energy and transforming body and mind. Chanting opens up blockages in the throat, where two important pathways of energy meet. It also moves internal energy through the jaws and up the face to the head. The sounds of the chant are designed to resonate with each internal organ, and the speed of chanting affects the movement of the diaphragm and breathing patterns. For example, fast chanting is designed to fan the rapid fires of the lower tan-t'ien; slow chanting is designed to draw the heat of the lower tan-t'ien slowly through the body.

Ritual, too, is incorporated into the techniques of internal transformation. The prostrations, bows, and walking patterns are designed to open blockages in the spinal column and move energy from the base of the spine to the top of the head. In addition, the alternation of kneeling, standing, prostrating, and bowing is an excellent way to strengthen tendons and bones, maintain flexibility and mobility, and keep the energy flowing.

Further Words on Ceremonial Taoism

Ceremonial Taoism is the Way of Devotion. Through devotion, a bond is formed between humanity and the sacred. The performance of a ceremony is a sacred act that seals a promise between humanity and the powers. The welfare of an individual, a community, and even a nation depends on the impeccability of the performance of a ceremony. The rituals are rites of renewal, and the ceremony is a sacred occasion in which humanity and deities come together to ensure that peace and harmony are maintained in all the realms of existence.

FURTHER READINGS

Book 2 of Henri Maspero's *Taoism and Chinese Religion* presents an account of the major and minor Taoist deities and contains brief descriptions of rituals associated with ceremonies for the major ones. However, some of Maspero's accounts of the status of some deities are questionable; for example, he states that nowadays the T'ai-i Ta-ti is a "petty god" and is not considered as an important deity presiding over the realm of the dead. This is incorrect. One has only to attend the Festival of All Souls (Chung-yüan) in any region of China, Taiwan, or Hong Kong to find that T'ai-i Ta-ti is given the title of T'ai-i T'ien-tsun and is the most important deity honored in that festival.

There are good descriptions of Taoist festivals in two of Michael Saso's books—in chapter 1 of *Taoism and the Rite of Cosmic Renewal* and chapter 7 of *Blue Dragon, White Tiger*. For material about Chinese cultural rites, see chapters 4, 5, and 6 in *Blue Dragon, White Tiger*.

Several chapters in Kristofer Schipper's *The Taoist Body* are especially pertinent in understanding Ceremonial Taoism. In chapter 2 he discusses the everyday beliefs of popular religion; in chapter 3 he discusses the notion of divinity and deity in Taoist beliefs; in chapter 4 he describes practices of local cults and the nature of priesthood in the Celestial Teachers sect and the nature of sacred scripture; and in chapter 5 he discusses the nature of Celestial Teachers rituals. Note that Schipper's account of Ceremonial Taoism is based on his experience with the Celestial Teachers tradition and should not be taken to represent the practices of all Taoist sects. Ceremonies differ widely among sects.

Further accounts of Taoist deities can be found in Livia Kohn's *The Taoist Experience*. See reading # 8, "Gods and Goddesses"; #45, "Celestial Garb"; and #46, "The Administration of Heaven."

10
Internal-Alchemical Taoism
The Way of Transformation

INTERNAL-ALCHEMICAL TAOISM is the Way of Transformation. Reborn in the union of the yin and yang energies, purified by the rising vapor, and tempered by the fires of the furnace, the internal alchemist emerges from the cauldron to be reunited with the primordial Breath of the Tao, the source of life.

Basic Ideas of Internal Alchemy

1. Before we were born, we were a part of the Tao. Formless and undifferentiated from the Tao, we were not subject to birth and death, and growth and decay. In this state, there is no form, no mind, no body, no sense, and no feeling.

2. When the generative energies of father and mother come together, energy from the Tao is drawn into the womb of the mother to form a fetus. The fetus represents a break, or separation, from the Tao: it has taken a form and is no longer undifferentiated from the Tao. However, enclosed in the mother's womb, the fetus has not made contact with the mortal world. Its energy is thus still pristine.

3. As the fetus grows in the mother's womb, it continues to differentiate and develop. When its form is complete, it exits the mother's body to become a separate entity. In its first contact with the world,

its internal energy is separated into three components: generative (ching), vital (ch'i) and spirit energy (shen). Simultaneously, mind and body begin to move away from each other.

4. As the infant grows from childhood to youth and adulthood, the three energies are dissipated. Generative energy leaks out with sexual desire; vital energy is lost with the development of emotions; and spirit energy is weakened with increased activity in the mind.

5. The ordinary person does not know that the leakage of the energies is the cause of ill-health, old age, and death.

6. The practice of internal alchemy begins with realizing that the leakage of energy is the cause of many physical and mental problems in life. Through internal transformations, energy that we were endowed with before birth can be recovered. We can attain health and longevity and return to the original undifferentiated state to be reunited with the Tao.

7. Longevity is recovering health and slowing down the aging process, and immortality is releasing the spirit to be reunited with the Tao when the body-shell dies.

8. Thus, longevity is a means to immortality, and prolonging life in the mortal realm gives us time to prepare to leave it in the proper way.

Major Symbols in the Language of Internal Alchemy

Taoist internal alchemy uses symbols and metaphors to describe internal transformations. Although some variations exist in the interpretation of the alchemical terminology, there is general agreement among contemporary practitioners on the meaning of the key symbols. Below is a list of the most commonly used alchemical terms and a brief explanation.

The Three Treasures are also known as the Three Flowers and the Three Herbs. They are the three internal energies in the body. When we emerge from the womb, the undifferentiated energy of the Tao is split into three components, ching, ch'i, and shen (see above). These energies are described as treasures because they are the foundations of health and longevity. Lose these energies and we lose health and life; gather and circulate them and we live a long and healthy life.

The Furnace, the Cauldrons, and the Tan-t'iens (Elixir Fields) are fields of energy in the body. The furnace, or stove, is in the lower tan-t'ien, or the lower elixir field. In the body, the lower tan-t'ien is in the region of the navel. There the fires needed for refining the internal energies are ignited. This is why this area of the body is called the furnace.

There are three cauldrons—lower, middle, and upper—and each is associated with one of the three tan-t'iens. The lower cauldron, or lower tan-t'ien, is where generative energy is gathered, stored, tempered, refined, and transmuted into vital, or breath, energy. The middle cauldron, or middle tan-t'ien, is where vital energy is gathered, stored, tempered, refined, and transmuted into spirit energy. In the body, the middle tan-t'ien is in the region of the heart and the solar plexus. The upper cauldron, or upper tan-t'ien, is where the spirit energy is gathered, stored, tempered, refined, and merged with the primordial vapor of the Tao. In the body, the upper tan-t'ien is situated between the eyebrows. Although the tan-t'iens have physical locations in the body, they emerge only when certain stages of the alchemical process are reached.

Each tan-t'ien is controlled by a gate. The gates are located along the spinal column. In the physical body, the lower gate is located in the spinal column between the kidneys, the middle gate is in the area of the spine between the shoulder blades, and the upper gate is in the area where the spine enters the skull. The gates are closed if there are blockages in the channel (the *tu* meridian) that runs up the spinal column. Thus, the gates control access to the tan-t'iens. Opening the gates allows the tan-t'iens to emerge and the three energies to be gathered, refined, and transmuted.

The Golden Pill or Golden Elixir is the Great Medicine. The Golden Pill is the product of compounding the generative, vital, and spirit energies after they have been refined. It is the primordial vapor of the Tao inside the body, as well as our connection to the energy of the outside cosmos. It is the energy that gives us health and life, and it is the key to the return to the Tao. The emergence of the Golden Pill or Golden Elixir is sometimes called "the Three Flowers gathering at the top of the head."

The Firing Process refers to the adjustment of the fires in the lower tan-t'ien for refining and tempering the internal energies gathered in the three cauldrons. Yang fire refers to fast breathing and it is used to direct the fire to the middle and upper tan-t'iens. Yin fire refers to soft, slow breathing and it is used to incubate the internal energy. Knowing when to apply fast and slow fires is crucial in internal alchemy. As in cooking and in preparing herbs, the substances will be burned if too much heat is applied, or will be undercooked if the heat is insufficient.

The Immersion of Fire in Water is also described as "using k'an to complete li." K'an is water and li is fire in the scheme of the pa-k'ua. The trigram for k'an is ☵ and for li is ☲. Using k'an to complete li means taking the solid line (yang component) in the k'an trigram and exchanging it with the broken line (yin component) in the li trigram to make the trigrams of ch'ien (sky) ☰ and k'un (earth) ☷, which are, respectively, solid yang and solid yin. In the internal-alchemical process, the immersion of fire in water refers to the vital energy sinking from the middle tan-t'ien and the vapor of heated water (generative energy) rising from the lower tan-t'ien. It is in this interaction of fire and water that the generative energy is refined and vital energy is transmuted. The result is the emergence of a new substance, called vapor (ch'i   , not ch'i, breath   ).

The Copulation of the Dragon and Tiger refers to the union of the yin and yang energies in the body. The dragon is yin energy and the tiger is yang energy. The union of yin and yang occurs at many levels. The back of the body is yang and the front is yin; the left side of the body is yang and the right side is yin; the upper part of the body is yang and the lower part is yin. Unification of yin and yang energies therefore entails dissolving all blockages and barriers that separate the front and back, left and right, and upper and lower parts of the body. When the blockages in the body are dissolved, the yin and yang energies will meet in the three cauldrons. Their union in the lower tan-t'ien is called the "dragon and tiger swirling in the winding river"; in the middle tan-t'ien it is called "the sun and moon reflecting on each other in the Yellow Palace"; in the upper tan-t'ien it is called the "the union of husband and wife in the bedchamber."

The Golden Raven and the Jade Rabbit are also symbols of the essence of yang and yin. The Golden Raven is the vapor of the sky and the Jade Rabbit is the vapor of the earth. When the Raven descends and the Rabbit leaps up, it signifies that a channel is open and the vapors in the crown of the head and in the abdomen can circulate. This is sometimes called the meeting of the Golden Boy and the Jade Maiden. It is a sign that the Microcosmic Orbit is open.

The Microcosmic Orbit is also known as the Waterwheel. The waterwheel moves the internal energy, or the waters of life. On one level, it refers to directing the flow of generative energy from the abdomen to the head; on another level, it is the flow of energy within the Microcosmic Orbit—a circuit that runs from the base of the spine to the top of the head, down the front of the body, and back to the tailbone of the spine. Two meridians make up the Microcosmic Orbit. The *tu* meridian begins at the base of the spine in a cavity called the *wei-lu*, ascends the spinal column, and ends at the palate, in the mouth. The *jen* meridian begins where the tu meridian ends and descends the front of the body to form a circular pathway, joining the tu meridian at the wei-lu.

Circulation of energy in the Microcosmic Orbit is called the Microcosmic Circulation or the Lesser Celestial Movement. There are three possible directions of flow of energy in the Microcosmic Orbit. One direction is clockwise: the flow is up the tu meridian at the back and down the jen meridian in front. Here, the generative energy is refined for the transmutation of vital energy and the vital energy is refined for the transmutation of spirit energy. This returns the generative energy to the head. A second direction of flow is counterclockwise: the flow is up the jen meridian and down the tu meridian. Here, the vital energy is created and nourished by spirit energy and the generative energy is created and nourished by vital energy. In the higher levels of cultivation, the flow of internal energy in both directions is simultaneous. A third possible direction is letting the energy flow out of the body. This is leakage. Leakage occurs through the orifices of the body (eyes, ears, nose, mouth, genitals, and anus). The causes of leakage are a weak constitution, injury, and craving.

The Macrocosmic Orbit is a circuit that consists of the Microcosmic Orbit plus the pathways that flow down the legs to the soles of the feet. Circulation of energy through this pathway is called the Macrocosmic Circulation or the Greater Celestial Movement. The circuit of energy begins at the base of the spine, goes up to the Point of All Gatherings *(chung-hui)* at the top of the head, down the front of the body, through the legs, and enters the soles of the feet at the Bubbling Spring Cavity *(yung-ch'üan)*. From there, the energy goes up the legs to return to the base of the spine.

The Nine Circulations of the Golden Pill refers to the circular and spiral motion of the internal energy in the body. The Golden Pill is the culmination of the transmutation of the generative, vital, and spirit energies. The Golden Pill is also the Immortal Fetus, the seed of the original spirit *(yüan-shen)*. This bundle of undifferentiated primordial energy tumbles in the tan-t'iens and spirals around the body.

Nine is the number of completion, and nine also describes the cycle and the period of time required for the energy to complete one circuit. The minor cycle takes three hours plus three quarter-hours to complete and the major cycle takes nine hours plus nine quarter-hours. Thus, the Nine Circulations of the Golden Pill describe the movement of the primordial energy of the Tao in the body.

The Immortal Fetus is the undifferentiated primordial vapor of the Tao that is produced when the transmutations of the three energies are complete. Initially a seed, it grows and develops in the lower tan-t'ien as a fetus grows in a womb. As it matures, it ascends the body and emerges from the top of the head, as energy is liberated from the body. This energy will eventually become reunited with the energy of the cosmos when the human shell dies.

Steps in the Alchemical Process

Practitioners of internal alchemy divide the process of transformation into stages, and the alchemical work performed at each stage serves as the foundation for the next stage. Sects differ on the emphasis of training in each stage, but in general they agree on what is accomplished in each step of the alchemical process.

THE LOWER STAGES: BUILDING THE FOUNDATIONS

External strengthening, or *wai-chuang*, works on the external structure of the physical body. In this stage, muscles, ligaments, and tendons are softened, joints are articulated, the spinal column is aligned, and bones are strengthened. Alchemical transformations are both physical and mental, and without the changes in the skeletal structure, changes in consciousness, energy, and spirit cannot occur. External strengthening therefore prepares the student for later stages of training.

External strengthening is the first step of training in internal-alchemical sects that focus on cultivating body before mind. Techniques of external strengthening include tendon-changing *(i-chun)*, massage *(an-mo)*, yoga-like *ch'i-kung* postures, calisthenics, and internal martial arts such as t'ai-chi ch'uan (see chapter 13 for a discussion of these techniques). The goal of this part of training is to revitalize the skeletal system and attain external health.

Internal strengthening, or *nei-chuang*, works on the internal structure and functions of the physical body. Once the skeletal system is sufficiently strong, work on the internals begins. This means massaging the internal organs, enhancing the circulation of blood, and stimulating the nervous system. Massaging the internal organs and stimulating the nervous system are accomplished by moving the spine. Since the spine is attached to the internal organs by a series of muscles deep within the body, gentle movement of the spine will shake the organs and massage them. Some forms of internal martial arts and calisthenics have been designed specifically for this purpose (see chapter 13). The goal of this part of the training is to revitalize the internal functions of the body and attain internal health. This is normally the second stage of training for sects that focus on cultivating body before mind.

Refining the mind, or *lien-hsin,* includes stilling the mind, cultivating quietude, minimizing desire, living in simplicity, and becoming uninterested in excitement and sensual stimulation.

Meditation is the typical technique used in this stage of training. Meditation can take the form of quiet sitting or standing, or involve physical movement like t'ai-chi ch'uan and walking meditation (see chapter 12 for a discussion of different methods of Taoist meditation). Changes in lifestyle and attitude are important in this stage of training: the student is required to minimize activity and lead a life of quietude and stillness.

For sects that focus on cultivating mind before body, this is the first step of training. Once the mind is stilled and attitude and lifestyle have changed, the body is cultivated with techniques of external and internal strengthening. For sects that focus on cultivating body before mind, this is the last step in building the lower foundations of the alchemical work.

THE MIDDLE STAGES: TRANSFORMING INTERNAL ENERGY

From here on, training in all sects of internal alchemy follows the same sequence.

Refining generative energy for the transmutation of vital energy. This stage of internal alchemy, *lien-ching-hua-ch'i,* focuses on gathering, refining, and transforming generative energy. In the physical body, the work is concentrated in the abdominal area around the lower tan-t'ien and the lower gate. In the mental domain, the work involves regulating and minimizing sexual desire.

Generative energy, or ching, is produced and stored in the lower tan-t'ien. Generative energy is drained from the body when it is used in procreation or when sexual pleasure is aroused. When generative energy exits the body, it is transformed from its pristine state into its mundane or contaminated state.

The first step in this stage of the alchemical work is to stop the leakage of generative energy by regulating sexual activity and desire. This allows the ching to be gathered and refined. External and internal health also facilitate the cultivation of generative energy. The production of generative energy is typically faster for people who are young and strong, slower for those who are old and weak; thus, some schools of internal alchemy have turned to methods of sexual yoga to enhance the collection of generative energy. Such methods are recommended for people who have problems producing this energy themselves. Sexual alchemy is not without its risks. When generative energy is gathered from a partner, no desire or pleasure must be present, or the energy will be dissipated rather than collected.

Once sufficient generative energy is gathered, it must be refined. This is the next step, and involves starting the fires of the furnace in the lower tan-t'ien. The furnace, or stove, is powered by water or generative energy. When the generator starts, heat is produced in the lower tan-t'ien. In internal alchemy, the term for this is *the birth of yang*. With the furnace in place, the next step is to set up the cauldron in the lower tan-t'ien. The cauldron is the container where the generative energy is collected, refined, tempered, and stored. Access to the lower cauldron is controlled by the lower gate, located in the spinal column between the kidneys. When the lower gate is open, the lower cauldron emerges and the generative energy can be refined. In traditional alchemical language, the term for the process described in this paragraph is *positioning the furnace and setting up the cauldron.*

Regulation of the fires of the furnace is the key to refining generative energy. As mentioned earlier, refining energy is like working in the kitchen. If the fire is too hot, the food will burn; if there is insufficient heat, the food will be undercooked. Moreover, applying the right amount of heat at the right time is critical. If hot fires are applied when warm fires are required, or vice versa, food and herbs will suffer.

The heat of the furnace is adjusted by regulating the breath. The movement of the diaphragm controls the depth of breathing and the capacity of the lungs determines the volume of breath. Thus, the entire respiratory system is called into play in the firing process. This is why it is important to develop and transform the structure and function of the body in the early stages of internal alchemy.

While refining is in progress, the cauldron must be sealed so that the energy will not leak out. This means that openings where the energy can dissipate must be closed. Any arousal of sexual desire will drain the energy from the body. Thus, while the internal herbs are gathered and refined, the senses must be still and sexual desire must be minimal.

The refinement of generative energy culminates with the transmutation of the ching into vapor. When the vapor rises to the middle tan-t'ien, the phenomenon is called *the blossoming of the Lead Flower.*

Refining the vital energy for the transmutation of spirit energy. This stage of internal alchemy, *lien-ch'i-hua-shen,* focuses on gathering, refining, and tempering vital energy. In the physical body, the alchemical work is concentrated in the middle tan-t'ien, or heart region. In the mental domain, this stage involves regulating emotions and moods, because vital energy is drained by emotional fluctuations.

Vital energy in the form of vapor, or ch'i, rises to the middle tan-t'ien after it has been transmuted from refined generative energy. There it is collected, refined, and tempered. Access to the middle tan-t'ien is controlled by the middle gate. When this gate is open, the middle cauldron emerges, and refinement of ch'i can begin. When alchemical work is focused on the middle tan-t'ien, the fires of the furnace in the lower tan-t'ien must be pumped to higher levels. This requires an even more effective respiratory system, because the breath has to be drawn to higher regions of the body.

Once the ch'i is refined, it must be stored. This requires sealing the cauldron of the middle tan-t'ien. At this point, the practitioner must be free from mood swings and emotional changes. Negative emotions such as anger, fear, sadness, and frustration are especially detrimental to the cultivation of vital energy.

The transmutation of vital energy culminates in the emergence of refined ch'i. When the refined ch'i rises to the upper tan-t'ien, the phenomenon is termed *the blossoming of the Silver Flower.* At this time, the pathways of energy between the lower and upper parts of the body are connected, and refined ch'i can move up and down the body in the Microcosmic and Macrocosmic Orbits.

THE FINAL STAGES: COMPLETING THE ALCHEMICAL WORK

Refining the spirit energy for the return to the Void. In this stage, *lien-shen-huan-hsu,* the refined ch'i rises to the upper tan-t'ien and is transmuted into spirit energy. In the physical body, this part of internal alchemy focuses on the upper tan-t'ien, which is located between the eyes. In the mental domain, it involves emptying the mind of thoughts, dissolving the duality of subject and object, and being in a state of total emptiness.

The completion of the refinement of spirit energy is termed *the blossoming of the Golden Flower.* At this time, all three energies in their purified form rise to the top of the head and merge to become one undifferentiated energy. This alchemical achievement is termed *the Three Flowers gathering at the top of the head.*

The return of the three energies—generative, vital, and spirit—to their original undifferentiated state is the emergence of the seed of the Tao. This undifferentiated vapor descends to the abdomen to form the immortal fetus. As with a physical fetus, the immortal fetus needs to be incubated in the body. As the immortal fetus develops, it churns, moves, tumbles, and grows big in the belly of the internal alchemist. The incubation period is termed *the ten months of pregnancy,* because it resembles the development of a fetus in a mother's womb. At this stage of training, the practitioner must be secluded in a quiet place and not be distracted. If a wrong step is taken, the immortal fetus will be lost.

During the ten months of incubating the immortal fetus, the practitioner continues to gather, refine, and circulate internal energy to nourish the fetus. The physical and mental health of the internal alchemist are of utmost importance, and great care must be taken to ensure that both the immortal fetus and the body that carries it are given proper nourishment.

Cultivating the Void to merge with the Tao. In this stage, *lien-hsü-ho-Tao,* when the period of incubation is complete, the immortal fetus emerges from the womb. It is now called the original spirit (*yüan-shen*). The maturation of the yüan-shen is likened to the growth of an infant to childhood, youth, and adulthood. As it matures, the yüan-shen leaves the lower abdominal area and enters the chest where it is fed by internal energy and bathed in vapor. Internal alchemy calls this stage *the Three Years of Breast-feeding.* Eventually, the yüan-shen rises to the head and exits the body at the top of the head. The yüan-shen begins to travel, leaving the body that had sheltered and nourished it. Initially the journeys are short; like a youth, it frequently returns to the shelter of home after its travels. However, with time, the yüan-shen will make longer and longer journeys, traveling to different realms to learn how to make its way back to the Origin. This is the education of the yüan-shen, as it prepares itself for the moment when it will leave the shell permanently. When the physical body dies, the yüan-shen is liberated and is once again merged with the undifferentiated energy of the Tao. This is the final stage of internal alchemy—returning to where we were before we were born.

Approaches to Internal Alchemy

While internal alchemists agree on general principles and the stages of transformation, they differ in the use of techniques. These differences have led to the rise of sects and programs of training that are sometimes conflicting.

There are two major approaches to internal alchemy: the Singular Path and the Paired Path.

THE SINGULAR PATH

The Singular Path is so named because the practitioners achieve their alchemical transformations without taking energy from a sexual partner. At the core of the Singular Path is the belief that internal energy, especially generative energy, is gathered and cultivated by regulating sexual activity and minimizing sexual desire. Practitioners of the Singular Path believe that the ingredients of immortality as well as the equipment for alchemical transformation are entirely contained within one's own body. Therefore, it is not necessary to use a sexual partner's body as a source of energy or a vehicle for alchemical transformation. Celibacy is not required by the Singular Path (except in some sects, such as the Lung-men sect of the Complete Reality School), but it is recommended that advanced practitioners refrain from sexual activity to conserve internal energy.

Of the sects that follow the Singular Path, some focus equally on cultivating body and mind (for example, the Hsien-tien Tao and the Wu-Liu sects); some emphasize cultivating the body (for example, the Wu-tang-shan sect), and some emphasize cultivating the mind (for example, the Lung-men sect). Today, one can learn the basic techniques of the Singular Path (such as meditation, calisthenics, and ch'i-kung) without being initiated into a sect. However, the highest level of internal alchemy is taught only to those who have made a lifetime commitment to a program of spiritual training within a particular sect.

THE PAIRED PATH (SEXUAL ALCHEMY)

In the Paired Path, sexual techniques are used to accomplish alchemical transformations. The practice of Taoist sexual alchemy, rarely understood, has been sensationalized and abused. Sexual alchemy has been a part of Taoist internal alchemy since the times of Wei Po-yang in the second century CE. It is different from the "bedchamber techniques" that advise the correct management of one's sexual and energetic resources. While the bedchamber techniques are methods for making the best use of sexual energy, sexual alchemy is designed to gather generative energy for the transmutation of ching into ch'i.

Taoist sexual alchemy is a technique for cultivating health and longevity. It is not a pursuit of pleasure. Pragmatics, not ethics or pleasure, govern its practice. Even in the seventh century BCE, it was known that the decay of health was associated with the loss of ching, or generative energy. Thus, medical treatises such as the *Huang-ti nei-ching (Yellow Emperor's Classic of Internal Medicine)* counsels that the conservation of ching is the key to health and longevity. Herein lies the paradox of the role of sexual techniques in cultivating longevity. If sexual activity leads to the loss of generative energy and health, how can health be gained by using techniques that involve sex?

The answer to this paradox lies in the act of sex itself. If sex is used to satisfy the desire for pleasure, it drains generative energy and is detrimental to health. On the other hand, if sex is used to gather energy from a partner to replenish one's own generative energy, it can enhance longevity.

How can one use sex to gather generative energy? The Taoist texts of sexual alchemy state that generative energy is produced in sexual arousal. However, if the arousal ends in ejaculation or orgasm, generative energy is dissipated from the body and lost. Thus, to conserve generative energy, one must be sexually aroused but not emit the procreative substance. In fact, in sexual alchemy, tremendous self-control needs to be exercised to turn the energy back into the body just before an ejaculation or an orgasm is about to occur. Moreover, sexual alchemy can be used to absorb generative energy from a partner. In this procedure, the practitioner is instructed to find partners who are strong, healthy, and youthful. This ensures that the generative energy gathered will be of high quality. Generative energy can be absorbed by withdrawing one's energy when the partner reaches the climax. This timely act will absorb the partner's energy and direct one's own energy back into the body. Needless to say, in this procedure one gains energy at the expense of the partner. The practice is not limited to men who use women to gain generative energy; women can also use the male seminal fluid to replenish ching by withholding the orgasm at the appropriate time.

Clearly, there is nothing romantic about Taoist sexual alchemy. The texts of sexual alchemy repeatedly warn practitioners not to be emotionally involved in the sexual act and to view the partner simply as a useful source of energy. The optimal way to gather energy from a partner is to have as many different sexual partners as possible. And, the healthier the partner, the more energy one can absorb. In the sexual act, there is no love, no pleasure, and no desire. This view is quite different from some contemporary views of Taoist sexual yoga that present the Paired Path as a way of strengthening the bond of love between two people. In the classics of sexual alchemy, this illusion is dissolved quickly.

Although labeled as a "crooked path" by internal alchemists of the Singular Path, sexual alchemy had always been a part of the Taoist arts of longevity. Practiced by the early alchemists, it was seen as one of the many techniques of longevity. It was practiced by the Shang-ch'ing Taoists in their religious rituals and by internal alchemists of the Sung dynasty (for example, by Chang Po-tuan), who regarded it as a pragmatic way of gathering generative energy, especially for those who are no longer young and healthy.

In Taoist internal alchemy, sexual yoga is a means only for gathering generative energy for the transmutation of vital energy. Sexual yoga will help the practitioner in the intermediate stage of internal alchemy, in which ching is gathered, refined, and transmuted. It will not take the practitioner to the advanced stages. In fact, internal alchemists acknowledge that ching gathered from a partner is mundane ching and must be refined before it can be transmuted into vapor, or ch'i. For the serious practitioner of sexual alchemy, the timing of the gathering is extremely important. Gather too much and too often, and the mundane ching will become stale or even turn toxic in the body.

In closing, it must be said that the practice of sexual alchemy is not without its risks. To do it properly, one needs the guidance of a teacher, and because traditionally these techniques have been practiced in secret, it is difficult to find a bona fide teacher. Moreover, to practice sexual alchemy, one must be totally free from sexual desire. Otherwise, the efforts of gathering energy will result in the loss of one's own energy.

Further Words on Internal-Alchemical Taoism

Internal-Alchemical Taoism is one the most rigorous paths of spiritual training. If the practice of Magical Taoism is likened to playing with fire, the practice of Internal-Alchemical Taoism is like climbing a cliff. The guidance of a teacher is needed for this path of spiritual training. Books, video, and audio tapes cannot replace a teacher. Without constant feedback and a systematic program of training, the practice of internal alchemy can be dangerous. A single wrong step can result in internal injuries.

The process of alchemical transformation can be long. Building the lower foundations is extremely important, and a student may spend many years working on external and internal strengthening. One cannot expect to circulate energy if blockages exist in the body, or if the mind is active and excitable, or if the senses are stimulated.

Even within Chinese society, the practice of internal alchemy has been guarded; around it, there has often been an air of secrecy. Teachers do not accept students lightly, and an attempt to find an appropriate teacher cannot be rushed. Although it is viable to have several teachers, this is not advised in the early stages of training. It is easier to follow one program of training while building the lower foundations. Also, at the lower and the middle stages of internal alchemy, some techniques are mutually exclusive, or even conflicting. For example, choosing the Singular Path will exclude you from using sexual alchemy, and vice versa.

To repeat an earlier warning: the practice of internal alchemy requires a lifetime of commitment. It is not simply a matter of taking some lessons in ch'i-kung or meditation. Practicing meditation, ch'i-kung, or calisthenics will no doubt enhance your health, give you inner peace, and help you cope with problems in your everyday life; it is not, however, synonymous with training in internal alchemy. The goal of internal alchemy is more than attaining physical health and mental well-being. It is a way of preparing the body and mind to return to the Tao when your time in the mortal realm is over.

FURTHER READINGS

Selections of internal-alchemical writings from the Taoist canon can be found in Livia Kohn's book *The Taoist Experience:*

Energies and Elixirs (reading no. 30)
Alchemical Transformation (no. 41)
The Inner Elixir (no. 42)
Gradual Dissolution (no. 43)

Lu Kuan Yü has translated a modern classic of internal alchemy, *Hsin-ming fa-chüeh ming-chih* (The Secrets of Cultivating Essential Nature and Eternal Life) The author of the original text, Chao Pi-ch'en, was a member of the Lung-men sect. Although Lu Kuan Yü's translation, titled *Taoist Yoga,* is a manual of internal alchemy, it is suggested that you do not use it as such. It is dangerous to practice internal alchemy without guidance. There are some inaccuracies in the glossary of this book: in the description of the Eight Meridians (p. 194), for example, *yang-yu* and *yin-yu* are not arm channels but leg channels. Lu seems to have confused the Twelve Vessels with the Eight Meridians. The Heart and Lung Vessels run down the yin side of the arm, and the Large Intestine, Small Intestine, and Triple Heater Vessels run down the yang side of the arm. For an overview of the Eight Meridians and Twelve Vessels, see any textbook or manual of traditional Chinese Medicine.

A short treatise on internal alchemy titled *Yü-huang hsin-yin miao-ching* (The Jade Emperor's Profound Mind-Seal Classic) has been translated by Stuart Olson, who also provides a commentary and explanation of the concepts of internal alchemy. Do not assume that the commentary is the definitive explanation of the text. Olson's title is *The Jade Emperor's Mind Seal Classic.*

An internal-alchemical interpretation of the *Ch'ing-ching ching* (Cultivating Stillness), by an anonymous nineteenth-century commentator who is influenced by the teachings of the Hsien-t'ien Tao sect, can be found in my book *Cultivating Stillness.*

There are two translations of the controversial *T'ai-i chin-hua tsung-chih* (*The Secret of the Golden Flower*). One is by Richard Wilhelm, who rendered the text into German, which was then translated into English by Cary F. Baynes. The other is a more recent translation by Thomas Cleary, *The Secret of the Golden Flower*. The text is controversial even among practitioners of Taoist internal alchemy. Generally considered to be a text influenced by the Complete Reality School, its authorship has been linked to Immortal Lü Tung-pin, anonymous Lung-men practitioners, and even the followers of Wu Chung-hsü, of the Wu-Liu sect. I agree with Cleary that Wilhelm's translation is inaccurate and is based on an incomplete Chinese text. Moreover, I find the Wilhelm-Baynes version too biased by Jungian psychology. Cleary's translation is from the complete text of the *T'ai-i chin-hua tsung-chih*, but he presents it as a text that interprets internal alchemy as the transformation of mind, similar to the contemplative type of internal alchemy taught by Liu I-ming. How should these teachings be interpreted? Herein lies the controversy of the text and its power. It is a text with multiple levels of meaning, and depending on the orientation of an individual's Taoist training and understanding of internal alchemy, it can be read in different ways.

The best way to clear up some of the misunderstandings about the branch of internal alchemy that uses sexual yoga is to look at original texts of sexual yoga and not rely on secondary sources or modern interpretations. This topic is frequently misunderstood and the practices are abused. You can find these texts translated by Douglas Wile in a book titled *Art of the Bedchamber: The Chinese Sexual Yoga Classics Including Solo Meditation Texts*.

At certain stages of development, the practice of internal alchemy is different for men and women. Wile's translation includes some texts describing techniques of internal alchemy for women.

11

Action and Karma Taoism
The Way of Right Action

THE SACRED POWERS reward those who do good deeds and punish those who do unethical deeds. This belief forms the core of Action and Karma Taoism. Of all the systems of Taoism, the teachings of the Action and Karma School are the least esoteric. They are concerned with issues in everyday life and the ethics of right action, without which higher levels of spiritual development would not be possible.

Historical Predecessors of Action and Karma Taoism

Historians credit the founding of the Action and Karma School to a book written by Li Ying-chang titled *T'ai-shang kan-ying p'ien* (Lao-tzu's Treatise on the Response of the Tao). The book was published during the Sung dynasty and its popularity inspired a movement in Taoism that brought the practice of Taoist spirituality out of hermitages, temples, and monasteries to the ordinary person who lives and works in society.

Although the Action and Karma School dates back only to the twelfth century CE, its teachings are rooted in traditional Chinese beliefs. The origins of the teachings lie in the notion that acts of goodness are in harmony with the Celestial Way (the Will of

Heaven) and that acts of malevolence are opposed to the Celestial Way. Thus, committing an unethical act is a transgression against the Celestial Way as well as against humanity.

With the emergence of Taoism as a philosophy, the Tao, or the Way, which is the law of the universe, became equated with the traditional idea of the Celestial Way. When Taoism was then developed into an organized religion, deities became the judges of human actions, giving rewards and meting out punishment according to the amount of merits and demerits accumulated.

Ideas of reward and retribution were present in Taoist thought as early as the Eastern Han dynasty. The *T'ai-p'ing ching* states, "Accumulate good deeds, and prosperity will come to you from the Tao." These ideas are further developed by Ko Hung, the great alchemist of the fourth and fifth centuries CE. In his *P'ao-p'u-tzu* (The Master Who Embraces Simplicity), Ko Hung writes:

> Those who wish to live the fullness of life must accumulate good deeds, be kind to others, practice charity and have compassion even for the creatures that crawl. They must help the poor, harm no living thing, rejoice in the good fortune of others and share in the suffering of others. They must utter no curses, look on the failure and success of others as their own, harbor no jealousy of their betters and conceal no unethical intentions behind good speech. In this way, they embody virtue and receive rewards from the deities. (From chap. 6, *P'ao-p'u-tzu*)

These words would be echoed eight hundred years later in the *T'ai-shang kan-ying p'ien*, the book that launched Action and Karma Taoism:

> If you are in harmony with the Tao you will advance. . . . Be kind and compassionate to all things. Be dedicated in whatever you do. . . . Help orphans and widows. Respect the old and care for the young. Do not hurt trees, grass, and insects.

> Share in the suffering of others. Delight in the joys of others.
> Help people in desperate need. Save people from harm. View
> the good fortune of others as your good fortune. View the
> losses of others as your own loss. (From chap. 4, *T'ai-shang
> kan-ying p'ien*)

Of retribution, Ko Hung says:

> When you interfere with another person's property, your
> wife, children, and other members of your household may
> suffer the consequences. Their lives may even be shortened.
> And if your wrongdoing does not bring death upon your fam-
> ily, they may suffer from floods, fires, burglaries, and other
> disasters. Therefore, the Taoists say that whenever a person
> has been killed wrongfully, vengeful killings will follow.
> Wealth gotten through unethical actions will lead to resent-
> ment. (From chap. 6, *P'ao-p'u-tzu,*)

Ko Hung took the ideas of reward and retribution further by drawing a relationship between health and longevity and ethical behavior.
Good actions can "starve out" monsters in the body that cause illness, whereas wrongdoings will encourage their development. In this
way, an individual's thoughts and actions can affect health and longevity.

The *Chi-sun-tzu chung-chieh ching* (Master Red Pine's Book of
Discipline), believed to have been written between the third and
fourth centuries CE, has in it a sophisticated system of thinking on
reward and retribution. It presents a logic and explanation for the
occurrence of fortune and misfortune and describes the role of deities and spirits in rewarding and punishing humanity. It also mentions the Spirit of the Hearth, or Kitchen Lord, who ascends to the
celestial domain to report the good and bad deeds of humanity, and
it links the destiny of individuals to the Celestial Lord of the North
Pole Star, a belief that is central to Action and Karma Taoism.

By the time of the Sung dynasty, the ideas of reward and retribution were firmly established in Taoist thinking. In the *Yun-chi ch'i-ch'ien* (Seven Bamboo Strips of the Cloud-Hidden Satchel), a collection of Taoist knowledge compiled in early Sung, health and longevity, fortune and misfortune, were clearly the consequence of an individual's actions. Not long after the publication of this compendium of Taoist knowledge, Li Ying-chang's *T'ai-shang kan-ying p'ien* appeared and inspired a school of Taoist thought that is still widely practiced today.

Principal Beliefs in Action and Karma Taoism

1. Good deeds bring reward and wrongdoings bring retribution. For every action, there is a response from the Tao. Thus, the *T'ai-shang kan-ying p'ien* says that "reward and retribution follow us like shadows."

2. Reward can come as wealth, prosperity, fame, success, achievement, and having filial descendants. Punishment can come as poverty, failure, disgrace, and having unfilial children. However, what makes the Action and Karma School different from Buddhism or even the traditional Chinese beliefs is that rewards can be health and longevity as well as wealth and prosperity, and retribution can be illness or shortening of the life span as well as poverty and misfortune.

3. There are deities and spirits whose job it is to monitor the deeds of each person. As noted in the chapter on Ceremonial Taoism, the Kitchen Lord is one of them. This guardian of the hearth reports the deeds of each member of the household to the Jade Emperor at the end of each year. Moreover, each person is born under the guardianship of one of the seven stars of the Northern Bushel (Big Dipper). On the first and fifteenth days of each lunar month, the first nine days of the ninth lunar month, and on the individual's birthday, the guardian star deity will report the deeds of the individual to the Jade Emperor. Finally, there are the three monsters who reside in the body who also report an individual's wrongdoings to the Jade Emperor.

4. The good and bad deeds of each individual are tallied, and the Jade Emperor, who is the Director of Destiny, rewards or punishes each person accordingly. Those who have done more good deeds than bad ones will be rewarded with prosperity, good health, and a long life; those who have done more bad deeds than good will have their life span shortened or have misfortunes given to them.

5. Reward and retribution can carry over to family and descendants; therefore, the actions of one generation affect the destinies of future generations.

6. Thoughts have as much leverage in determining reward and retribution as actions. Thinking an unethical thought is equivalent to doing an unethical deed.

7. Repentance can redress the wrongs that have been done, if the individual keeps the promise of refraining from doing unethical deeds in the future.

The Significance of Action and Karma Taoism in Taoist Spirituality

Action and Karma Taoism is nonmonastic, nonpriestly, and nonsectarian, but its teachings are adopted by many Taoist sects. For example, the *T'ai-shang kan-ying p'ien,* the foremost scripture of Action and Karma Taoism, is studied by initiates of the Complete Reality School, the Hsien-t'ien Tao sect, and the Wu-Liu sect. All the schools of Taoism—Magical, Ceremonial, Divinational, and Alchemical, as well as modern practitioners of internal alchemy—view ethics and right action as the foundation of spiritual development. To those who do not wish to be affiliated with any sect, Action and Karma Taoism offers a moral code and a method of cultivating health and fulfilling spiritual needs. Since this school does not require a temple or monastic environment for the transmission of its teachings, it is the most accessible form of Taoism practiced today. Most importantly, Action and Karma Taoism brings the teachings of the Tao to daily living and defines what it means to walk the path of the Tao while we are in the mortal realm.

FURTHER READINGS

The *T'ai-shang kan-ying p'ien* is generally regarded as the text that launched Action and Karma Taoism. You can find a translation of this text and stories that were inspired by the *Kan-ying p'ien* in my *Lao-tzu's Treatise on the Response of Tao*, which also contains a detailed discussion of the history of the Action and Karma School and the influence of Buddhism, Confucianism, and Chinese folk religion on its teachings.

PART THREE

TAOIST PRACTICES

12
Meditation

TAOISTS USE MEDITATION to cultivate health and longevity and to attain the highest level of spiritual development, the union with the Tao. In the early stages of spiritual development, meditation is used to clear the mind, minimize desire, balance the emotions, and circulate internal energy. In the later stages, it is used to help the practitioner to be united with the Tao, the undifferentiated origin of all things.

Forms of Taoist Meditation

For many people, all forms of meditation are alike. Practice one and you've practiced them all. However, different spiritual traditions have different approaches to meditation, and not only are Buddhist and Hindu forms of meditation different from the Taoist, but even within Taoism there are different kinds of meditation. Different sects practice different styles of meditation, and within the same sect the form of meditation changes as one progresses in practice.

There are twelve kinds of Taoist meditation practiced today. They are summarized briefly below in twelve subsections.

THE METHOD OF INTERNAL OBSERVATION

The Internal Observation method originated in the T'ang dynasty. It is influenced by T'ien-tai Buddhism and is very similar to vipassana meditation. The practitioner initially watches and attends to the rise and fall of thoughts, emotions, and sensations. As the practitioner becomes mindful of these phenomena, he will realize that their existence and the problems they generate are caused by the activity of the mind. Were the mind to be still, there would be no problems.

The next step is to stop the thoughts, emotions, and sensations before they occur. Once the practitioner becomes adept at watching the rise and fall of mental activities, he becomes familiar with their patterns of occurrence and can anticipate and stop them before they arise. When thoughts, emotions, and sensations are stopped, the mind becomes still. In stillness, it becomes clear. In clarity, it becomes bright—and this brightness is the radiance of the Tao within.

The method of Internal Observation does not require the practitioner to focus on anything during meditation; nor are there mantras or visualizations. In fact, the distinct feature of this style of meditation can be described as "the mind is used to defeat the mind." Through mindfulness and attention to the activity of the mind, the mind becomes empty.

There are no specific physical postures associated with this style of meditation, although most practitioners prefer to sit with legs crossed. It is possible to meditate sitting on a chair, or while walking or standing. Since there is very little physical demand, this form of meditation is suitable for people of all physical conditions. Moreover, because the procedures are simple and straightforward, Internal Observation can be practiced with minimal supervision, once you have learned it from a master.

Today, this style of meditation is practiced by many people, both Taoist and non-Taoist, who do not have the time or inclination to commit to the more demanding forms of Taoist meditation.

THE METHOD OF FOCUSING ON THE CENTER

The method of Focusing on the Center is sometimes called centering. In this form of meditation, attention to the outside world is gradually withdrawn until the practitioner no longer has attachment to the sights, sounds, and events of the outside world. When the causes of thoughts, emotions, and sensations cease to stir the mind, the mind becomes still, and centering can begin.

There are several definitions of *the center*. Some practitioners regard the Yellow Palace in the middle tan-t'ien, the area around the solar plexus, as the center; others say that the center is intangible and cannot be localized in the body, and that it is the state of mind that intuits the balance or the center of the nature of things, and this balance is the Tao.

Unlike the method of Internal Observation, this style of Taoist meditation requires the practitioner to focus on something, although practitioners disagree on what is the focus. It does not require the practitioner to adopt specific physical postures during meditation, however, and thus, like the Internal Observation method, is suitable for people of all physical conditions.

THE METHOD OF HOLDING THE ONE

Also known as Guarding the One, Holding the One originated in Shang-ch'ing Taoism, where Holding the One refers to keeping the Oneness of the Tao within. In the original Shang-ch'ing practice, Holding the One involved visualizing the various manifestations of Lao-tzu or other deities, which are images of the Tao. These visualizations serve to keep the deities or the guardian spirits within. In modern practice, however, the method of Holding the One no longer requires visualization.

The key to this meditation lies in dissolving the duality between the self and the world so that oneness can be attained. In the early stages, the practitioner first stills the mind and body so that no thoughts, emotions, or sensations arise. Once the stillness is attained, the "mind of the Tao" will emerge. The mind of the Tao is consciousness that is rooted in the Tao and sees all things as one. With continued practice, the experience of oneness will take hold, and the union with the Tao is achieved.

This form of meditation is favored by sects that focus specifically on cultivating the mind. It does not require the practitioner to adopt specific body postures, but during the practice, the body and mind must remain still, for any movement will destroy the experience of oneness. Because this requirement is central to the practice, the physical demands are more rigorous than those of Internal Observation or Focusing on the Center. To maintain physical stillness, the body must be relaxed and the skeletal structure must be strong. This style will be difficult for people who do not have the skeletal strength, especially in the spine, to hold the body in one position over a period of time that can sometimes last for several hours.

THE METHOD OF STOPPING THOUGHTS AND EMPTYING THE MIND

Stopping Thoughts and Emptying the Mind is similar to Zen meditation. The practitioner sits in silence and empties the mind of thoughts, desire, and emotions. Unlike Internal Observation, where the mind watches the rise and fall of mental activity, the goal here is to extinguish the mind altogether, without using aids such as visualization, mantra, or even passive observation. To the practitioners of this style of meditation, any activity of the mind, passive or active, is the work of mischief by tricksters and monsters. Therefore, to attain complete emptiness of the mind, the practitioner must cut off all attachments cleanly and abruptly.

This form of meditation is used by both the northern branch of the Complete Reality School and the Hsien-t'ien Tao sect in the early stages of spiritual training. Once the practitioner has attained the stillness of mind, other forms of meditation are used to take the practitioner through the intermediate and advanced stages of internal alchemy.

THE METHOD OF RECOVERING THE REAL MIND

In Recovering the Real Mind, the original or real mind is cultivated. The real mind is the Tao mind, the consciousness capable of directly intuiting the nature of the Tao. It is sometimes called Original Mind.

This method originated in the Complete Reality School. The

practitioner enters this stage of training after the mind is emptied of thoughts. Freed from the domination of analytic thinking and idle internal chatter, the practitioner can now develop another kind of stillness. In this stillness, not only are thoughts extinguished, but the mind and body begin to develop a natural tendency toward stillness. This development is reflected in everyday life, as the practitioner, unexcited by events, has no desire to stimulate the senses or arouse the mind.

Although this method originated in the Complete Reality School, today it is practiced by people who wish to cultivate physical health and mental clarity but do not have the time or inclination to commit to the long and arduous training demanded by internal alchemy. No specific physical posture is required, although many practitioners prefer to sit cross-legged or in the half-lotus yoga posture. It is also possible to do this kind of meditation sitting in a chair. Therefore, this method can be practiced by people of all physical conditions.

THE METHOD OF FOCUSING ON THE CAVITIES

Focusing on the Cavities requires the practitioner to draw attention away from things external and focus on a certain cavity in the body. The main difference between this method and the method of Focusing on the Center is that there is no reference to centering and balance.

There are two kinds of focusing. The first involves awareness and directing attention to a particular cavity in the body. This kind of focusing is used to calm the emotions, stop stray thoughts, and minimize sensations. In the advanced stages, another kind of focusing, which involves directing internal energy to an area, is practiced. Concentration of energy in an area of the body can be used to break a blockage or gather energy in a tan-t'ien to be refined and transformed.

Depending on the stage of spiritual development and the practitioner's health needs, different cavities are focused on. For example, in the early stages, the focus is directed to the cavity known as the Life Gate (*ming-men*). As the internal alchemical process advances, the lower, middle, and upper tan-t'iens become, in turn, the point of focus. Sometimes, if a practitioner has a particular problem, more obscure cavities are focused on.

Focusing on the Cavities is practiced by sects that use meditation to facilitate internal alchemy. It is favored by the members of the Wu-Liu sect, who view the Life Gate as the key to initiating the process of internal alchemy. Because this method is used to facilitate alchemical transformations, frequent instruction and supervision are required. Also, because this method involves moving internal energy, the proper physical and mental foundations must be built before it can be practiced. Typically, a relaxed body, a strong spine, articulated joints, softened tendons, and a mind emptied of thoughts and desire are prerequisites. The postures are demanding, and the practitioner is required to maintain them for a considerable period of time, so that certain alchemical processes can be completed. This form of meditation is generally not taught to novice practitioners.

THE METHOD OF VISUALIZING THE VALLEY SPIRIT

In Visualizing the Valley Spirit, the practitioner visualizes an image and then slowly merges with it. This technique is most similar to the original Shang-ch'ing methods of visualizing the images of guardian deities and spirits. It differs, however, from classical Shang-ch'ing practice in that here the visualizations are not of deities. In this form of meditation, the visualized images include the Kun-lun Mountains (used to channel energy through the spinal column); the Yellow Palace (to gather and transform vital energy in the middle tan-t'ien); the Sea of Energy, or *ch'i-hai* (to light the fires of the internal stove and gather and transform generative energy in the lower tan-t'ien); and, ultimately, the Valley Spirit (to gather and transform spirit energy in the upper tan-t'ien). Visualizing the Valley Spirit is the highest stage in this type of meditation.

This style of meditation is rarely practiced. I know of no major Taoist sect that practices this form of meditation.

THE METHOD OF EMPTYING THE MIND AND FILLING THE BELLY

Emptying the Mind and Filling the Belly is another method used in facilitating internal alchemy. Emptying the mind is letting the fires of desire sink, and filling the belly is letting the abdomen be filled with energy. Taken together, the dual process is called *immersion of fire in water*.

Sinking the fires of desire is minimizing attachment to objects, be they material things, thoughts, or emotions. Filling the belly is cultivating and storing energy in the lower tan-t'ien. The latter can be accomplished by controlling the breath, by taking energy from a partner in sexual alchemy, or by absorbing the essences of the sun, moon, and mist.

This form of meditation is usually practiced in combination with other techniques. It requires formal instruction and supervision, and should be attempted only if the practitioner is ready to make a long-term commitment to Taoist internal alchemy.

THE METHOD OF UNITING INTENTION WITH BREATH

Of all the forms of Taoist meditation, Uniting Intention with Breath is the one most linked to patterns of breathing. In the early stages, the practitioner focuses on the movement of the breath, sometimes counting breaths and sometimes just paying attention to inhalation and exhalation. Initially, the breathing follows a normal pattern, and the practitioner simply uses it to focus the mind.

Once the mind is focused and detached from the outside world, the pattern of breathing will begin to change. This change is not under the conscious control of the practitioner; rather, it is a function of the state of mind. When the mind is still, breathing will slow down and become soft and deep. This is called fetal breathing because it resembles the breath of the fetus inside the womb.

When yin reaches the height of its development, yang emerges. Thus, when the mind has attained complete stillness, it will be set in motion. This movement is not ordinary mental activity directed toward objects in the world, but an intention with a purpose. Called true intention *(chen-i)*, this intention is capable of moving internal energy. When intention moves, energy is circulated; when it is still, energy is gathered and stored.

In even more advanced levels of development, the duality between the practitioner and the universal energy of the Tao is dissolved. When there is no separation between inside and outside, there will be only one breath, and this breath is the Breath of the Tao, the source of life. The practitioner is breathing not just with nostrils, lungs, diaphragm, or even with the tan-t'iens; the entire body is one breath, rising and falling with each inhalation and exhalation as the practitioner becomes the Breath of the Tao.

Sometimes this method of Taoist meditation is mistakenly equated with ch'i-kung breathing exercises. Ch'i-kung works with tangibles and manipulates substances that have form, such as breath and internal energy. The method of Uniting Intention and Breath works with the formless, for the Breath of the Tao is intangible. There is no active manipulation or direct control of the movement of breath; rather, different patterns of breathing emerge as a result of changes in an individual's state of mind. Therefore, we can say that Uniting the Intention and Breath is a method that uses meditation to transform breath and internal energy.

This form of meditation is difficult to practice, because it is hard to tell whether one is trying to control the breathing or letting it happen. Therefore, this method should be practiced only under constant supervision, making it suitable only in a monastic type of situation.

THE METHOD OF GATHERING AND CIRCULATING
THE LIGHT OF THE SPIRIT

Gathering and Circulating the Light is described in the controversial *T'ai-i chin-hua tsung-chih* text (see page 189). It is divided into two stages: gathering the light of the spirit and circulating the light.

Before the light of the spirit can be gathered and circulated, it must be born and developed. Spirit is the original spirit *(yüan-shen)*, or the immortal fetus; thus, this method is used only in advanced stages of internal alchemy.

To let the original spirit emerge, the knowledge spirit *(shih-shen)* must be tamed. The knowledge spirit is the mischievous, analytical, scheming mind. It is attached to worldly things and is responsible for violent mood swings, and thus prevents us from seeing the Tao. To cultivate the original spirit, one must first overcome the knowledge spirit and then use it to help the original spirit to develop. Simultaneously the practitioner must prepare her body for conception of the immortal fetus. This involves strengthening and softening the skeletal system, regulating all the functions of the body, and gathering, conserving, and transforming generative, vital, and spirit energy. In other words, the lower and intermediate stages of internal alchemy must have been completed (see chapter 10) before the original spirit can emerge.

When the immortal fetus is conceived, original spirit is born. Initially, the light of the original spirit is dim, and the practitioner has only a vague experience of its presence. As the original spirit is nurtured by internal energy, it becomes strong and its light brightens. When the original spirit is fully developed, the practitioner is bathed in a golden light. Light emanating from the body is then gathered and drawn within. With time, the light becomes less dazzling and takes on a soft but radiant glow. This is the time for circulating the light. At first, the circulation follows set pathways: inside, it follows the meridians; outside, it hovers around the practitioner. In the advanced state, the circulation does not follow any pathway but is diffused throughout the body, spreading like smoke. This also happens outside the body, as the practitioner feels that he or she is enveloped by a diffused golden light.

This form of meditation is typically practiced by sects affiliated with the Complete Reality School. Since the method of Gathering and Circulating the Light is practiced in the highest levels of spiritual training, it is not possible to learn it without building the proper foundations of internal alchemy. In Complete Reality training, this form of meditation is taught only to the highest initiates.

THE METHOD OF DRAWING THE LIGHT INWARD

Drawing the Light Inward is another form of meditation practiced in advanced stages of spiritual development. After the foundations of internal alchemy are complete and the original spirit is developed, the practitioner uses this method to nurture it.

During meditation, the practitioner gathers the light into three spots ∴ when he or she experiences a light hovering around. The spot on the top is drawn into the area between the eyes. This region is also known as the third eye, the upper tan-t'ien, or the Mysterious Cavity. The spot in the lower left is drawn into the left eye, and the spot in the lower right is drawn into the right eye. In this way, the lights of the sun, moon, and stars are united with the light inside, and the barrier between the internal universe of the practitioner and the external universe of the cosmos is dissolved.

As the light enters the practitioner, the body becomes weightless and the mind becomes clear and empty. When filled with the light, the bones, muscles, tendons, and internal organs are nourished by the primordial energy of the Tao. Body and mind are renewed, and in a state of bliss and ecstasy, the practitioner is merged with the timeless and undifferentiated state of the Tao.

The method of Drawing the Light Inward is used by internal alchemical sects that have synthesized Complete Reality and Shang-ch'ing practices. Since this method is practiced in advanced stages of spiritual training, it is not available to novice practitioners. Moreover, as a technique of internal alchemy, it requires formal instruction, frequent supervision, and a lifetime of commitment and discipline.

THE METHOD OF RETURNING TO EARLIER HEAVEN

This method is exclusive to the Hsien-t'ien Tao sect. It consists of seven stages. In each stage, a specific area of the body is focused on and transformed.

The seven cavities, in their order of focus, are:

1. The lower cavity. This is the center of the lower tan-t'ien. Specifically, the focus is on a spot three Chinese inches (about two and a half inches) below the navel.
2. The front cavity. This is the Sea of Ch'i, or ch'i-hai. The cavity is one and one-half Chinese inches below the navel.
3. The back cavity. This is the Life Gate, or ming-men. It is a position on the spinal column between the kidneys and is an important junction in the tu meridian.
4. The middle cavity. This is the center of the middle tan-t'ien. It is also known as the Central Palace (*chung-t'ing*), or Yellow Palace, and is at the solar plexus.
5. The upper cavity. This is the center of the upper tan-t'ien, between the eyes, called the Bright Hall (*ming-t'ang*). The sequence 1 through 5 is used to open the Microcosmic Orbit.
6. The lowest cavity. This is the Bubbling Spring, or yung-ch'üan, a cavity located in the sole of the foot. When the practitioner has completed this stage in the training, the Macrocosmic Orbit is opened.
7. The Mysterious Gate. This is also called the Earlier Heaven Gate, the Gate of the Limitless, or wu-chi, and the Original Cavity. It has no form and does not exist if the practitioner has not reached this stage. This cavity materializes only when the original spirit is conceived, and it is the gate to the union with the Tao.

In Hsien-t'ien Tao meditation, stages 1 through 6 are involved with form and action. The cavities are areas in the body that can be localized and focused on. Stages 1 through 6 are called Later Heaven (*kou-tien*) Meditation, after the separation of sky and earth, because they work on a body and mind that are separated from the Tao. In stage 7, the practice is not tied to form or action. The cavity cannot be localized and there is no focus. Stage 7 is called Earlier Heaven (hsien-t'ien) Meditation, before the separation of sky and earth, because it works on a mind and body that are connected with the Tao.

Other than focusing on the cavities, the Hsien-t'ien Tao method of meditation also requires the practitioner to adopt specific body postures. These include sitting cross-legged, in single (half) lotus, and in double (full) lotus. There are also hand positions, including putting the palms on the knees or holding them together to form a t'ai-chi pattern. One of the most difficult positions in this form of meditation involves supporting the body with the knuckles of both hands while the body is in full lotus and elevated above the ground. All in all, the postures of Hsien-t'ien Tao meditation are the most rigorous, because the sect places equal importance on the cultivation of body and the cultivation of mind.

Further Words on Taoist Meditation

Many people practice meditation for mental relaxation and the reduction of stress. Some practice it to cultivate spiritual sensitivity, enhance physical health, and prolong life. However, Taoist meditation is not only a technique of health and longevity; it is a tool for attaining a union with the Tao, of which health and longevity are the by-products.

Today, one can learn Taoist meditation for health and relaxation without being initiated into a Taoist sect or having to commit to a lifetime of training in internal alchemy. Twelve methods of Taoist meditation have been described in this chapter. Instruction in the first five is often given in weekend courses or at seven-day retreats. These methods are relatively safe to practice on your own, once you have been given formal instructions. However, it is advisable to attend follow-up courses, to receive feedback.

The final seven methods described are used to take the practitioner to the highest levels of development in Taoist spirituality. These forms of meditation are usually practiced together with techniques that strengthen the skeletal system and regulate the internal physiology. Only those who are ready to commit to a rigorous and disciplined program of training should consider learning these forms of meditation. Initiation into a sect is usually required, and constant supervision from a teacher is necessary.

The practice of Taoist meditation requires commitment, patience, and discipline. The physical, mental, and spiritual benefits of meditation can occur only when the practitioner accompanies practice with the appropriate lifestyle and attitude.

FURTHER READINGS

Although some of the following readings on Taoist meditation are written as instruction manuals, do not use them as such without the guidance of a teacher.

Two chapters in Lu Kuan Yü's *The Secrets of Chinese Meditation* discuss two forms of Taoist meditation. Chapter 5 describes a style of meditation attributed to Yin-shih Tzu, a twentieth-century Taoist practitioner. Chapter 7 describes a form of Taoist meditation that uses quiet sitting together with breathing exercises to accomplish the Microcosmic Circulation. Lu's book is useful in comparing Buddhist and Taoist forms of meditation, as he discusses Zen and T'ien-tai meditation in other chapters.

Livia Kohn has two chapters on Taoist meditation in her *Taoist Meditation and Longevity Techniques*. "Guarding the One: Concentrative Meditation in Taoism" contains a thorough discussion of the meaning of Holding the One in Shang-ch'ing Taoism; "Taoist Insight Meditation" gives a good introduction to the *nei-kuan* (inner observation) or *ting-kuan* (concentrative observation) type of meditation. The chapter on insight meditation also contains a translation of a nei-kuan classic *T'ai-shang lao-chün nei-kuan ching* (Lao-tzu's Treatise on Internal Observation).

Another classic treatise on nei-kuan, Ssu-ma Ch'eng-cheng's *Tso-wang lun* (Sitting in Oblivion), is translated in Kohn's *The Taoist Experience* (reading 31, "Observing Life").

13

Techniques for Cultivating the Body

In Taoist practice, cultivating the body is integral to spiritual development. Union with the Tao is not possible without physical health. There are also practical considerations for cultivating the body. Strength and flexibility in the muscular and skeletal systems and a healthy internal physiology are required for advancing into the higher levels of Taoist spiritual training. The procedures used for cultivating the muscular and skeletal systems are known as techniques of external strengthening; those used for cultivating the internal physiology are called techniques of internal strengthening.

Below is a brief discussion of the most commonly used Taoist methods of external and internal strengthening. Be advised that it is not safe to practice these techniques or similar ones without formal instruction from a qualified teacher.

Techniques of External Strengthening

TENDON-CHANGING

The most effective method of strengthening the muscular system is tendon-changing (i-chin). Translated literally, i-chin means transforming or changing the tendons. In traditional Chinese physiology, chin include ligaments, muscles, fascia, nerve fibers, and the soft tissues in the body. Tendon-changing therefore means transforming both the surface and deep structures of the muscular system.

The goal of tendon-changing is to recover dynamic movement in the muscles, ligaments, and tendons. A soft tendon is a strong tendon; a relaxed muscle with a good supply of blood is a healthy muscle. A soft and relaxed muscular system can respond faster than one that is hard and tense.

Tendon-changing methods typically involve alternating stretching with letting go. With repeated practice, the tendons, ligaments, muscles, and tissues will regain their dynamic buoyancy. Moreover, techniques of tendon-changing are also designed to rotate the joints and introduce movement to muscle groups not used in normal everyday activity. With time and practice, the muscles, tendons, ligaments, and fascia will become soft and bouncy, and the skin will be shiny and rosy. Circulation of blood in the muscular system will be enhanced, and the healing of cuts and bruises will be facilitated.

MARROW-WASHING

The premier method of strengthening the bones is marrow-washing *(hsi-sui)*. Marrow-washing refers to three processes: cleansing the marrow, regulating marrow content in the bones, and changing the shape and structure of the bone. Cleansing the marrow is replacing unhealthy marrow with healthy marrow. The result is like that in a marrow-transplant, but in marrow-cleansing the replacement is the result of processes occurring within the body. Regulating marrow content in the bones is balancing the calcium content so that calcium is neither concentrated nor deficient. Changing the structure of the bone involves changing the shape of the bone to optimize its load-bearing capacity and softening the bone to protect it from fracture.

All marrow-washing exercises begin with applying the correct amount of pressure to the bones and joints. Specific movements are used to control the pressure exerted on the bones. The movements are typically slow and smooth and require relaxation and control. To do the exercises of marrow-washing, the muscle groups, tendons and ligaments must be strong, and the joints must be articulated. A seldom-known technique of changing bone structure involves grinding and hitting the bones. Here the joints and bones are rubbed and knocked against surfaces so that they are pushed into the desired position and shape. Needless to say, these movements require precise execution, or injuries can occur.

When marrow-washing is complete, the bones will be soft, and when pressure is applied to them, they will give way like a sponge. The amount of calcium in the bones will be regulated, and the bones will get bigger and heavier.

Techniques of Internal Strengthening

The goal of internal strengthening is to improve the health of the internal organs, increase the efficiency of the physiological systems, and enhance the circulation of internal energy.

REGULATING BREATH

Breath sustains life, and proper breathing can enhance health and prolong life. In general, regulating the breath refers to breathing without conscious control or awareness, and directing the breath refers to conscious control over the movement of the breath and the rate of breathing.

In the Taoist arts of cultivating the body, there are nine patterns of breathing: nostril breathing, mouth and nostril breathing, mouth breathing, natural abdominal breathing, reverse abdominal breathing, perineal breathing, tortoise breathing, fetal breathing, and breathing with the entire body.

In nostril breathing, the mouth is closed and the nose is used for both inhalation and exhalation. This kind of breathing generally occurs during meditation in which stilling the mind is the object of the practice. It is a soft and slow kind of breathing.

In mouth and nostril breathing, the mouth is closed during inhalation and air is let in through the nose. In exhalation air is let out through the mouth. This kind of breathing generally occurs in meditation associated with lighting the fires of the lower tan-t'ien.

In mouth breathing, the mouth is used during both inhalation and exhalation. This kind of breathing occurs when breathing through the nose is difficult or not possible. In general, it is recommended only for individuals who have respiratory problems that prevent use of the nostrils.

Abdominal breathing is deep breathing. The air is channeled into the abdominal area and the entire trunk of the body is involved in the breathing. This kind of breathing requires much diaphragmatic action. Moreover, the internal organs must be pliable enough to move out of the way when the diaphragm presses down to let the air sink into the belly. Deep abdominal breathing should occur naturally and without effort. If forced, abdominal breathing can cause injuries. Natural abdominal breathing, reverse abdominal breathing, tortoise breathing, and fetal breathing are all types of abdominal breathing.

In natural abdominal breathing, the belly expands during inhalation and presses in during exhalation. In reverse abdominal breathing, the belly presses in during inhalation and expands during exhalation. These two kinds of breathing occur at intermediate stages of internal alchemy and are usually associated with fanning the fires of the lower tan-t'ien and tempering the internal energies in the upper, middle, and lower tan-t'iens.

In perineal breathing, the area around the perineum rises up during exhalation and drops down during inhalation. This kind of breathing is associated with the Microcosmic and Macrocosmic Circulations, and acts to pump the internal energy through the two circuits.

In tortoise breathing, the breath is so light that it is almost nonexistent. Called tortoise breathing because it resembles a tortoise's way of breathing when the animal is inside its shell, such breathing occurs naturally at advanced stages of internal alchemy. It is said that the tortoise lives a long life because of this form of breathing.

Fetal breathing is the combination of tortoise breathing and abdominal movement synchronized with inhalation and exhalation. It is named after the manner in which a fetus breathes inside the womb. This kind of breathing also occurs at advanced stages of internal alchemy and is typically associated with the conception and nourishment of the original spirit, or immortal fetus.

Finally, there is breathing with the entire body. This is the most advanced form of breathing and it occurs when the practitioner is at the highest stage of spiritual development, in union with the Tao. When the entire body is involved in breathing, the number of inhalations and exhalations is minimal. The duration of each cycle is long: initially, there will be sixteen to twenty cycles per minute; in the most advanced levels, there will be only three to four cycles per minute.

DIRECTING BREATH

In directing the breath, the practitioner guides the flow of breath in the body, initiates fast or slow breathing, and concentrates on the act of inhaling and exhaling. However, the control is never forced: it is the intention that initiates and directs the movement of breath. Once such control sets in, breathing becomes natural.

The most elementary method of directing the breath is to become aware of the breath by counting the number of inhalations and exhalations while breathing. This technique is generally used to stop stray thoughts or draw the mind away from what is happening outside; however, this method should be abandoned once the mind is focused, or the practitioner can become too dependent on an active process in quieting the mind and will never attain the true stillness of nonaction.

An intermediate form of directing the breath involves holding the breath for a period of time before expelling or inhaling it. This method is similar to some forms of breath control found in yoga. This technique is used to allow the breath to reach every part of the body and be absorbed into the deep tissues, internal organs, and bones before the dead air is expelled. Needless to say, this kind of breath control requires a strong diaphragm and an efficient respiratory system. Without such strengths, there will be insufficient oxygen intake during inhalation, and holding the breath will produce more harm than benefit.

The most advanced form of directing the breath is to let the intention guide the breath—a method known as *tao-yin* (literally, guiding and directing). When the mind is empty of thoughts, true intention emerges. In Taoism, true intention originates from the original spirit and has a direction and purpose. In this method, the practitioner initiates the intention and lets it guide the movement of the breath. Once the intention is initiated, there is no conscious control. The movement of the breath follows opened pathways in the circulatory system and flows naturally in the body. For this technique to work properly, the mind must be clear and emptied of thoughts, and the body must be relaxed and positioned in an appropriate posture. The elementary stages of this method require the practitioner to sit cross-legged. The more advanced techniques call for half-lotus and full-lotus positions.

The intention and the breath can be directed to several locations in the body, the destination depending on the stage of training. The three gates along the spine, the three tan-t'iens, or energy fields, the Bubbling Spring at the sole of the feet, the Golden Gate (an acupuncture point at the ankles), and the Point of a Hundred Gatherings *(po-hui)* on the head are typical locations to which the breath can be channeled. Typically, when blockages in the gates must be opened, breath and intention are directed to those areas. When the internal fires of the stove are lit and generative energy is collected and refined, intention and breath are directed to the lower tan-t'ien. Similarly, intention and breath are directed, as required, to the middle and upper tan-t'iens when alchemical work is performed on the vital and spirit energies.

CH'I-KUNG POSTURES

Ch'i-kung postures are designed to facilitate the circulation of internal energy (translated literally, *ch'i-kung* means the work of internal energy). Although many people consider breathing exercises, stretching exercises, and meditation as forms of ch'i-kung, traditional Taoist practice understands ch'i-kung as the natural flow of internal energy in the body when certain physical and mental conditions are present. Quieting the mind and moving the diaphragm do not necessarily imply circulation of energy, although they can help the practitioner build the foundations for it.

Internal energy (ch'i) can circulate only when certain physical and mental conditions are met. These prerequisites are built by external and internal strengthening and are developed over a period of years. In the Taoist arts of cultivating the body, certain physical postures can be used to kick-start the circulation of energy or to facilitate and maintain the flow. These are called ch'i-kung postures. However, if the foundations of external and internal strengthening are not built, the kick-start and the maintaining mechanisms will not work.

There are many ch'i-kung postures; the most basic and important are those that are incorporated into the daily activities of sitting, standing, walking, and sleeping. Thus, cultivating the body can occur in every facet of life.

Sitting postures. The sitting posture is the most common ch'i-kung posture. There are several forms. The practitioner can sit upright on a chair, with the upper body straight and relaxed. The eyes are open but not focused. The legs are placed in front and the palms are relaxed and resting on the lap. In natural cross-legged sitting, the practitioner sits on a flat surface or on a cushion folding the legs in a natural way. The body is upright and straight and the hands are placed on the knees or are clasped together near the navel. In half-lotus sitting, the practitioner sits cross-legged with one leg in lotus position (that is, the leg is brought up to the opposite thigh in such a way that the sole of the foot is turned up). In full-lotus sitting, both legs are in the lotus posture. The palms of the hands are placed on the soles of the feet.

Standing postures. In the free-standing posture, the practitioner stands balanced, with equal weight on both legs. The feet are parallel and the legs are straight, but the knees are not locked. The body is straight; the eyes are open but not focused; and the arms dangle along the side of the body.

There are several arm positions in the standing posture. In the hands-pressing-down posture, the practitioner stands as in the free-standing posture except that the arms are positioned in front. Common arm positions are holding the circle (that is, the arms curl in); bending at the elbow, as if holding a large ball; straightening the arms in front of the body and pressing down with the palms; and positioning the hands as if they are holding a small round object in front of the body.

The walking posture. In the walking posture, the body is straight and upright and the shoulders are relaxed. In walking, one foot is placed forward, heel first. The foot is rolled down, allowing the weight to shift from the heel to the middle of the foot. When the weight is spread equally across the sole, the foot rolls again to shift the weight to the toes. Simultaneously, the heel of the other foot contacts the ground and the weight is rolled from the heel to the rest of the foot. The first foot is then lifted off the ground to begin the next step. The cycle is repeated. The most important thing about the walking posture is that the walk should be as natural as possible.

Sleeping postures. There are several kinds of sleeping ch'i-kung postures. Most of them originate from Chen Hsi-yi. The most common ones are lying on the back, lying on the side, and lying semi-inclined. When lying on the back, in bed, the practitioner lies flat, with arms and legs relaxed and spread out. The eyes can gaze upward or be closed. When lying on the side, the upper part of the body is straight and the arm under the body is hooked upwards. The hand of this arm can be placed on the pillow with the palm resting against the face. The other arms rests gently on the upper side of the body. The leg lying underneath is straight and the other leg is slightly bent. In the semiinclined posture, the practitioner is half-sitting, half inclined on the bed. The upper part of the body rests gently against the head of the bed. Both legs are stretched out and the arms rest gently on the legs.

All these ch'i-kung postures affect the circulation of internal energy. If the tendons and muscles are soft and the circulatory pathways are open, these postures will facilitate the flow of energy; if the tendons are contracted and the pathways blocked, the postures can injure the muscular and skeletal systems or the internal organs.

Therefore ch'i-kung postures should be learned and practiced only under the supervision of a teacher qualified to prescribe the correct posture for the student's stage of development.

ABSORBING ENERGY FROM NATURE

The primordial energy of the Tao is present in all of nature. Of all the things in nature, it is said that the sun, moon, stars, mist, rocks, and earth have the highest concentration of energy. A person who can absorb energy from these sources will attain health and longevity.

The Shang-ch'ing Taoists were the first to describe and experiment with the techniques of absorbing energy from nature. They visualized the images of the sun and moon and directed the rays of the images through the mouth into the body. In Shang-ch'ing practice, this was called *ingesting the essence of the sun and moon.* Today, people who practice absorbing energy from nature no longer visualize the images of the sun and moon. Instead, they gaze directly at the sun, moon, and stars to absorb the essence of these celestial bodies.

In this method, it is assumed that the practitioner has undergone the required alchemical transformation in the sensory organs so that sustained viewing of the sun will not damage the eyes. Gazing at the sun to absorb its essence is very different from watching an eclipse. The very use of glasses, goggles, and the like, prevents the energy of the sun from entering the body through the eyes. Thus, the precautions are different from those for viewing an eclipse; the practitioner must have built the necessary foundations and attained the physiological transformations in the sensory organs if this method is to be practical.

Absorbing light from the celestial bodies can replenish spirit energy. This is because when earth and sky were separated in creation, spirit energy, being light, ascended skyward and was collected in the celestial bodies. When absorbing energy from the sun, the practitioner begins by gazing at the sun at sunrise or sunset, when the disk of the sun is just above the horizon. At these times, the rays of the sun are less strong and will not overwhelm the gazer. The advanced practitioner absorbs the essence of the sun when it is strongest, at the zenith. The optimal time for absorbing the essence of the moon is when it is full, and the best time for absorbing the essence of the stars is when the sky is clear and there is no moon.

Mist floats between earth and sky and is the vapor of the Tao. It can replenish ch'i if it is absorbed into the body. The Shang-ch'ing Taoists called this *eating vapor*. Not all mists, however, should be absorbed. There are mists that carry vital energy and mists that carry destructive energy; absorb the wrong kind and one could become ill, or even die. Mist that envelops the land so that the sky is invisible carries positive energy because it connects sky and earth. On the other hand, mist that forms a low bank above the ground is poisonous. This is stagnant mist and it should never be absorbed.

Rocks and soil also have high concentrations of energy. When earth and sky were separated in creation, generative energy, being heavy, descended and sank into the ground. Therefore, it is said that absorbing the essence of the earth will replenish generative energy. When absorbing earth energy, the practitioner presses the soles of both feet against the ground, or lies down with the back flat against the ground. Practitioners usually start by absorbing energy from ground covered with grass. The grass acts as a cushion so that the earth energy will not overwhelm the beginning practitioner. With time and experience, the practitioner can absorb energy from bare earth. Eventually the practitioner can absorb energy directly from rocks and stone—the most powerful source of earth energy.

Absorbing energy from nature is a method of internal strengthening for advanced practitioners of internal alchemy. The barriers between the internal universe of the individual and the external universe of the cosmos must be dissolved before the body can absorb energy from the environment and use it to replenish the energy within. This means dissolving the duality of subject and object and refining the internal energy so that it is as pristine as the energy of the Tao in nature. The sense organs, especially the eyes, must have undergone transformation before they can gaze at the sun and not be damaged. Moreover, the bones must be changed through marrow-washing before they can absorb energy from an external source. In other words, this method is viable only when the lower and intermediate foundations of internal alchemy have been built. If these techniques are practiced prematurely, severe internal injuries can result. Never practice absorbing energy from nature without the guidance of a qualified teacher.

Techniques that Work on Both External and Internal Strengthening

MASSAGE AND KNEADING

In the Taoist arts of health and longevity, massage and kneading are called *an-mo* (*an* means pressure and *mo* means stroking). Today, massage generally refers to pressure being moved around an area; kneading refers to applying pressure to one spot. Pressure can be applied continuously or discontinuously; thus, the techniques include hitting and knocking.

Massage and kneading can work on external or internal strengthening, depending on how they are applied. They can also be performed by one individual on another or by the individual on herself.

When massage and kneading are used for external strengthening, they can relax tight muscles, expand contracted tendons, and soften hardened tissues. They can also be used to align skeletal structure and direct the flow of blood into areas of the body that lack circulation. Although massage and kneading can provide temporary relief from stiffness, they are not effective in producing permanent changes in the muscular and skeletal system; in the Taoist methods of cultivating the body, massage and kneading of the muscular system are therefore always accompanied by techniques such as tendon-changing, marrow-washing, or the internal martial arts.

When massage and kneading are used to work on internal strengthening, the results are more permanent. Internal organs can be strengthened by massaging and kneading the surface and deep tissues. Typical areas of the body where moving pressure is applied are the areas around the kidneys and the lower abdomen. Massaging and kneading the three gates along the spinal column can help to open blockages in these areas. One massages the Life Gate between the kidneys to open the lower gate, the area of the spine between the shoulder blades to open the middle gate, and the area where the spine enters the skull to open the upper gate. Other areas commonly massaged to allow energy to flow to the head are the temples, the jaw, and the back of the skull.

Sometimes an area of the body is hit or knocked so that circulation can get through. Performed correctly, hitting and knocking send vibrations deep into parts of the body that are not easily accessible. Probably the most famous example of this technique is knocking the teeth together. This is used to loosen the jaw, open the cavities in that area, and send bursts of energy into the head.

TAOIST CALISTHENICS

Taoist calisthenics are movements that combine stretching, controlled breathing, massage, and kneading. Modern writers have labeled them calisthenics since no technical name had been given to this method by the traditional Taoist practitioners; however, these movements should not be equated with modern calisthenics. Western calisthenics are primarily exercises of stretching, but these traditional Taoist exercises combine stretching and massage with the circulation of energy. To avoid confusion, in the discussion below I shall use the term Taoist calisthenics to refer to exercises that have been developed by Taoists to work on both external and internal strengthening.

The earliest form of Taoist calisthenics is probably the Five Animal Exercises. The five animals—tiger, leopard, dragon, snake, and crane—have external and internal qualities that, if developed in humans, can enhance health and longevity. The tiger is valued for its strong bones, the leopard for its dynamic tendons, the dragon for its ability in stretching the spine, the snake for its flexibility in moving the spine, and the crane for its capacity to store internal energy. The original set of the Five Animal Exercises was designed by Hua-tuo, the father of Chinese medicine, but was lost when the physician burned his books in the prison of the tyrant Ts'ao Ts'ao in the third century BCE. Other forms of the animal exercises were developed by the fang-shih of the Han dynasty.

By the time of the Sung dynasty (eleventh century CE), there were Taoist calisthenics based on animal movements, yogic postures from India, and exercises attributed to the immortals. (These can be found in the *Chi-feng sui* [Red Phoenix Calisthenics], a collection of Taoist exercises originated by Chen Hsi-yi.) Some of these movements are designed to facilitate the circulation of energy; some are used to deal with specific health problems; and others are meant to be practiced at different times of the year to prevent illnesses associated with the change of seasons (figs. 13.1 and 13.2).

The body must be flexible and agile for the practice of Taoist calisthenics to be effective. Some movements and postures are quite demanding, and injuries can occur if the body is forced into these positions prematurely. Do not try to learn Taoist calisthenics without the guidance of a teacher.

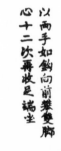

FIGURE 13.1. Taoist calisthenics: "Stretch the arms outward and grab both feet. Count to twelve, then draw the legs in, and stand up— from the *Chi-feng Sui* (Red Phoenix Calisthenics), a text of the Hsi-yi sect (Yi-men), founded by the followers of Chen Hsi-yi.

血舒茲安脇前側閉庚
也筋三腰伤起氣桑
骨五力攸左然
而次能骨定右拳敬
安止除節使攞如
神亦腹皆氣腳熊戲
養能脹響能安身

FIGURE 13.2. Taoist calisthenics: "Stop the breath and hold the fists like a bear. Rotate left and right, keeping the feet steady. Straighten the chest to let the breath move both ways. Hold on tightly and you will hear the joints and bones crack. Repeat this three or five times. This technique exercises the bones and tendons, quiets the spirit, and cultivates energy in the blood"—from the *Chi-feng Sui* (Red Phoenix Calisthenics), the Bear Posture of Keng-sang.

Today, Taoist calisthenics are practiced for general health and to cultivate the body for higher levels of spiritual development. Whatever the application, Taoist calisthenics are most effective techniques for cultivating the body, combining physical conditioning with the circulation of internal energy.

INTERNAL MARTIAL ARTS

In Taoist spiritual training, the internal martial arts are tools for external strengthening, internal strengthening, and the cultivation of mental focus and stillness. The movements in the internal martial arts are usually slow and controlled (hsing-i ch'uan is an exception). Initially, the movements stretch the tendons, articulate the joints, soften the muscles, and improve general circulation. In the intermediate stages, the movements can be used to exercise the spine by rotation and alternating stretching with letting go. When the movement of the spine is articulated and the abdominal muscles and deep tissues are softened, the movement of the spine will massage the internal organs, moving them gently as the spine rotates, expands, and contracts. In the advanced stages, the movements can be tuned to set the tan-t'iens in motion to refine the internal energy. Eventually, the internal energy will circulate in synchroneity with the movements, as the practitioner attains a sense of stillness in movement and movement in stillness.

There are four styles of internal martial arts. The best known and most widely practiced is t'ai-chi ch'uan (the Ultimate Fist). Less known are pa-k'ua chang (Eight Trigrams Palm) and hsing-i ch'uan (Form and Intention Fist). The least known is a system called liu-he pa-fa (Six Harmonies and Eight Methods).

Of all these forms, liu-he pa-fa is said to be the most internal because its movements are designed to penetrate the superficial layers of the body and exercise the internal organs. Its movements are rigorous and demanding, and of all the forms of internal martial arts, it is probably the most difficult to learn and practice. Founded by Chen Hsi-yi, the Taoist sage of the Northern Sung dynasty, the liu-he pa-fa system consists of sixty-six movements divided into two halves. The first half focuses on stretching the tendons and articulating spinal movement; the second half uses the movement of the spine to massage the internal organs.

The most popular form of the internal martial arts is t'ai-chi ch'uan. Reputed to have been founded by Chang San-feng, the Taoist internal alchemist of the Yüan and Ming dynasties, this set of movements is physically less demanding and does not have the power of liu-he pa-fa in massaging the internal organs. There are many styles of t'ai-chi ch'uan. Some styles focus more on the martial applications; others are more oriented toward health. Be aware of this difference when looking for instruction in this internal martial art.

Pa-k'ua chang is a series of movements in which the practitioner walks in patterns of circles. While walking, the spine is straight, the pelvis is sunk slightly into the hip joints, and the knees are slightly bent. *Chang* means palm: in pa-k'ua chang, the hands are never rolled into a fist. Pa-k'ua chang is an excellent technique for rolling and rotating the spine and exercising the lower spine and the tail-bone. Moreover, the circular movements help to develop agility and strength in the lower part of the body, thus allowing the upper part of the body to be relaxed and the internal energy to flow. However, these benefits can occur only when the legs are strong, the pelvic joints are open, and the spine has reached a certain level of articulation.

Hsing-i ch'uan is the probably the most martial of the internal martial arts. Involving pounding, thrusting, and hitting with bursts of movement, hsing-i ch'uan often gives the impression that it is nothing but fighting with fists and knuckles. However, the movements of hsing-i ch'uan can train the spine to move in the most intricate ways and the tendons to respond to the slightest change in intention; it thus offers a kind of training not available in the other forms of internal martial arts.

The Use of Herbs and Foods

Many practitioners of the Taoist arts of health use foods and herbs to supplement their training. The use of herbs and special foods must go hand in hand with the practitioner's condition of health and stage of spiritual development. If foods and herbs are used inappropriately, internal injuries can occur.

In Chinese herbology, herbs can be divided into three main groups: those that have curative properties, those that are used as preventive medicine, and those that facilitate the gathering and circulation of internal energy.

Herbs with curative properties are prescribed to counter illness or strengthen the constitution. They include herbs that women take to replenish blood and energy lost during childbirth. Herbs that act as preventive medicine can help to maintain general health and strengthen the body's immune system. As a child I took such herbs regularly. The third group, those that affect the circulation and collection of internal energy, are usually taken in conjunction with a program of spiritual training. These herbs have powerful effects, and should be taken only under the guidance of a teacher or doctor. Some herbs are only suitable when the practitioner has attained both internal and external strength, and others are effective only if the blockages in circulatory pathways are opened. At best, taking the wrong herbs will be a waste of resources, as the body will reject what it cannot absorb. However, some herbs can be harmful if they are ingested inappropriately. The best approach to the use of herbs is to consult with the teacher of the program you are studying.

Many people are curious about the role of foods in Taoist spirituality. The general rule of thumb is to let the body decide what foods it can take, rather than trying to control diet with preconceived ideas. One of the aims of Taoist training is to cultivate an intelligent body. Once the body has attained an awareness of its health, it will naturally reject foods that are unhealthy for it. Techniques of cultivating the body often require the practitioner initially to expend a lot of energy. It is not uncommon for appetites to increase in the early stages of external and internal strengthening. A practitioner locked into the social conventions about dieting and keeping calories down may not reach the higher stages of spiritual development. With time, however, as the internal physiology becomes more efficient, the body will not need as much food to maintain a healthy level of internal energy. Also, as the body is cleansed and the energies are refined, there is a natural inclination to stay away from meat and fatty foods.

Contrary to popular belief, vegetarianism is not required in Taoist practice. The Lung-men sect of the northern branch of the Complete Reality School is one of the few monastic groups to abstain from meat. Almost all of the internal-alchemical sects agree that abstinence from meat should be natural, not forced. On certain feast days, especially during the major festivals of the deities, it is customary to abstain from meat for purposes of purification. The observance of these dietary rules is especially important for practitioners of Ceremonial Taoism. The role and meaning of vegetarianism on the feast days will be discussed more fully in the next chapter.

FURTHER READINGS

Some books in this list are manuals on ch'i-kung, Taoist calisthenics, and other types of physical and mental exercise. I recommend them to offer more information on methods of cultivating the body. But if you wish to learn the techniques described in these books, or in this chapter, first get formal instruction from a reliable source. Neither the author nor the publisher of this book is responsible if injury should result from practicing the techniques described.

Book 11 in Henri Maspero's *Taoism and Chinese Religion*, titled "Methods of Nourishing the Vital in Ancient Taoist Religion," gives a good historical perspective of the techniques of breath control and regulation, yoga-like ch'i-kung postures, Taoist calisthenics, massage, and assorted methods of internal alchemy.

Ch'i-kung as a technique of longevity is discussed in two chapters of Kohn's collection *Taoist Meditation and Longevity Techniques:* "Gymnastics: The Ancient Tradition," by Catherine Despeux, and "Qi For Life: Longevity in the Tang," by Ute Engelhardt. In the same collection, "The Revival of Qi: Qigong in Contemporary China," by Kunio Miura, gives a brief and clear discussion of modern ch'i-kung practice.

Kohn's collection of translations, *The Taoist Experience*, has several sections on ch'i-kung postures, regulating the breath, and the use of foods and herbs:

Breathing for Life (reading #17)
Gymnastics (# 18)
Drugs and Diets (# 19)

Translations of some texts of the Taoist canon on breath control and circulation of energy are in the two volumes of *The Primordial Breath*, by Jane Huang and Michael Wurmbrand.

The Essence of T'ai-chi Ch'uan: The Literary Tradition is a collection of classical and modern treatises on t'ai-chi ch'uan translated by Benjamin Lo. The collection includes Chang San-feng's classic *T'ai-chi ch'uan ching* (Treatise on T'ai-chi Ch'uan) and other short discussions on t'ai-chi ch'uan by anonymous writers and modern t'ai-chi ch'uan masters.

To get a feel for some of the many techniques of Taoist calisthenics and yoga-like ch'i-kung postures, see William Berk's *Chinese Healing Arts: Internal Kung-fu*. Berk's book describes each of the forms, including the Seasonal Ch'i-kung Postures, the Five Animal Forms, and the Twelve Devas, and includes a list of herbs and a brief discussion of the theory of Chinese medicine.

A description of the basic forms of i-ch'uan is in Y. P. Dong's *Still as a Mountain, Powerful as Thunder*. I-ch'uan, a form of standing ch'i-kung, is a practice to cultivate body and mind simultaneously; it is also used to enhance the practice of two internal martial arts, liu-he pa-fa and hsing-i ch'uan—thus combining elements of meditation, ch'i-kung, Taoist calisthenics, and internal martial arts.

The Taoist arts of longevity being intimately tied to the theories of health and human physiology found in traditional Chinese medicine, I include a recommendation for reading on the topic. The best exposition on Chinese medicine is in two ancient treatises; one is translated by Ilza Veith as *The Yellow Emperor's Classic of Internal Medicine*; the other is translated by Wu Jing-Nuan as *Ling Shu, or The Spiritual Pivot*.

14

Rites of Purification, Ceremony, and Talismanic Magic

TAOIST RITES OF PURIFICATION, ceremony, and talismanic magic involve highly ritualistic behaviors. The rituals ensure that the practitioners are in a proper state of mind and body when they encounter the sacred powers.

Rites of Purification (Chai)

In ancient times, people purified themselves before participating in sacred ceremonies. Purification cleanses body and mind, and makes us worthy to communicate with the powers of the universe. In Taoism, the process of purification is called *chai*, and the rites of purification became known as the rules of chai in Taoist practice.

Today, in the West, many people equate chai with vegetarianism, because the word is now associated with the Buddhist dietary rule of abstaining from meat and with foods served in vegetarian restaurants. In Taoism, however, chai does not simply refer to a diet of vegetarian foods: chai is a set of purification rites that must be performed before the sacred ceremonies are conducted. Some of these rites are older than Taoism, and can be traced back to the days when the shaman-kings of ancient China honored the powers of sky and earth and gave thanks to them at spring planting and autumn harvest.

The Taoist rites of purification are divided into two categories: those that prepare the participants for the ceremonies and those that purify the ceremonial grounds. Rites in the first category prepare participants in sacred ceremonies by clearing the mind, cleansing the body, and making the spirit ready to merge with the Tao. Purifying the mind includes the practices of seclusion, quieting the mind, and minimizing activity. The chai of purifying the body consists of abstinence from sexual activity and observing dietary regulations. The most common diet observed in the purification rites is abstinence from meat and dairy products. This form of vegetarianism is only one part of the chai of cleansing the body; other dietary regulations include fasting, inhaling mist and vapor, swallowing the light of the sun, moon, and stars, and feeding on the Breath of the Tao.

For the Great Services, or *chiao*, purification usually begins three days before the ceremonies and continues throughout the festival; for the Ritual Gatherings *(fa-hui)*, purification begins one full day before the ceremonies; for the Feast Day *(tan)*, purification is observed on that day alone. (See chapter 9 for listings of the Taoist festivals.)

Some Taoist practitioners, especially the higher-level initiates, observe the rites of purification not only during the major and minor festivals but for several months of the year as well. Taoist practices of purification are never ascetic and practitioners are not forced to commit to long periods of purification in preparation for a ceremony. The lay practitioner who wishes to participate in a Feast Day ceremony need only observe the rules of purification for that day, although the more serious participants will begin at sunset the previous day. Participants in the Ritual Gatherings and Great Services—typically higher-level initiates of a priestly or monastic order—are usually prepared to observe the more demanding rites of purification. Even so, only the individuals of highest spiritual attainment, normally those who lead the ceremonies, are committed to the most rigorous forms of purification (the aforementioned fasting, or swallowing the light of the celestial bodies).

The chai of purifying the ceremonial grounds involves clearing the negative elements from the area by chanting, lighting lamps, and offering incense and special foods. All ceremonies are preceded by a ritual that purifies everything in the ceremonial area—the altar, the ground, the air, and the people. Rituals of purifying the ceremonial grounds differ among Taoist sects, but the rationale behind them is the same: all are designed to make the environment a suitable place for human beings to meet the sacred powers.

Ceremony (Chiao)

Taoist ceremonies are traditionally called chiao. In the early Chou dynasty, the chiao were ceremonies in which the emperor made offerings to the spirits of the sky and earth. The two oldest ceremonies were associated with spring planting and autumn harvest. The Spring Planting Ceremony was performed in early spring before the fields were plowed. In this ceremony, petitions were sent to the spirits of the sun, rain, clouds, winds, and earth, asking them to bring gifts of sunshine, rain, and fertility. The Autumn Harvest Ceremony was performed in the early fall and was a ceremony of thanksgiving.

As Taoism became an organized religion, the rituals of these two ancient ceremonies were modified and incorporated into Taoist ceremonies that honored the visits of the deities to the earthly realm. The earliest Taoist ceremonies were recorded by the Celestial Teachers in the *San-yüan chai* (Purification Rites for the Festivals of the Three Seasons). During the Northern Wei dynasty (circa fifth century CE), K'ou Ch'ien-chih, the founder of the northern sect of the Celestial Teachers, revised the old liturgies and added musical notation to them. Around the same time, Liu Hsiu-ching, the patriarch of the southern sect, wrote the *San-p'ien chai-fa* (Three Treatises on the Purification Rites), laying down standards of chai and chiao that are still followed today. By the time of the T'ang dynasty, different rites of purification were associated with different types of ceremonies, and each ceremony had its own set of rituals and liturgies. This large collection of chai and chiao was edited by Tao Kuang-t'ing, a liturgist of the Era of the Five and Ten Kingdoms (907–960 CE), into the *Hsüan-men k'o-fan ta-ch'üan* (Complete Collection of the Taoist Ceremonies). This authoritative work became the foundation of all Taoist ceremonies for centuries to come. From the T'ang dynasty onward, chai (purification) and chiao (ceremony) were inseparable. Although the word chiao is now used to refer only to the Great Services, the spirit of the chai and chiao of ancient China is found in all Taoist ceremonies.

Three kinds of sacred ceremonies are practiced by Taoists today: the Golden Ceremony, the Jade Ceremony, and the Yellow Register Ceremony. The Golden Ceremony consists of silent meditation, announcement of the names of the participants, renewal of the bond with the sacred powers, the three prostrations and audience with the deities, the nine prostrations and audience with the deities, an altar dedication ritual, petitioning for forgiveness, and thanksgiving.

The Jade Ceremony consists of the nine prostrations and audience with the deities, silent meditation, announcement of the names of the participants, three prostrations and audience with the deities, chanting of scriptures, asking the powers for merciful judgment, and comforting the dead. The Golden and Jade Ceremonies were patterned after the most ancient rituals, and in them we find the remnants of the Chou dynasty sacred ceremonies.

The Yellow Register Ceremony consists of rituals that were developed after Taoism had become an organized religion. This is the most complex ceremony, and the rituals were revised throughout the Wei, Chin, Sui, T'ang, Sung, Yüan, and Ming dynasties. In the Yellow Register Ceremony, special rituals honor the deities and spirits, teach the living, comfort the dead, and make peace with the ghosts. There are also liturgies of repentance on behalf of the living and the dead, liturgies that have the power to liberate the dead from suffering in the underworld, and liturgies that deliver humanity from calamity and disaster. During the reign of the Ch'ing dynasty emperor Ch'ien-lung (1736–1795 CE), the rituals of the Yellow Register Ceremony were collected and published. Included in this collection are instructions for building altars for special occasions, protocols for announcing the names of participants and presenting the list of petitions, procedures for conducting morning and noon services, and rituals for setting up and closing the altar. There are also rituals for inviting to the ceremonial grounds the celestial deities, the guardians of the underworld, and the dead. Finally, there are instructions on how to write talismans and use mudras (hand gestures), and how to circumambulate the altars and dance the gait of power for the flight to the stars.

The Taoist Altar

At the center of Taoist ceremony is the altar. The altar is an image of the Tao and the spiritual center of a sacred space. Although the arrangement of the altar varies among Taoist sects, and different rituals call for special arrangements of ceremonial objects, the significance and symbolism of the objects on the altar are the same.

An example of the basic arrangement of an altar of the Hsien-t'ien Tao sect is shown in figure 14.1. The principal objects on the altar, along with a brief explanation of their symbolism, are described below.

A *sacred lamp:* This is the light of wisdom. It is also the Golden Pill or Elixir of Immortality. The lamp is usually placed in the center of the altar in front of the patron deity of the temple or the deity being honored in the ceremony. The lamp symbolizes the original spirit, which is the light of the Tao within. It is never extinguished.

Two candles: To the left and right of the sacred lamp are two tall candles. They represent the light of the sun and the moon in nature and the two eyes in the human body. The sun and moon are emanations of the light of the Tao, and the eyes are windows to the mind. If the mind is not tainted by dust, original nature will be bright; the light of the Tao will shine within, and the eyes will not be covered by the dust of the mundane world.

Tea, rice, and water: Directly in front of the sacred lamp are three cups. The cup in the center holds grains of uncooked rice; the cup to the left contains water; the cup to the right contains tea. Tea symbolizes yin, or female generative, energy; water symbolizes yang,

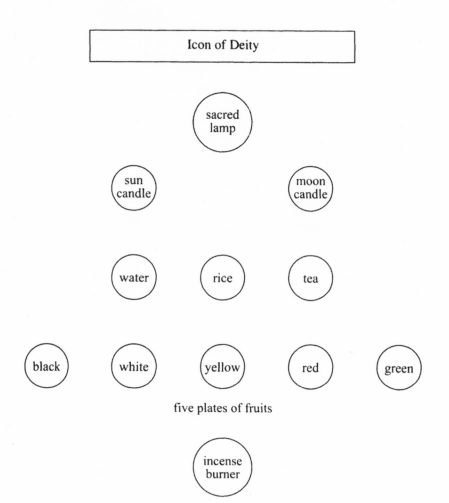

FIGURE 14.1. A Taoist Altar. Basic arrangement of a typical Taoist altar of the Hsien-t'ien Tao and affiliated sects. The five fruits represent the five elements.

or male generative, energy. Rice symbolizes the union of these two energies, because it receives the yang energy of the sun and absorbs the yin energy of earth.

Five plates of fruit: The five fruits represent the five elements: wood, fire, earth, metal, and water. Each element is associated with a color. Wood is green, fire is red, earth is yellow, metal is white, and water is black. In the creative cycle, wood gives rise to fire, fire burns to create earth (ashes), earth nourishes metal, and, where metal is found, there is water. In the destructive cycle, metal cuts wood, wood (in the form of tree roots) chokes earth, earth restricts the flow of water, water extinguishes fire, and fire melts metal. In the body, wood is the liver, fire is the heart, earth is the spleen, metal is the lungs, and water is the kidneys. When the five elements are in a creative cycle, the internal organs nourish each other and the body is in good health.

An incense burner: The incense burner is typically placed in the center of the altar in front of the five plates of fruit. This is the stove, or the lower tan-t'ien, where internal heat is generated to purify and refine the generative, vital, and spirit energy. The three energies are symbolized by three sticks of incense. The burning of the incense symbolizes the refinement and purification of the internal energies. The rising smoke and falling ash also symbolize the separation of pure energy from mundane energy. On another level, the sticks of incense represent the human body. As the smoke rises and the ashes fall, we reconnect ourselves with the sky and earth and become a channel for the flow of energy between the realms above and below.

On the altar, the sacred lamp, which is the symbol of original nature, is closest to the deity. Arranged progressively away from the deity are the two candles, the tea, rice, and water, the fruit, and finally the incense burner. This arrangement shows that the entrance to the Tao begins with purifying the three internal energies, reconnecting the body with sky and earth; when the energies are refined, they are gathered in the five viscera to nourish the body, a process represented by the five plates of fruit; as spiritual development continues, the yin and yang energies copulate—represented by the cups of tea, rice, and water; when the original spirit emerges, the Tao shines within and a golden light hovers around the eyes— represented by the two candles. Finally, the original spirit, symbolized by the sacred lamp, is cultivated to return to the void and merge with the Tao—the deity in the icon.

Talismans

Talismans are scripts of power, and the use of talismanic magic in Taoism dates back to the Eastern Han (circa second century CE), when Celestial Teacher Chang Tao-ling (see page 3) used talismans to heal the sick and ward off evil spirits. By the time of the Six Dynasties, talismans were used by the Celestial Teachers for exorcism and protection against malevolent spirits. The Shang-ch'ing Taoists used talismans to help them fly to the celestial realm, and the alchemists hastened the production of the elixir of immortality with them. Today, talismans are also used to purify ceremonial grounds for ceremonies.

To draw a talisman, one has to have skill and power, and not all Taoists are trained in this practice. Only practitioners of Magical Taoism and leaders of ceremonies are adept at this art; in fact, practitioners of Ceremonial Taoism who are not involved in the magical arts can draw only those talismans specific to the rituals used in the ceremonies. The drawing of talismans in ceremonies is taught to an initiate only when he or she is ready to lead a ritual.

The following passage is included in the book only to show the reader what is involved in drawing a talisman. Please do not copy the talismans or try to use them. Preparing or placing talismans incorrectly can incur wrath from the sacred powers. The only way to learn talismanic magic is to be apprenticed into a sect of Magical Taoism or to become a leader of rituals in a sect of Ceremonial Taoism.

A talisman consists of a string of words embellished with special symbols. The typical talisman is a strip of yellow paper with words and symbols written in red ink. In some talismans, the deities are invoked by the writing of their names on the talismans; in others, the script contains words or symbols of command or power.

There are two major styles of talismanic writing: ancient seal script and common script. The ancient seal script, which is a form of archaic Chinese writing, is found in the Shang-ch'ing, Ling-pao, and Celestial Teachers talismans. The common script talisman is preferred by the modern Mao-shan sorcerers and the Kun-lun sect.

Figures 14.2 and 14.3 show the two kinds of talismanic scripts. The Ling-pao and Celestial Teachers talismans date back to the Eastern Han and the Chin dynasties; the Kun-lun talismans are from the turn of the century—i.e., about a hundred years ago. For ease of describing talismanic writing, I shall use the Kun-lun talismans as examples. They are written in modern Chinese and are the easiest type of talisman to comprehend.

Kun-lun talismans that invoke the power of the high deities have three V-shaped marks at the top (fig. 14.4). In writing the talisman, these marks are drawn first. When the first mark, the one top center, is drawn, the writer utters, silently, "The first mark moves sky and earth." The second mark, the one on the left, is accompanied by the silent incantation, "The second mark unleashes the power of the patriarch's sword." The third mark, the one on the right, is accompanied by, "With the third mark, may all malevolent spirits and destructive powers be banished a thousand miles away."

At the bottom of the talismanic strip are words and symbols of power. The symbols at the bottom of the talismanic strip shown in figure 14.4 (see talisman at left) are said to have the power to open the celestial gates, block the passage of malevolent spirits, open the gates of the underworld, and defeat the armies of evil. A symbol that is said to enhance the power of the talisman consists of wiggly lines or lines with loops that run down the length of the strip. These lines are usually drawn surrounding the words of command to focus and gather power (figure 14.3).

Special preparations and procedures must be followed in drawing a talisman. First, the writer of the talisman must undergo purification rites. These include abstaining from meat, sex, and all forms of intoxicants and stimulants for at least a day before the talisman is prepared. This is why the Mao-shan sorcerers, who need to prepare and use talismans frequently, abstain from alcohol and lead a celibate life. It is also why many practitioners of Kun-lun magic are vegetarians. In addition to the abstinences, incantations are chanted to purify body and mind. Sometimes, an altar is erected, and incense, fruit, and wine are offered to the powers before the writing begins.

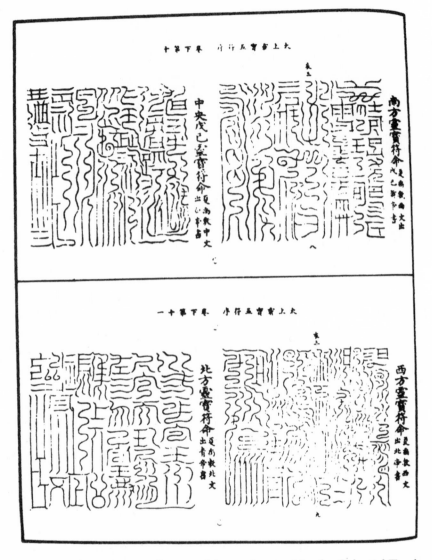

FIGURE 14.2. Ling-pao talisman of protection used by the Celestial Teachers sect, from the *T'ai-shang ling-pao wu-fu ching* (The Highest Revelation of the Five Talismans of the Sacred Spirit). The talisman in the upper right protects the user from malevolent spirits from the south; the one lower right, from the west; the one upper left, from the center; and the one lower left, from the north.

FIGURE 14.3. Kun-lun talisman of healing. This talisman invokes the power of the Jade Emperor. The triangle with horizontal line that appears at the bottom of the talisman is a symbol used to enhance the talisman's power.

Moreover, the talismans should be written only during certain hours of the day. The hour of tzu (11:00 PM to 1:00 AM) is the best time for preparing talismans, followed by the hour of wu (11:00 AM to 1:00 PM). On four days of the year it is not suitable to prepare talismans: the ninth day of the third lunar month, the second day of the sixth lunar month, the sixth day of the ninth lunar month, and the second day of the twelfth lunar month.

Not all talismans are written on paper. Some, especially those used in ceremonies, are symbols traced in the air with a stick of incense or the tip of a wooden sword. Because there is no visible trace of writing, these talismans are called formless talismans.

Many details of talismanic writing and magic are beyond the scope of this book. Even today, the preparation and use of Taoist talismans is accessible only to those who are initiated into the practice of Taoist

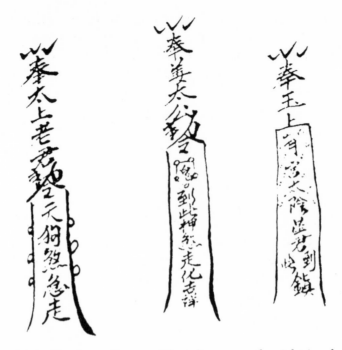

FIGURE 14.4. Kun-lun talismans. The talisman on the right invokes the Celestial Lord of the Lunar Yin for protection. The talisman at center invokes a legendary sorcerer and magician of the Shang dynasty, Kiang Tzu-ya, to transform malevolent forces into benevolent ones. The talisman at left invokes the T'ai-shang Lao-chün, the patriarch of Taoism, to chase away a baleful star named the Dog Star. In Chinese astronomy, a solar eclipse is referred to as "the Sky Dog eating the sun" and this talisman also invokes protection from evil spirits during an eclipse.

magic and sorcery and those authorized to conduct ceremonies. However, this section will enhance readers' appreciation of talismanic writing and introduce them to a Taoist practice that is generally not accessible to Westerners.

This chapter completes our armchair journey through the Taoist spiritual landscape. Some readers may wish to seek spiritual guidance in the Taoist path; others may feel that a curiosity has been satisfied. To those who want to learn more about Taoism and its practices, I would say: Your next step is to seek formal instruction. To experience the fullness of Taoist spirituality, one must leave the security of intellectual speculation and venture into practice. Reading a book can inspire you to take a spiritual journey, but book knowledge cannot replace spiritual experience. My hope is that this book has opened up the Taoist spiritual terrain and given you a direction and the initiative to explore it.

FURTHER READINGS

For a brief review of the chai-chiao services, see section q in chapter 7 of Michael Saso's *Blue Dragon, White Tiger*. Saso describes the purpose and meaning of the chiao, with special regard to the people of southern China.

A more detailed presentation of the chiao performed by the Celestial Teachers sect can be found in Saso's other book on Taoist ceremonies, *Taoism and the Rite of Cosmic Renewal*.

Translations of Taoist precepts and monastic vows are in reading #13, "Precepts and Prescriptions," of Livia Kohn's *The Taoist Experience*.

APPENDIXES

The Dynasties of China

Dates for the Chinese dynasties are those adopted by textbooks of Chinese history published in Hong Kong. Note that the dynasties of China did not always occupy the same geographical regions. Some dynasties overlap in time, and there were periods of political chaos where no ruling house was in control.

Hsia	2205–1765 BCE
Shang	1766–1121 BCE
Chou	1122–225 BCE
Western Chou	1122–770 BCE
Eastern Chou	770–221 BCE
Spring and Autumn Period	770–476 BCE
Warring States Period	475–221 BCE
Ch'in	221–207 BCE
Han	206 BCE–219 CE
Western Han	206 BCE–8 CE
Eastern Han	25 CE–220 CE
Three Kingdoms	220–265 CE
Wei	220–265 CE
Shu	221–263 CE
Wu	222–280 CE
Chin	265–420 CE
Western Chin	265–316 CE
Eastern Chin	317–420 CE
Six Dynasties	420–589 CE

Sui	589–618 CE
T'ang	618–906 CE
Five Dynasties and Ten Kingdoms	907–960 CE
Sung	960–1279 CE
Northern Sung	960–1126 CE
Southern Sung	1127–1279 CE
Yüan	1271–1368 CE
Ming	1368–1644 CE
Ch'ing	1644–1911 CE

The Dynastic Era Ends

Republic of China	1911–1949 CE
People's Republic of China	1949–

Appendix 2
Map of China

The Yang-tze, one of China's two great rivers, divides China into two regions—north and south. From the eighteenth century BCE (Shang dynasty) to the third century CE (Eastern Han), the mainstream of Chinese civilization lay in the central and lower regions of the Yellow River valley. Notice that the Spring and Autumn states of Ch'i and Lu (where Confucius and Mencius lived and taught) are located in the northern region of China, near the mouth of the Yellow River. The state of Ch'u, home of the Ch'u shamans Lao-tzu and Chuang-tzu, is located in the central part of the Yang-tze valley, and Wu and Yüeh are situated along the southeastern coast. The modern cities of Beijing and Shanghai are shown to give an idea of distance. Notice also that Szechuan (the Land of Shu) and Yunnan (where Chang Tao-ling first acquired a following) are even farther from the mainstream of Chinese civilization.

A third point to notice is that the Eastern Chin dynasty, where the Shang-ch'ing Taoists and the southern branch of the Celestial Teachers cult flourished, occupied a region where the Spring and Autumn states, Ch'u, Wu, and Yüeh, were located. The areas where the Shang-ch'ing Taoists were most active coincided with the old lands of Wu and Yüeh.

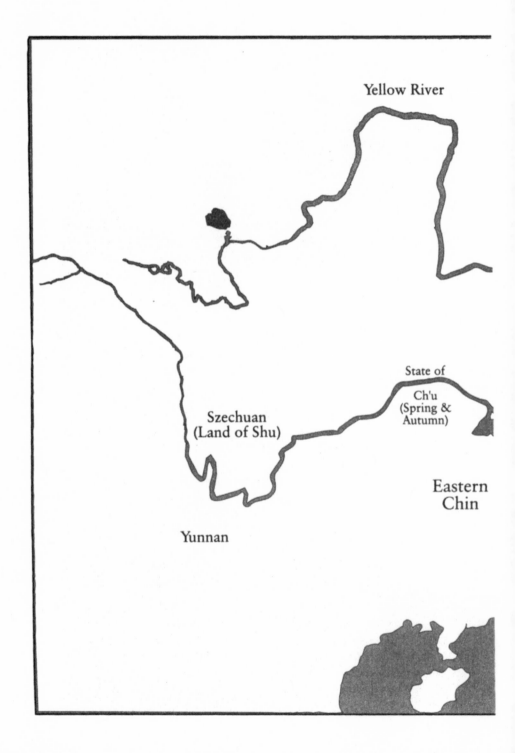

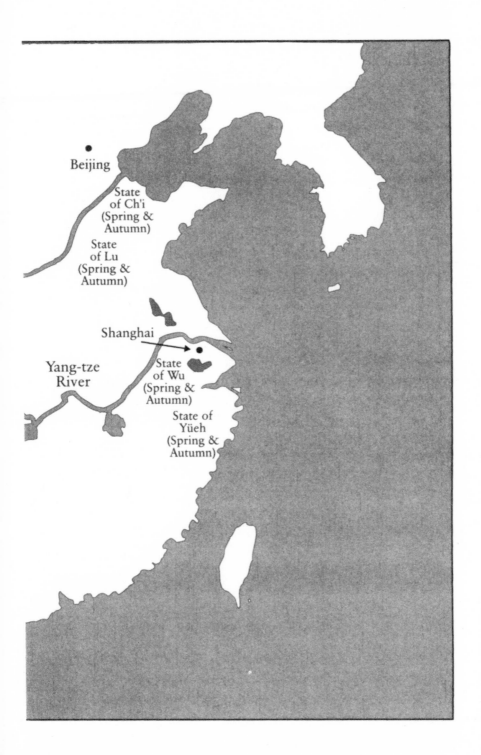

Beijing

State
of Ch'i
(Spring &
Autumn)

State
of Lu
(Spring &
Autumn)

Shanghai

Yang-tze
River

State
of Wu
(Spring &
Autumn)

State of
Yüeh
(Spring &
Autumn)

APPENDIX 3
Bibliography of Further Readings

Berk, William. *Chinese Healing Arts: Internal Kung-fu*. Culver City, Calif.: Peace Press, 1979.

Chang, Wing-tsit, trans. and comp. *A Source Book in Chinese Philosophy*. Princeton: Princeton University Press, 1963.

Cleary, Thomas, trans. *The Inner Teachings of Taoism*. Boston: Shambhala Publications, 1986.

————. *The Taoist I-ching*. Boston: Shambhala Publications, 1986.

————. *Understanding Reality*. Honolulu: University of Hawaii Press, 1987.

————. *The Buddhist I Ching*. Boston: Shambhala Publications, 1987.

————. *Awakening to the Tao*. Boston: Shambhala Publications, 1988.

————. *I Ching: The Tao of Organization*. Boston: Shambhala Publications, 1988.

————. *I Ching Mandalas*. Boston: Shambhala Publications, 1989.

————. *The Book of Balance and Harmony*. San Francisco: North Point Press, 1989.

————. *Back to Beginnings*. Boston: Shambhala Publications, 1990.

————. *Vitality, Energy, Spirit: A Taoist Sourcebook*. Boston: Shambhala Publications, 1991.

————. *Further Teachings of Lao-tzu: Understanding the Mysteries*. Boston: Shambhala Publications, 1991.

————. *The Secret of the Golden Flower*. San Francisco: HarperCollins, 1991.

DeWoksin, Kenneth. *Doctors, Diviners, and Magicians of Ancient China: Biographies of Fang-shih*. New York: Columbia University Press, 1983.

Dong, Y. P. *Still as a Mountain, Powerful as Thunder*. Boston: Shambhala Publications, 1993.

Eliade, Mircea. *Shamanism*. Princeton: Princeton University Press, 1964.

Harner, Michael. *The Way of the Shaman.* San Francisco: HarperCollins, 1990.

Hawkes, David. *The Songs of the South.* New York: Penguin, 1985.

Henricks, Robert G. *Lao-tzu Te-tao-ching.* New York: Ballantine, 1989.

Huang, Jane, and Michael Wurmbrand. *The Primordial Breath,* vol. 1. Torrance, Calif.: Original Books, 1987.

———. *The Primordial Breath,* vol. 2. Torrance, Calif.: Original Books, 1990.

Kohn, Livia, ed. *Taoist Meditation and Longevity Techniques.* Ann Arbor: University of Michigan Press, 1989.

———. *Taoist Mystical Philosophy.* Albany: State University of New York Press, 1991.

———. *Early Chinese Mysticism.* Princeton: Princeton University Press. 1992.

———, ed. *The Taoist Experience.* Albany: State University of New York Press, 1993.

Lo, Benjamin. *The Essence of T'ai-chi Ch'uan: The Literary Tradition.* Richmond, Calif.: North Atlantic Books, 1979.

Lu, Kuan Yü. *The Secrets of Chinese Meditation.* New York: Samuel Weiser, 1964.

———. *Taoist Yoga.* New York: Samuel Weiser, 1970.

Maspero, Henri. *Taoism and Chinese Religion.* Amherst: University of Massachusetts Press, 1981.

Needham, Joseph. *Science and Civilization in China,* Vol. 5:3. Cambridge: Cambridge University Press, 1976.

———. *Science and Civilization in China,* Vol. 5:5. Cambridge: Cambridge University Press, 1983.

Olson, Stuart. *The Jade Emperor's Mind Seal Classic.* St. Paul, Minn.: Dragon Door Press, 1992.

Robinet, Isabelle. *Taoist Meditation.* Albany: State University of New York Press, 1993.

Saso, Michael. *Blue Dragon, White Tiger: Taoist Rites of Passage.* Washington, D.C.: Taoist Center, 1990.

———. *Taoism and the Rite of Cosmic Renewal.* Pullman: Washington State University Press, 1989.

———. *The Gold Pavilion: Taoist Ways to Peace, Healing, and Long Life.* Boston: Tuttle, 1995.

Schipper, Kristofer. *The Taoist Body.* Berkeley and Los Angeles: University of California Press, 1993.

Veith, Ilza. *The Yellow Emperor's Classic of Internal Medicine.* Berkeley and Los Angeles: University of California Press, 1972.

Ware, James R. *Alchemy, Medicine, and Religion: The Nei P'ien of Ko Hung.* New York: Dover, 1966.

Watson, Burton. *The Complete Works of Chuang-tzu.* New York: Columbia University Press, 1968.

Wile, Douglas. *Art of the Bedchamber: The Chinese Sexual Yoga Classics Including Solo Meditation Texts.* Albany: State University of New York Press, 1992.

Wilhelm, Helmut. *Heaven, Earth, and Man in the Book of Changes.* Seattle: University of Washington Press, 1977.

Wong, Eva. *Seven Taoist Masters.* Boston: Shambhala Publications, 1990.

———. *Cultivating Stillness.* Boston: Shambhala Publications, 1992.

———. *Lao-tzu's Treatise on the Response of the Tao.* San Francisco: HarperCollins, 1993.

———. *Lieh-tzu: A Taoist Guide to Practical Living.* Boston: Shambhala Publications, 1995.

———. *Feng-shui: The Ancient Wisdom of Harmonious Living for Modern Times.* Boston: Shambhala Publications, 1996.

Wu, Jing-nuan. *Ling Shu, or The Spiritual Pivot.* Washington, D.C.: Taoist Center, 1993.

Index